Left

"There is no one quite like Bernard-Henri Lévy in America. He's a star and a philosopher: a brave activist who puts himself in harm's way. This is a writer who is adept at raising important issues and treating them with intelligence and verve." —*San Francisco Chronicle*

"*Left in Dark Times*—Lévy's blend of memoir, dissection of the 1970s New Philosophy movement that made him famous, and call for a left-ism that's neither infantile nor robotic—demonstrates the acuity of his antennae, and his good fortune in reflecting current events." —*The Chronicle Review*

"Vastly compelling." —*The Plain Dealer*

"Lévy embarks on a long excursion into what Diderot may have been the first to call *l'esprit d'escalier,* all the fine rejoinders that occur to one only when one is descending the stairs and it's just too late.... It's hard not to wish him well in striving to purge the left of its demons." —*The New York Times Book Review*

"[*Left in Dark Times* is] a mixture of political autobiography, polemic and plea." —*The Economist*

"Lévy drops the hammer against self-styled 'progressives' and ignorant moral relativism." —Timeoutnewyork.com

"Alternately ponderous, angry and impassioned [*Left in Dark Times* is] an attempt to hold tight to the left, a left Mr. Lévy considers himself bound to." —*The New York Observer*

LEFT IN DARK TIMES

LEFT IN
DARK TIMES

A STAND AGAINST THE NEW BARBARISM

BERNARD-HENRI LÉVY

Translated by Benjamin Moser

RANDOM HOUSE
TRADE PAPERBACKS
NEW YORK

Published in the United States by Random House Trade
Paperbacks, an imprint of The Random House Publishing
Group, a division of Random House, Inc., New York.

RANDOM HOUSE TRADE PAPERBACKS and colophon
are trademarks of Random House, Inc.

Originally published in hardcover in the United States
by Random House, an imprint of The Random House
Publishing Group, a division of Random House, Inc.,
in 2008.

LIBRARY OF CONGRESS CATALOGING-IN-
PUBLICATION DATA

Lévy, Bernard-Henri.
Left in dark times : a stand against the new barbarism /
Bernard-Henri Lévy ; translated by Benjamin Moser.
p. cm.
ISBN 978-0-8129-7472-0
1. Right and left (Political science)   2. Totalitarianism.
3. Political ethics.   I. Title.
JC480 L48 2008
320.5—dc22   2008023464

Printed in the United States of America

www.atrandom.com

9 8 7 6 5 4

Book design by Barbara M. Bachman

Can a French philosopher's reflections on his intellectual journey shed any light on American dilemmas? What can he, as he wrestles with his own political roots and convictions, possibly have to say to Americans in the midst of their national controversies and momentous decisions?

Of course, there is the portrait of Nicolas Sarkozy that opens this book, a French president who, in morphing as he has from a questionable but imposing statesman to a quaint, Warholian character, may now interest only folklorists, or students of political curiosities.

And there are the subsequent pages in which I try to retrace the ideological and political history of a generation—my generation—which was the last in Europe to believe in the great Revolutionary tale and which was also the first to deconstruct its foundations. The United States never having believed in all that talk of a new man, of history broken in two, or of the regeneration by violence of humanity's failures, I understand that this intellectual journey, my rereading of the Cambodian Revolution or the dissenting movements of the 1960s, might all seem remote.

But my true purpose in this book goes well beyond these preliminary considerations.

In advancing a "critique of neoprogressive reason," I attempt to address all those who have been led astray on both sides of the Atlantic, in both of our countries. And what I mean by this is a critique of those who, inspired by the desire to create a heaven on earth, were—and are, more than ever—led to a flirtation with darkness, barbarism, and hell.

Are the values of individual freedom compatible with the idea of equality, without which, as we have known since Tocqueville, no democracy can endure? And if so, under what conditions?

Are human rights Western or universal? Does their Western birth mean that they are strictly limited to their original home—or are they natural rights that can therefore legitimately be called upon to migrate beyond their birthplace?

Have the neoconservatives ruined or corrupted the idea that democratic values are universal? Or have they simply damaged those values, weakened them, temporarily discredited them: and if so, for how long?

Does anti-Semitism have a future? If so, what will it look like? Who in the United States or Europe is most vulnerable to the new type of virus through which the most ancient of hatreds is transmitted—and perpetuated?

What about anti-Americanism? Is it coming from the Right? the Left? the gray area that separates them and where they collide? Is the term a kind of password in America and Europe to say something else—and if so, what?

Why has the concept and criticism of Empire, and even anti-imperialist activism, ended up hiding and denying today's sufferings and wars, from Bosnia to Rwanda to Darfur? Why, in other words, is anti-Americanism among the most efficient vehicles for reactionary thinking in our time?

What is Islamo-progressivism? How is it that great minds seem so reluctant, in the face of Islamic radicalism, to defend human rights, and especially women's rights? Wouldn't being a real progressive mean lending a hand to those forces in the Muslim world, those dissidents male and female, those rebels who refuse to march to the orders of something that looks a lot like a new version of fascism? Wouldn't it oppose the totalitarian Islam of a loud minority with the enlightened Islam that so many democrats and secularists from Karachi to Algiers, from Sarajevo to Jakarta, demand?

How can one be both antitotalitarian and antifascist? Proud of the achievements of antiracist struggles yet intolerant of the petty chauvinisms and separatism that are their degenerate form?

How can we keep faith with the memory of the anticolonial movement while still dismissing those fools who, in the name of that same faith, cannot imagine the very idea that decolonized peoples might themselves be dabbling in forms of barbarism, casting those who are shocked by such barbarisms into the abyss of neocolonial ideology and nostalgia?

These several questions are really just parts of the same one. This single, and ultimately simple, question concerns the monsters that the new laboratories of what we in Europe call Leftism and what Americans call liberalism are giving birth to.

And on the other hand, it's about what liberalism ought to do, what it should be and should become, in order to rid itself of its ghosts as well as to elevate itself to the highest, most noble aspects of its heritage. Criticism that will help it rediscover its foundations. . . . Make a selection—the original meaning of the word "criticize"—in order to reshape a discourse aware of the dangers facing it in the current desert. . . .

Many of us, here and elsewhere, in the United States as in Europe, can identify with this program. In my generation and the one that came after it, there are more and more people who have not given up any of their hopes, who haven't sworn off or changed their pantheon, who share the same veneration for the memory of Martin Luther King, Jr., or Rosa Parks—but who refuse the slightest compromise, under whatever pretext, with bigotry and hatred.

I hope these pages can contribute to the effort to clear things up.

I hope these pages can contribute, modestly but solidly, to the reconstruction of a universal movement of free spirits worthy of the name.

Neither resignation nor defeatism: it's time to fight back.

Contents

Introduction

It's January 23, 2007, at three in the afternoon. On the front page of *Le Monde,* my old friend André Glucksmann, who has fought alongside me for the past thirty years, has just published an article announcing his support of the UMP candidate Nicolas Sarkozy. The telephone rings. It's the candidate himself: the smooth, treacly voice can scarcely contain his joy at Glucksmann's beautiful, lyrical text.

"So you've seen *Le Monde . . . ?*"

I ought to say that Nicolas Sarkozy and I have been friendly since he was first elected mayor of Neuilly in 1983. Because of family circumstances, I happened to be registered to vote in that suburb of Paris. He had a list drawn up of voters who might be useful to him. And he found that among them was the author of *Barbarism with a Human Face.* I was invited to lunch at city hall. I immediately took to the very young, incredibly decisive kid who during our first meeting was—already!—trying to understand how a man like me could possibly disagree with him. Other lunches followed over the years. Trips to the mountains. Countless excursions through the desert. Indeed, when I look back at the already long career of the sixth president of the Fifth Republic, I'm not sure why I get the idea that it was an uninterrupted series of trips through the desert culminating in a victory parade. I gave him ammunition for a debate with Tariq Ramadan. In a conversation during the Clearstream affair, in which he was accused of financial irregularities, with his face inches from my own, his voice trembling in rage and emotion, I heard him say: "Whoever did this to me, I'll hang him myself—you understand me? personally hang him!—from a pitchfork." A final meeting, in December 2006, in Marrakesh, with Claude Lanzmann, where I tried to explain to Sarkozy (which goes to show what I know!) that you don't get to be president by spending too much time as France's top cop! In other words, there was something that, despite the genuine disagreements, unchanged by the passing years, eventually became a kind of friendship.

"You've seen *Le Monde*?" he says again, in that tone of scarcely concealed triumph that I know so well. "You saw your friend's article about your friend?"

"Yes," I answer. "Of course I did. It's good. It's courageous. I'm happy for you because . . ."

He interrupts me: a note of disappointment and mistrust creeps into his voice.

"Courageous? Why courageous?"

"Because he's taking a risk. People are going to beat up on him about this. So it's courageous."

His mistrust gives way to a sudden annoyance and then, quickly, to a show-offy tone which over the years he's still never quite learned to rein in—the tone I'd heard a few years before, when a number of biographies began to be written about me: he made a point of telling me that not seven but a grand total of *eleven* books were going to be published about him, and that the palm of martyrdom, the title of the most attacked man in France, the crown of the most victimized Christ in Europe, was his and his alone.

"You don't get it," he went on. "Courage has nothing to do with it. Because a lot of people from the Left are joining forces with me. Lots and lots, you'll see . . ."

"Fine," I agreed. "Not courageous, all right. Let's say daring. Taking the risk, before all these other people you're talking about, of shaking things up. It has a certain charm . . ."

He cuts me off—once again smooth and accommodating, the whole swaggering production.

"Let's get to the point. What about you? When are you going to

write your little article for me? Huh, when? Because Glucksmann is
fine. But you, after all, you are my friend."

"Oh, me . . ."

"Well?"

"You don't need me. You already have so many people. All those
polls have you elected before the fight's even started. Isn't there one out
this morning giving you a fifty-five-percent lead?"

"The problem isn't the polls," he answers, even treaclier than before, and such a bad actor! "It's not about getting elected. I mean getting elected, fine, but thanks to the people you respect and care about.
So I'll repeat the question: When are you going to join up with me?
When are you going to do it for me, write a nice little article?"

"You know very well," I said, feeling more and more uncomfortable.
"We've talked about it a hundred times. Personal relationships are one
thing. Ideas are another. And no matter how much I like and respect
you, the Left is my family and . . ."

"What?" he says in a suddenly rough voice, almost angry, but an
anger that could be yet another acting job. "Emmanuelli, your family?
Montebourg, your family? These people who've spent thirty years
telling you to go fuck yourself? Do you really think I'm an idiot or do
you really believe what you're saying, that these people are your family?"

"Yes, well, I'll grant you . . . It's true it might seem strange and those
people haven't always been easy on me. . . . But that's just how my life
is. . . . That's life. . . . Once again, I'm still your friend. . . . Part of me wishes
you every success in the world . . . but I've always voted for the Left and
I'm voting for the Left this time too."

"Listen . . ."

The tone becomes friendly again. Charming. But underneath the
apparently acted and over-sonorous solemnity of his "Listen" (*"Écoute"*),
in the way he emphasizes the *t,* sticking his tongue—I can see it almost
as if I was standing in front of him—through his teeth and then jerking
it quickly backward, like the snapping of a rubber band, in the sleazy
way he lets it be understood that we're going to take our time, lay it all
out on the table, and finally reach an agreement, you know, just to clear
up something that can't be more than an unfortunate misunderstanding:

something I suspect he got from Jacques Chirac, but which doesn't really suit him.

"Listen . . . Let me refresh your memory . . . *Dangerous Purity* . . . Does that ring a bell, *Dangerous Purity*?"

"Of course."

"Then it's a simple question. Was it Emmanuelli, your family, who talked about your book *Dangerous Purity* in 1994? Was it Arnaud Montebourg, your family, who went on the television back then to talk about *Dangerous Purity*?"

"No, true enough. What a memory you have! You're the one who defended the book. And I know it very well. But that doesn't have anything to do with this. Nothing. Because . . ."

"Of course it has something to do with this! And anyway . . ."

He pretends to be catching his breath.

"And anyway, I'm sure you know a lot of other officials who spoke about Chechnya the way I did last Sunday?"

He had in fact called me ten days before, early in the morning, a few hours before he was about to give a major speech: he wanted to make sure that I would be "all ears" because he was going to say things that would make people like me feel "authorized" to vote for him.

"We'll see," I said. "The campaign's just beginning. And . . ."

"And anyone else who's said that Darfur shouldn't be seen as a little detail of the history of the twenty-first century? Anyone else, except for me, who's said that we can't allow the century to open with another genocide?"

"We'll see, Nicolas, we'll see. I think the biggest mistake my friend Glucksmann's made is deciding too early on, and with so much enthusiasm, without waiting for your opponents, especially Ségolène Royal, to lay out their cards. . . ."

"Madame Royal's cards . . . pffff . . . Let's talk about her cards. . . . The main thing I've heard her do is praise Hezbollah and talk about how fine the Chinese justice system is . . ."

"That's true. For now, that's partly true. But you have to see the context . . . her actual words . . ."

He cuts me off again—but this time, with an impatience he takes no trouble to disguise.

"Come on. Stop quibbling. Be courageous, my dear Bernard. Be courageous, get out of bed. . . ."

"It's three in the afternoon."

"I know. As a manner of speaking. I mean: take your hand, give it to me, and together we'll make a revolution, you'll see. . . . You're not going to work against me, at least?"

Now I hear the clannish, feudal, possibly brutal Sarkozy that his opponents have denounced, and which I never wanted to believe in: a man with a warrior vision of politics, who hystericizes relations, believes that those who aren't with him are against him, who doesn't care about ideas, who thinks interpersonal relations and friendship are the only things that matter. . . .

I also note another old trait that time has not cured him of, and which makes him the prototype of the "Sartrean subject" that a few years before, in another book, I had tried to sketch: say everything; hold nothing back; a person who would blurt out everything, really everything, that pops into his head—Does it occur to him to go back to the Place Beauvau, to the Interior Ministry, in order to avoid the low blows of his fake friends, who are in the pocket of Dominique de Villepin?—Well then, he'll say: "I'm going back to the Place Beauvau, to the Interior Ministry, in order to avoid the low blows of my fake friends, who are in the pocket of Dominique de Villepin"! If it occurs to him that the place of an intellectual is by his side, in the great revolutionary army he is raising to change France at long last, then he comes right out and says it, unafraid of being rejected, devoid of false embarrassment or modesty; "Sartrean subject" indeed, because he's the only being I know who is quite as "stripped of inner conscience."

I mutter a few banalities about the role of writers, who aren't there to throw their arms around politicians but to ask questions, criticize, oppose. I tell him to give my best to Cécilia. Wish him good luck in the tough battle ahead. At which point the future president of France hangs up and leaves me, I must say, highly perplexed—caught between two feelings, both very troubling, because, on that day at least, both are equally indisputable.

The first was that I wouldn't join him and that I'd vote for the Left once again.

But the second was that, unfortunately, he was right when he said that, on the questions of Darfur and Chechnya, as well as several other matters that have always been close to my heart, the Left to which I had stayed faithful was behaving strangely.

At that point, this book began.

PART ONE

WHAT'S LEFT
OF THE LEFT

1.

And Upon This Ruin . . .

Why didn't I vote for Sarkozy?

Why was I so profoundly convinced, then, that it was literally impossible for me to vote for that man?

First of all, some of the reasons concerned things I knew about him, things that many voters would soon discover.

A kind of feverishness that seemed incompatible with the job.

An indifference to ideas, a cynicism, that has led to incredibly brutal flip-flops on certain important matters (Russia, for example).

An ability to live in denial, which we would see during his grotesque and devastating reception of Colonel Gadhafi in Paris.

The pragmatism—a better word is opportunism—we saw soon after his victory, when, like a kid set loose in a candy store and told: "Here you go! It's all yours! It's free! Take what you want!," he literally took it all, working his way through every bin, snatching up all the most desirable items. The icon Kouchner. The wise Védrine. The knights of Mitterrand's Holy Grail, whom, when Sarkozy was a young minister, he confessed to admiring. Totems of the Left. Literary and show business legends. Who's the patron saint of the Socialists? Blum? Then bring me Blum! The Christ of the Communists? Guy Môquet? Then bring him to me—not, of course, Guy Môquet himself, the seventeen-year-old

Resistance hero killed by the Nazis, but his last, beautiful, heartbreaking letter to his parents! And the queen of today's victims? Who wears the dark crown of contemporary suffering and martyrdom? Ingrid Betancourt, you say? Then go fetch them right away, the Betancourt family, and bring them to my palace!

I didn't deny that all this could have its good sides. Nor that, precisely because of his appetite, Nicolas Sarkozy might have some surprises up his sleeve. All I knew was that he had a strange and worrying way of operating. I also knew that he had an almost deformed memory. People usually have a memory. It can be complex, contradictory, paradoxical. But it's their own. It is, in large part, the foundation of their identity. Sarkozy, however, is a hijacker of other people's memories. He lays claim to everyone's memory, which finally means he has no memory of his own. Our first memory-free president. The first of our presidents to wish all ideas well, because he really is indifferent to them. And that is why, if one man in France today incarnates—or claims to incarnate—that famous "post-ideological age" in which I cannot bring myself to believe, then it is Nicolas Sarkozy, sixth president of the Fifth Republic.

None of that subtracts, I repeat, from the charm of his character. Nor, once again, from my personal liking of him. But that was the first group of reasons that prevented me from supporting him.

A SECOND GROUP WAS more essential.

Because it had to do with my very being, with my fundamental political identity—something in me bolted at the double idea: first, of rushing to the rescue of someone who I guessed was going to win anyway (Ah! The defectors already rushing in! All the flatterers, the followers, of whom you could say, as of Juvenal's courtesan, that no cheese can make them retch!); and second, equally, of not voting, as I have for my entire life, for what is known as the Left.

A reflexive vote?

Mechanical?

Had my thinking really become so Pavlovian that, as I'd just said to him, the Left was my family and you don't betray your family?

There was probably some of that.

And that's exactly what I say when, a few days later, questioned by a French weekly embarking on its umpteenth report on the "rightward drift" of French intellectuals,[1] I remarked that "I belong to the Left out of orientation and almost genetically; the Left is my family and you can't change families the way you change shirts."

Except that, put that way, this argument is frankly pathetic—and even goes against some of my most basic convictions.

I'm not crazy about the word *family*, first of all.

I don't like the ugly mafia whiff it acquires when applied to politics.

I hate the idea that goes with it, that you always have to choose the "family" in the event of conflict—over, for example, the truth: ah! the holy horror of "families" one finds in all the writers I admire ... the even greater horror, Louis Aragon thunders, in his *Defense of the Infinite,* of those "chosen" families, spiritual families and therefore political families ... the family one subjects oneself to out of free will—he explains as one who knows—the family of the spirit and the heart! It's "as if you had chosen your own tomb" ... as if you'd renounced any "morality," any "human greatness." ... Nothing but tuberculosis spreads quicker through families than this kind of lie ... and when the lie has won the day, when the family of spirit is irremediably corrupted, when the party of the heart no longer fulfills the hopes we've invested in it, doesn't the right thing to do become to betray it exactly as much as—Aragon, again—it has betrayed itself?

And I know better than anyone that everything in the movement of the world and of ideas has broken down, cracked, and sometimes nullified the famous split between Left and Right that has structured French politics for a century—a split that has become harder and harder to believe in.

Let's go over it again.

The words "Right" and "Left" have long been used to denote the most recent form of the struggle between the old and the modern:

though it no longer makes much sense to say, with a straight face, that the Right is condemned to be the "old" and that the Left necessarily represents the "modern," as it's been a while since, to borrow a phrase from Roland Barthes, I've been "indifferent about being modern."

"Right" and "Left" have been seen as two opposing attitudes toward this old belief, no longer exactly in "modernity," but in Progress, which was the catechism of former centuries: here again, the criteria have shifted; the main issues have been overturned by an increasingly conservative Left and a Right that no longer flinches at the sacred word of progress; and for the author of *Barbarism with a Human Face*—for one who stepped into the public debate more than thirty years ago by denouncing and deconstructing the "reactionary idea of Progress"—that's not really the question either.

We've believed, or wanted to believe, that the Left stood out for the distance it put between itself and powerful interests in general, and moneyed interests in particular—while the Right was in bed with them; that the Left was free whereas the Right was bought and paid for; that the Left was for average people while the cruel Right was dedicated, under a more or less transparent disguise, to its awful "class politics" which were "making the poor poorer"! As if the Right was completely undemocratic. . . . As if this new age of democracy, under the reign of Opinion, wasn't precisely the age that made disguises impossible, that tore off masks . . . As if, in this age of all-powerful visibility and transparency at every level, any political force could crudely, clearly, cynically present itself as being on "the side" of money and power and in so doing abandon the people and its votes to the other side . . . As if, with the joint triumph of the desire for vengeance, truth, and purity (these three forms, always leading to the worst, of what Nietzsche called the will to power), anyone could present a platform that was not, from top to bottom, from Right to Left, an appeal to what Nietzsche, again, called the greatest number . . . As if the structure and regime of the Benthamite Panopticon had been overturned ages ago: no longer slaves under the master's eye but the master himself, every master, under the intractable eye of a people who holds all the cards . . . Or as if, in the new planetary celebritocracy that has taken the place of oligarchy, the rules of the game had not changed entirely: the celebrities under the eye of the people, of its implacable demands and desires, beginning with the desire to cut off the heads of the powerful or, in any case, to appear to—the rule applies to Europe, but almost even more to the United States, as we saw during the misadventures of Bill Clinton, the personal attacks against Hillary, then Obama, and, in general, by the rise of the "political junkie."

There was, finally, the question of the revolution. Since the French Revolution, the word "revolution," the pure signifier, was, in France at least, the most serious political dividing line. The Left wanted it; the Right feared it. The Left, even and especially if they hated its provisionary guises, kept alive the dream of society in a happier incarnation and thought that this was exactly what made one a Leftist—the Right was made up of those people whose political outlook meant methodically putting down each and every revolution. That time, too, is past. And, for reasons I'll come back to, we have entered a period in which, as Michel Foucault once told me,[2] the question "Is the revolution possible?" has given way to a more troubling and much more radical question: "Is the revolution desirable?" And now, especially, the answer has become "No," a clear "No," not desirable at all, or, in any case, only for very few people. Who in the contemporary political landscape still openly dreams of wiping the slate clean? of a radical new beginning? of history split in two? of society as a blank page upon which the poem of the New Man will be inscribed? Europe has ended up aligning itself, in this matter, with realism, pragmatism, and, finally, American humility—and that is excellent news.

Anyway, that's all behind us now. All those benchmarks, all those parameters, have finally come crashing down. As have references to that "socialism" of which I wrote, thirty years ago, at the end of *Barbarism with a Human Face,* that I dreamed that in a dictionary of the year 2000 we could finally read the definition: "Socialism, n., cultural genre, born in Paris in 1848, died in Paris in 1968." May '68 is far off. And now 2000 as well. And even if the dictionary doesn't exist, even if so many socialists keep clinging to their socialism as an old actor clings to a repertory role, the most clear-sighted among them know that nothing good can come for the Left without breaking with much of their history, and even with their name.

Yet despite all this—despite that weighty tendency that Nicolas Sarkozy would exhibit by inviting, as he'd told me, leftist personalities to join him once he was elected, not only in the government, but in a whole range of commissions and positions of power and influence; despite the fact that, contrary to every expectation, the personalities thus invited would all, or almost all, answer his call; despite a stampede unprecedented in the history of the Republic, which is hard to attribute either to opportunism, impatience, to the desire to serve no matter what, or even to an epidemic, which fits so well with the current mood of political skepticism and unbelief—despite all that, I believed—and I still do—that there are still reasons to remain on the Left.

Why, then?

What's left of the Left?, as Nick Cohen would say.[3]

What am I thinking, clinging to a political identity which everything seems to indicate is being reshuffled and is even wasting away? Why am I turning my back on a man who nevertheless has real merits—first, of being a real living creature in a political universe so often populated by "the living dead" (Tolstoy) or by ghosts; second, of having the ambition, which is after all worthy, to get rid of this bubble, this microclimate, this state of psycho-political exception in which France has lived for decades and which was suffocating the country; third, to have weakened the National Front by embracing it and thereby accomplished something—we can agree on this—that so many men and women, including this author, have considered urgently necessary for the last twenty years; fourth, and finally, to plan (and, in the first months of his reign, he mostly kept the promise) to break with the leprosy that was, under all the Gaullist and Socialist governments for the last fifty years, France's "Arab Policy," and to move closer to the United States and Israel—all things I can only, once again, be thrilled to see?

I'll skip the hackneyed answers.

I'll skip—once again—the too-easy "defense of the oppressed."

I'll skip—I think it was the novelist Françoise Sagan who came up with the notion—the idea that "In the case of any given injustice, the man, or woman, of the Right will say it's inevitable; the man or woman of the Left will say that it's intolerable."

I'll skip the so-often-rebutted notion: "Only people on the Right wonder if there is a difference between Right and Left, and what it is."

I'll even skip—since it seems so obvious to me—the decisive role of what we once called "the social question": the scandal of extreme poverty . . . and the even greater scandal that is our consent to this misery . . . and the fact that, one day, I am sure, this consent will seem as mysterious and as odious as the consent of the Athenian democrats to slavery. . . .

RATHER, IN RETROSPECT, I realize that I was thinking about three certainties on that day.

To be "on the Left"—or, as an American would say, "liberal" or "progressive"—means three main things to me.

Primal Scenes

The first is fidelity to a certain number of images.

Yes, images.

They vary with each person.

They vary even more for people of different nationalities.

In my case, that day, a rush of images flashed through my mind almost as soon as I hung up the phone.

Of Léon Blum with his fist raised, July 14, 1936, facing his working-class people with his overly elegant suit, his glasses, and his dignified moustache, with the look of a successful man betraying his class, an attitude that long seemed to me one of the good definitions of the word *aristocracy*.

André Malraux, in the same period, at Garches, I think, during another rally—his jacket is too well tailored; his right hand seems to be praying; his left hand, in his pocket, makes him look extremely insolent; the presence of Communist apparatchiks Thorez and Duclos sitting aghast in the second row, behind the magnificent dandy, only adds to his insolence—this image, though I'm not sure why, moves me more than the more famous snapshots of him posing in front of the flying coffins of the España squadron.

Malraux, once again: 1945; the first poster of his film about that same war in Spain; a stylized fighter in the foreground, machine gun in hand, the other hand reaching for a yellow and red sun that he seems to be trying to stop, like Joshua, but which is hurrying on; a plane above his head, as in a child's drawing; and the column of fighters lined up behind him, who look like they're about to attack the sky itself.

My own father in the same war, a young Republican volunteer in a shabby uniform, with an old gun, during a mild spring, under an intense and dramatic sky, an avalanche of light on a rocky, thorny landscape, and, in his eyes, under his cap, a pride, a haughtiness, maybe even including a bit of irony, which never left him and which a part of me has always liked to think was acquired there, among those troops.

My father once more, in the other war, the next one, the one for which the Spanish Civil War was just a dress rehearsal: anti-Nazi, not anti-German; Free French, an oxymoron in those dark days; those days in which being both Free and French was a furtive, clandestine notion— yet one that was greater than France itself: in those days I can't properly speak of images: just that bundle of documents dated July 19, 1944, and signed by General Diego Brosset, commander of the First Motorized Infantry Division, that "citation" of the soldier André Lévy, leading the charge at Monte Cassino: "an ambulance runner ready, day and night, no matter what the mission; who evacuated the wounded beneath mortar fire with a total disregard for danger and returned again and again to gather up the wounded under violent enemy fire."

Me myself, about twenty years old, in Bangladesh, my mind in the past, regretting having been born so late, feeling that I'd been born into the wrong time and in the wrong country: was I worthy of my illustrious ancestors? I was finished with the liberal moment; sick of the whole comedy: it may not have been the best time in my life, but I still wanted to change things a bit: this was surely not the struggle of the century, not the salt of the earth, but it was an oppressed people crying out, and just like the elderly Malraux I had to choose its side.

Me again in Portugal, in the summer of 1974, in boiling but glorious temperatures, the light slowly combusting in the evening on Marquês de Pombal Square, where a fervent but calm crowd, resolute but peaceful, was burying the evil spirits of Salazarism.

Portugal once again, the next summer; young captains courageous;

Otelo de Carvalho as a baroque, Shakespearean actor; life bursting out everywhere; uprisings without anger or sad passion; the end of the market of hatred; barracks and monasteries transformed into winter palaces; basins emptied of their fountains, in the deserted and respect-fully preserved castles; girls with champagne-colored necks and joyous shoulders; endless nights; stars for every night; the spinning suns of my dreams of a true and great life; a hundred flowers with the thousand colors of a memory come to life; incense and dizziness; lights without fires; lost orientations; a unique, unbalanced geography; Paris, for ex-ample, reduced to the status of a distant province of a fifth empire whose capital was here; Dominique de Roux, the adept of Céline, ele-vated to the rank of a great red conspirator giving Malaparte's *Technique of the Coup d'État* to one person and Trotsky's *Military Writings* to another, and, yet another day, running through the newspaper kiosks of the city, especially around all the barracks, and buying up all the copies of *Libéra-tion,* which was, with Jean Daniel's *Le Nouvel Observateur,* the favorite paper of the young captains and which published, that morning, an ex-posé about his own extremist past on the other side; we still didn't know how to resuscitate bodies, said Malraux, whom he didn't like, but we were starting to figure out how to resuscitate dreams.

Still later, in Italy. And, in Italy, the university amphitheaters filled to overflowing, overheated, wherever I came, at the invitation of the Lotta Continua collectives, to preach against terrorism—which meant trying to explain to these rudderless young people, on the edge, that the temptation of armed struggle was, at this point in time, a fascist temp-tation. Bologna, Milan. Shouts. Raised fists. Terrible, exalted condem-nations. Embittered fervor. "Lévy we'll shoot you in the head," graffiti in pink letters which, in the sun, looked like tears of blood, on the façade of the University of Rome. These free agents who were said to come to the Aula Magna with .38s under their coats. The day I had to fight my way in and out of the room. The devil in their faces. Naked ni-hilism. The mystery of these girls, crazed virgins, full of charms and ha-tred, bitter, budding murderesses. Red Italy? Black Italy? The two, of course. Black because red. Fascist because terrorist. The scowl of left-ism. Its dead soul. Its dark shadow. Why do you think, you fools, that I got involved in the Battisti case, the repentant terrorist who had been in France for twenty years, with the formal consent of Mitterrand, and who was odiously arrested by Sarkozy's France?

Or again in Mexico. The first Mexico: Artaud; Tarahumaras; Chiapas in the days before Subcomandante Marcos; ragged, nameless despair; the unidentified century; the Left without rhetoric; the evil of globalization, but the real one, the real deal, the one which correctly acknowledges that there are many worlds and that misery is deeper in some than in others.

The second Mexico: ten years later; another time; on a speaking tour with my New Philosophy friends, including André Glucksmann; Octavio Paz leading the way, with his old Indian head and that look in his eyes like a thoughtful beast; the armada of communism refusing to back down; violence, once again; the bomb threats in Guadalajara; the time I had to calm the ruckus by coming up with a Soviet who, throughout the whole evening, allotted speaking times, with an implacable equity, five minutes here, five minutes there, between the people in the room and the orators who had confiscated knowledge; where was it, the real Left—was it these half-baked demons who whipped themselves up into a fury if anyone dared attack Castro? Or was it us, simply trying, according to the principles of that internationalism which was the best of progressivism, to let the voices of the Eastern European dissidents be heard by people who couldn't get Chile and the overthrow of Allende out of their minds?

Or, of course, Bosnia. No longer images, here, but a film. No longer snapshots but a long, slow dance. It's no longer something from a past that refuses to move on, but a burning present, with colors and smells mingling, and which, twelve years later, I have never managed to mourn properly. The baying of terrorized men. The grating cry in the distance signaling a dead body. The tarlike texture of coffee left in abandoned bunkers. The image of Samir, on our way down a bombed-out Grondj Hill, throwing himself on top of me and probably saving my life. The image of Zlatko Dizdarevic, in one of those endless conversations that helped us pass the time when the guns were thundering too loudly and we didn't want to show how scared we were: "The Left," he said, his laughter bursting out like that of an annoyed giant, "the Left, I'll tell you, means just saying no to hell." Or again, the image of that group of intellectuals, atheists in the catacombs, who did not want to leave their city and talked about Sartre while the snipers were targeting them. Images . . . Images . . . All images piled up in my memory, blending into one another, blurring: so close, so close, and yet I'm surprised, sometimes at night, like a thief in my own haunted house, to have to go back to my notes to nail one of these images down.

Or, finally, in the United States. That American Left of which it's popular to say, even in America, that it doesn't exist, that it's a contradiction in terms, etc.—and which nevertheless gave me (I can't help it) some of the most enduring images in my little Olympus: the battle for civil rights . . . Rosa Parks . . . Dr. King . . . the marches against the Vietnam War and the young people who back then were an example of insurrection for the whole world . . . Bob Dylan and Joan Baez, *political* idols of my youth . . . that wind of rebellion and freedom that blew there first and that didn't arrive in Europe until much later, its strength much weakened . . .

so that's where we are.

I'm speaking of myself, of course. But what I'm saying applies to everyone—including here, in the United States, where, for example, the little international club of Bosnia's friends had its very special members: Susan Sontag, Christopher Hitchens, John Burns. I hope the ones I forget can forgive me. Because all of us have memories that are dear to us. All of us are what we are because of the dead who live on in us, and the living that enlarge us. And for each of us, for each new political adventure, it is the images, solid as flesh, specific even when they blend with others, that make us what we are, that stay with us, that follow us.

Could it be that when people get involved in politics, they're trying to keep their youth alive, and that, once they're involved, they tend to join families?

And does my insistence on sticking with a Left that has done everything to empty itself of its substance mean I'm clinging to yesterday rather than today, to nostalgia rather than to the future, to a time gone by rather than to the present day—the old story of the mature man who watches the burial of the young man he once was and who wears himself out, one last time, trying to resemble him?

Yes, maybe.

But not only.

I don't think that's all there is to it.

Since, as strange as it may seem when one looks back over the creaky ruin it has become, the Left, too, was once young.

As unimaginable as it may seem to one who considers "that great backward falling corpse which the worms have already started to chew" (Sartre, in his 1960 preface to Paul Nizan's *Aden, Arabie*),[1] the Left has always been both very old and very young. And that's how it is today, and how part of it remains: as old as those ruins we must demolish, like those apartment blocks in the *banlieues*; as young as hope, when it is something bigger than our own lives. And it is this youth, this not-yet-dead part of itself, this idealism that it still bears, whatever one says about it, whatever it says about itself, that I am thinking of when—looking back over these scenes, and others as well, many others—I say I belong to "the" Left: these images that come and go in my intimate existence, that touch a very distant chord, that give us our truths.

But that's not enough, of course.

And if I'd only been thinking about that, if I merely had that gallery of snapshots in mind, if my attachment was only to a novel from another age, if I was only keeping faith with those Spaniards, those Maquisards, that magnificent father, those Portuguese, those rebellious, insubordinate Americans, then I'm sure the future president would have brought up at least two objections, if our conversation had gone on any longer.

First objection. Those images belong to everyone. Nobody has a monopoly on being haunted or inspired by them. These bright specters are like the dybbuks of Jewish folklore who jump from one soul to the next, their very liberty refuting the silly, predictable notion that we own our own ghosts. Remember Romain Gary's novel *The Dance of Genghis*

Cohn, in which the dybbuk of a no-name Jew invaded the mind of a former Nazi and drove him mad. But Nicolas Sarkozy . . . This man, a
right-winger, to be sure, but not the devil and not a Nazi . . . It's true
enough that nobody can forbid anyone to be haunted by the image of
André Malraux in Spain, of Léon Gambetta in his balloon, or of Jean
Jaurès pleading for the love of country and world. Nobody can forbid a
candidate from carrying with him the last words of Guy Môquet, that
seventeen-year-old Communist Resistant gunned down by the Nazis
at a moment when—October 1941—his party was barely emerging from its class collaboration with the uniformed proletarians of
the Wehrmacht. And nobody can regret that the first decision of the
candidate-cum-president was to have these words read out, at the beginning of every school year, in every class in France, by teachers who,
before him, would clearly never have dreamed of doing so. We can have
different gods and still worship the same saints. And worshipping
saints, being illuminated by a quick flash of images, is not enough to
make an identity.

Second objection. Alongside these images are others. And when I
see my friends gloating, when I hear these temple guardians exhorting
their flocks to unbreakable fidelity, telling the story of their family
without a single stain, illustrated from one end to the other like an illuminated book of hours, I can't help thinking about other pictures, less
flattering, less glorious, less bursting with power and life, but, alas, no
less real, and which show the other side. Guy Mollet, cigarette in his
mouth, jowls drooping a bit like the old Jean-Marie Le Pen. François
Mitterrand, the other one, the first one, from the governments of the
1950s, who was pacifying the Algerian *djebels* with flamethrowers, his
hair black and thick but his mouth limp, his eyes strangely more dead
than in photographs taken twenty or thirty years later, his flat and
boneless face, as if his cynicism was a kind of inner leprosy that had
eaten away his features. Blum himself, in those newsreels where he's
gasping for breath, with a broken voice, his hand jerking around in
front of his lips as if it were trying to chase off the words that are coming out of his mouth, or trying to push far away from himself the blood-
drenched words already echoing back—Blum, yes, explaining that the

Spanish Popular Front is going to die, that my father's comrades-in-arms were going to die like rats in the streets of Barcelona and that the French Popular Front wasn't going to lift a finger to save them. Those American Democrats who rallied to Bush in 2000, as they had to Nixon thirty years before, and rallying more generally to the worst racist ideas of the clans of the Old South—what claim do those people still have to be called Democrats? And then the image of dishonor itself, which was the long involvement of the Left, the European Left, with Stalinism, which haunts me too—because it was the Left once again that accepted the worst crimes of the most Mafioso Communism, whose prattle stifled the cries from the Russian, Cuban, and Chinese gulags, which in France, before the National Front, created the detestable concept of a "threshold of intolerance," wading through the blood of innocents, sticking its nose right into the manure, allowing itself to reflect all the infamies that a human face can reflect, while still claiming to be the Left—what a disaster!

In other words, images aren't enough.

If we're going to compare images, I'd have to agree that there are as many images in my head that shame the Left as there are that do it proud.

And if all I had were these images, the magic lantern we all have at the back of our minds to project our beloved shadows, then I wouldn't be able to choose a side—weren't they, or some similar to them, the reason a third Lévy—my friend Benny Lévy, an ex-revolutionary convert to a well-informed and even orthodox Judaism—the reason he said to me, in one of our last conversations: "I've never been on the Left; I've been a Maoist; I've been as revolutionary as anyone else; but on the Left, a leftie, related to all those ghosts you've mentioned, a relative of all those wretches who always liked to imagine themselves belonging to the family of murderers, no thank you, I'd have done a lot of things in my life but that, never, never . . . !"

But anyway. Those are my images. They made me who I am and will never leave me. And no matter what anyone says, they are what first come to mind when I say that I am loyal to the Left.

My Primal Scenes

Then there are the events.

Yes, I said to myself on that afternoon, as I was turning over in my head the future president's half-affectionate, half-threatening words: being on the Left means something more than those moving images, which can be misleading and even false: it means a certain number of "great" events, of "historic" events, as the saying goes, which serve as great, very great, markers of our identity.

These events are rare.

They are exceptional, in the literal sense of the word.

Each of them pierces our very being, bursts through our ordinary days, interrupts our well-ordered existence.

It's wrong, moreover, to say "historic"; you can say "historic events," but that isn't it: it would be better to say "nonhistoric"—and still better to describe such events as "ahistoric" or even "antihistoric," since they so upend the laws of normal history that history, reasserting itself, resists and opposes them.

A characteristic of these events that we'll therefore call "historic" or "ahistoric," the quality that, according to Heidegger, distinguishes them from events that he rightly calls "natural," is that we can never say, "That's it; it's over; it's run its course; its meaning is settled; we now know how it went and what it meant"—and that is why they are such great markers of our identities.

So what are these events, precisely?

What events do we have in mind when, as I do, we stubbornly cling to this big corpse that the Left already was in the days of Sartre and Nizan, and of which the least we can say is that it hasn't been resuscitated since?

Here, too, it all depends on your personal history.

If you're German, for example, and consider yourself an heir of the "traitor" and "antifascist" Willy Brandt.

Or if you're Italian and you recall Amadeo Bordiga, or the writers Leonardo Sciascia, Pier Paolo Pasolini, or Alberto Moravia.

Or Spanish, inspired by the antifascist Civil War of 1936.

Or, once again, American, shaped by the teachings of Eugene V. Debs, Norman Thomas, Michael Harrington, Irving Howe—and haunted, still, by the memory of Rosa Parks, of Martin Luther King's peaceful marches, by the struggles and protests against the Vietnam War, by the memory of the democratic movement in Chile and the man who dug its grave, Kissinger; or by the election of John Fitzgerald Kennedy.

For a Frenchman—the situation I am most familiar with, of course, and for which I take myself as an example, though everyone can fill in his or her own examples—for a Frenchman these events are common knowledge.

Maybe it's no longer, as it was in the nineteenth century, the French Revolution—although . . . it's not so clear, after all, that the debate on the French Revolution has lasted long enough. . . . In a country where, two centuries later, the question of whether to call the Vendée massacres a genocide is still current, we can't take for granted that we're completely at peace with that supreme event. . . . And the truth is that, even today, I have to admit that Mao Zedong was at least partly right when he famously quipped, apropos of the "lessons" he drew from the "revolution of 1789": "It's still too early to say." It might not be 1848 either, nor the separation of church and state, nor the Commune— gigantic events, to be sure, outside the normal flow of history, to a certain extent untimely, because they cannot be reduced to their contexts or conditions, these moments that broke with previous history, these interruptions in time that were also long-standing concentrations, themselves once red lines that people fought about, which tore apart and oriented generations of men and women—though . . . are we entirely sure that those questions, too, are dead and buried? Could we swear that the repercussions of those shocks cannot still be felt in the discussions about, for example, the critical situation of our *banlieues*?

But anyway . . . When I speak of events that still separate ideological and political families, when I try to think of the specific events that, on that day, consciously or not, I had in my memory and which kept me from being able to say yes to the future president, I'm really thinking of just four events that, along with those images, have made me who I am.

THE FIRST IS VICHY, that sinister nightmare from which France has clearly had trouble waking. Should it? Should we—first question— forget Vichy's crimes and write them off in the name of passing time? And should we—second question—just say that those were tough times for France, that the intrigues in the headquarters of Pétain's regime in Vichy were sheer pandemonium—to borrow a term from Mitterrand's last phase—and put it all into perspective, contextualize them, and, at the end of the day, justify them? The question was already being asked the day after the regime fell. And on that same day, voices could be heard saying that yes, you had to understand, excuse, let off the hook, let the dead bury the dead and keep Frenchmen from attacking and hating one another: France was a smoking ruin, France was a sewer, and it's a clever person indeed who knows whom to trust in a gutter. France had been defeated, France was no longer itself during those terrible years, during that parenthesis, and, as André Mornet, prosecutor in the Pétain case, said, we had to "erase them from our history." . . . I think the opposite. I think that the crimes for which Vichy took the initiative (and we know that many of them were on its own initiative) can never be excused. I think that the only way to free ourselves is not by forgetting them but by keeping them alive in our memory (I don't think we should give an inch on the "duty of remembrance" described by Primo Levi, theorized in the eighties and so often de-nounced today). And above all, I think (this is the biggest dividing line) that if these crimes are inexcusable, and if we have to keep their memory alive, then Vichy was not just another name for good old French conservatism, or for a slightly muscular authoritarianism, or for a nationalist distraction—but that it was, in the strict sense of the word, fascism.

THE SECOND IS the Algerian War. France is still emerging from the painful debate which the party of the former and the future president had taken the initiative to begin, and which centered around a law or-dering future school curricula to recognize "the positive role of the French presence overseas, and especially in North Africa." Enough re-pentance! this right wing was saying. Enough beating our breasts over a few crimes we may have committed here or there! We built schools and hospitals, we built kilometer after kilometer of highways and railroads, we brought those backward peoples the miracle of the Enlightenment, coveted by the whole world: doesn't that justify taking a few liberties with the law? The crimes, especially, of the Front de Libération Na-tionale, its leaders' cynicism, the disaster of the one-party socialism built on the ruins of the French endeavor and resulting in such a huge amount of pain and death: doesn't that put our own mistakes into per-spective, and excuse them? Well, I don't think so. I don't like the idea that my neighbor's crimes excuse my own. I don't, once again, think that this is a debate on which compromise is possible. Algeria, an ad-venture which began with the horrors of "smoking people out" with suffocation and fire, with racially determined roundups, and other mass crimes committed by Bugeaud's hellish legions; which continued with the Indigence Code, the daily humiliations of the so-called native populations, and then the Sétif massacre which was the real cause, nine years later, of the actual war; and which concluded, fifteen years later, at the Villa Susini or elsewhere, with the cries of the people tortured by Generals Aussaresses and Massu . . . I refuse to call that adventure a work of civilization. Here again, what I favor is not dwelling on the crime but creating a constructed, well-informed, organized memory of it. I call the Left those who believe that colonialism, the submission of one people to another people's law, a collective servitude that is always written with the red ink of the blood of individuals, is perhaps not the only crime in the history of humanity, to say the least; and obviously not one that excuses other crimes committed in the same places by anti-colonial liberation movements—but who believe that it is still a crime; a great crime; and an inexcusable one at that.

MAY 1968. I am not a fervent veteran of May '68. I was one of those people who, the day after, emphasized that the notion that "the beach was beneath the paving-stones" could be naïvely naturalistic and utopian. And far be it from me to join those who, forty years on, try to summon the "spirit of May." But there are two major ways to see that event. There is the France that cannot quite get over it and vomits up all that history—cultivating, meanwhile, the nostalgia for an ordered society, with natural and agreed-upon authorities, it supposedly over-turned: May '68 as a black hole sucking up everything that was most solid in the patriarchal, reactionary, archaic France of the Gaullist and pre-Gaullist age. And there is the France that, for the same reasons, sees it as a happy moment: new rights; new freedoms, novel power, for women to do what they wanted with their bodies, and to choose whether they would be mothers; modernity; perhaps the true moment when modernity entered our country; joy; poetry; yes, a real moment of poetry, but in acts; passions communicated; impatiences shared; "in-flamed disorders" (Antonin Artaud, *Héliogabale*); a nocturnal journey through cruelty and madness; throwing dice against the sky; letting them crash to earth; watching, between earth and sky, a wave of insub-ordination that we'd capture and channel through our heads; the cops will never again go through our souls, our hearts, and our bodies; art against culture; life against survival; all those lives, cracked, intimidated, or just faded into premature old age, which awoke for the springtime. A world that doesn't change its foundations but its tastes; the taste not for getting but for giving; ah, how dumb is the idea of a sensual, preda-

tory May '68, inventor of consumer egoism, when it was exactly the opposite, a true moment, in fact, of giving and of giving back! And not to
mention (I'll come back to this, since it's obviously the essential point)
the moment of the final struggle with "doddering Moscow," of the
break with all those old European Communist parties tossed into the
dustbin of what we were starting to call red fascism—without even
mentioning the birth, at that moment, of the Left's, and the masses',
antitotalitarianism, which had been seeking its expression for the previous fifty years . . .

AND FINALLY, LONG before all this, at the turn of the previous century,
"the Affair," the real one, the only one: one that was, François Mauriac
would say, the inaugural scene of "an ongoing civil war."

Contemporary French history begins here. Dreyfus's innocence was
clearly established. But the extraordinary thing was that a whole fac-
tion of the political classes, along with important sectors of public
opinion, acted as if innocence didn't matter, and that asserting it could
only weaken the Army, the State, Order, and thus the country, even further. The Right, therefore, grouped together those whose highest values were Tradition, Authority, Nation, the Social Body and, along with
these values, hatred of intellectuals, democracy, Parliament. The Left
included—besides the opposite of all those values—all those who defended one man's rights, and thus the Rights of Man, and everything
that went along with them: freedom; truth; the critical mind-set; secular government; "when the *raison d'État* loses its way, bring reason back to
the state"; when the individual with no collective importance is threatened with being ground under by the collective, take, instinctually, the
side of the individual. Read *Notre jeunesse* by Charles Péguy. Bernard
Lazare's *J'accuse,* which stood as a model for Zola's. Thirty years later,
Léon Blum's *Souvenirs sur l'affaire. The Jewish State* by Theodor Herzl,
whose experience covering Dreyfus's trial led him to spark the national
liberation movement that eventually led to the creation of Israel. And
read what that other intellectual wrote, Charles Maurras, founder of
the Action Française, who places race and nation above any truth; and

who could only utter, half a century later, when a verdict was handed down condemning him for collaboration with the Nazis, his famous phrase: "This is Dreyfus's revenge." Mauriac was right. It's all there. It all begins there. And France, a century later, returns there: every time one side starts to prefer injustice to disorder; every time the other side stands up against the injustice—no matter how minor, or apparently harmless, or costly to repair. That is the fourth event.

IT'S TRUE THAT NONE of these events can completely justify the clear division of Right and Left.

We know, for example, that the pro-Dreyfus forces recruited on the Right as well, and that a significant portion of the Left (Jules Guesde, but also Jean Jaurès) took their time in getting involved in what sounded to them like yet another internal quarrel of the bourgeoisie: Ah, that hatred of the "Jewish plutocracy" in the Left of the day! Its distaste at having to take the side of a representative of what the socialist Édouard Drumont called "Jewish France"; and the hideous remark of the founder of *L'Humanité,* Jean Jaurès, who, returning from a trip to Algeria in 1895, grumbled about a kind of socialism that expressed itself in the "slightly restrictive" form of anti-Semitism![1]

We know that some figures involved in France's May '68 weren't exactly on the Left: there was my friend Benny Lévy, head of the Parisian Maoists at the beginning of the seventies; but there was also Maurice Clavel, a herald, if that's what he was, of what he called "the rebellion of life" and who, everyone knew, was an admirer of Maurras and a fervent Christian and who—he certainly said it often enough!—knew of only one revolution, the one that began two thousand years before on the day of the Pentecost, under the aegis of a certain Jesus of Nazareth; and there was *Combat,* the *Combat* of Philippe Tesson, who would soon send me to cover Bangladesh, for a paper that, during those days of general strikes and riots, was being sold only in the streets of the Latin Quarter. Who, today, remembers *Combat?* Who remembers the marvelous, unique echo chamber it was for the student uprising of those weeks? And who, among those who do remember it, also remembers that a few years earlier the same paper had also opened its columns to writers who favored a French Algeria?

We also know that the colonial question divided the Left as much as the Right, then and now.

And things are almost worse when it comes to Vichy. There were so many socialists, neo-socialists, syndicalists, anarchists, Left pacifists, and sometimes Communists, who, as if they wanted to unleash complete confusion, took part in its crimes. . . . The constant *question* of Vichy, which, forty years later, reserved such new and strange surprises for us: a left-wing president, François Mitterrand, telling us that "in his soul and his conscience" he knew that neither "the Republic" nor "France" had "anything to do with that"; a right-wing president, Jacques Chirac, who, on July 16, 1995, at the Vél d'Hiv in Paris, finally called the infamous crime by its name by mentioning the "enduring debt" of a France that "did not keep its word" and "committed an irreparable crime."[2]

I understand very well, in other words, that none of these events is enough to separate the left wing from the right. I am aware that these events themselves—along with their memory—are split by the same dividing line that they purport to draw.

And part of me says that it might not be one situation or another that draws the line, which clearly notes where it goes, and which sees whether it can be drawn through ourselves.

But another part of me resists, and refuses, the erasure of old landmarks—so much so that, over the course of the following weeks, something else would become more and more obvious to me: the validation, by Nicolas Sarkozy himself, to an extent that I could never have imagined, of the idea that these "great" events are what will continue to draw the lines in the future.

WE'RE NOT THERE YET—but still . . .

I'll skip over Sarkozy's Dreyfusism, even though his various initiatives, like the "selective immigration" policy, the creation of the Ministry of Immigration and National Identity—even the communitarian bent we started to note in the candidate's declarations about, for example, the Islam of France—are not exactly heading toward the defense of universal values that is, according to Julien Benda's *The Treason of the Intellectuals,* the essence of Dreyfusism.

But I am thinking of Sarkozy's strange declarations, strange and strangely pervasive,[3] which effectively state that France "didn't invent the Final Solution" (which, put this way, is obviously not wrong); that it didn't "give in to the totalitarian temptation" (which, on the other hand, is wrong, and means nothing more and nothing less than exculpating those French policemen who, on the morning of July 17, 1942, went to arrest the Jews in their neighborhoods, taking care "not to forget the little ones"); and that it "did not commit crimes against humanity or genocide" (wrong again, since arresting and deporting French citizens whose only mistake was having been born Jewish meets, in and of itself, the definition of genocide as defined not only in the Penal Code but also in the Nuremberg trials). It doesn't matter what the future president does. It doesn't matter how often he heaps praise on the martyrs of the Plateau des Glières or on the young Guy Môquet, shot by the Nazis. It doesn't matter that, on July 21, 2007, he went with Simone Veil to pay his respects at the Holocaust Memorial and that he and his prime minister make unambiguous statements. The fact remains, and will always remain, that he campaigned on those words. The fact remains, and will always remain, that by doing so, he helped negate the work of one or two generations who struggled to preserve that memory.

As for colonial affairs, I'm thinking of his attitude, from campaign stop to campaign stop,[4] in dwelling on the theme of "French pride" and promising "never to linger in the demagoguery of repentance"; in claiming that our country "also owes its greatness" to the men and women who were both "witnesses to and actors in" this "civilizing mission unprecedented in our history," meaning the colonial mission; and by constantly repeating that if France has a moral debt it's toward the French Algerians and the Algerian soldiers in the French army who were "cowardly abandoned." There, once more, our opinions diverged. There, once again, I found myself unable to vote for someone who felt no debt toward the three to four hundred thousand Algerians killed in a war that, for many long years, did not dare speak its name.

Finally, I'm thinking of President Sarkozy's embrace, like no other politician's before him, of the fearful, oversensitive, and wounded France that sees the source of all its troubles in May '68—I'm thinking of those crowds at his campaign rallies practically swooning at the very idea that someone finally dared to say out loud what they'd been thinking to themselves for the last forty years. . . .[5] How could men or women of the Left allow themselves, once again, to vote for a man who, throughout his entire campaign, insisted that he saw May '68 as the beginning of our contemporary "cynicism"; the secret inspiration of the "delinquents and the rioters"; the origin of the "crazy cult of money"; of the reign "of short-term profit and rudderless financial capitalism"? How could one support a president outrageous enough to say, at one of his final rallies,[6] that he only had two days left, not a single day more, to "liquidate once and for all" the values and the legacy of the very event that had, among all its other merits, illuminated the connection, the axis, between the two fascisms, brown and red? "Liquidate": a strange choice of words. "Finish off" that moment of real clear-eyed thinking, right when they were sowing confusion everywhere, what a strange idea . . . This platform didn't amuse me. It sent a chill down my spine.

But once again, my own personal case hardly matters.

The main thing is that these gestures and words made it hard to believe that the old debate was over.

The main thing is the very fact that Sarkozy thought he had to give three revisionist readings of three major, epoch-shaping events.

If we needed another reason, there it was: in the France of the early twenty-first century, being on the Left, believing that the question of Right and Left was not entirely meaningless, was not giving an inch on the questions of Vichy, the crimes of colonialism, May '68, or, of course, the legacy of Dreyfus.

Act, Then Listen

And then, finally, there are reflexes.

Yes, after saying that the Left is shaped by images and events, I have to add that it is also shaped by reflexes.

NOT OPINIONS, CONVICTIONS, life philosophies, visions of the world. Real reflexes. But a reflex is never just a reflex; nor, even less, an instinct; since nothing is more intelligent, more charged with culture and memory, than a good and sure reflex—since reflexes are blocks of petrified memory, thought, and knowledge.

Which reflexes, then?

Where do they come from? How are they created?

At the end of the day it's the same thing.

Pure deductions from earlier events, and from those great encounters of memory and history.

Just as famous laws bear the name of the speakers who proposed them, the reflexes I am speaking of, the great reflexes that make up our identity, bear the name of the scenes or the events where they were born.

One example of a reflex born of these primal scenes (the scene, in this case, which I borrow from my family's history, of Jews, Moroccan fusiliers, people of every color, fighting in the same battalions of the Armée d'Afrique during the Second World War): my almost physical incapacity to separate the fight against anti-Semitism from the fight against racism. I know they are different. I know that they are theoretically different, because their objects are different (anti-Semitism and racism differ, we have known at least since Freud, in that the hatred of the "small" difference is something different from the hatred of the "greater"). And I know that powerful interests are working to make sure they stay different on a practical level too (all those new anti-Semites who hate Jews—I'll come back to this—in the very name of antiracism). But in my heart of hearts I also know that I'll never buy that. I know that for me it would be the most bitter defeat to have to accept that difference. I know that I will remain faithful to the decision I made almost a quarter of a century ago, when, together with Coluche, Simone Signoret, and others, we sponsored an antiracist initiative whose first vow was to mourn equally for an attack on a Jew, an Arab, or a representative of any other minority. I know indeed that I will do everything humanly possible to join those two struggles, which, despite their differences, are equally urgent. Are you yourselves, my American friends, resigned to breaking the pact that united, in a single cause, your own Jewish and black minorities? Would you happily give up the sacred, magnificent, and vital union that made your country great? Don't you, in other words, realize how disastrous it would be to allow "competition between victims" to triumph over the "solidarity of the shaken" so dear to the Czech dissident philosopher Jan Patočka? Another example of a reflex since—let's say—my Portuguese years: the trouble I have putting struggles for freedom at the expense of struggles for equality, or the reverse. I know, of course, that this, too, is problematic. I know everything that, in theory, could divide the two. And when I began this book, I was emerging from a literary and political season in which the company of Tocqueville—and more specifically the Tocqueville who journeyed to America—had made me aware, just in time, of the progress of an idea of equality that could eventually take over from liberty (just as, on the other hand, I heard a worldwide defense of the idea that the limitless progress of liberty could eventually produce

new, growing, unacceptable inequalities). Well, my reflex (and here
again, it is really a reflex) is to do everything, truly everything, to stave
off anything that might seem fatal in this double accusation. My reflex
(immediate, unconditional—only after which come theories and ratio-
nalizations) has always been and still is not to accept the sacrifice of
one ("First freedom; we'll worry about equality later"—the battle cry of
the ultraconservatives, enemies of the Welfare State, convinced that
those poor bastards need to fend for themselves when they're sick,
homeless, or unemployed) or the paralysis of others ("Equality first;
since what good is freedom if it's only on paper, and comes at the price
of too many injustices?"—the old Marxist anthem updated by people
like Walden Bello, Naomi Klein, Arundhati Roy, and other apostles of
John Holloway—like "deglobalization"). So being on the Left, for me, has
always meant seeking, at all costs, and even despite apparent impracti-
cality, the double crown of freedom and equality, which—in France as
in the United States and Great Britain—reflects the best of the Enlightenment and its legacy, one simultaneously feeding off of, and opening
onto, the other, a liberal torpedo in the egalitarian granite, a demand for
equality in liberal logic, the two-headed eagle of the desire for emancipation which can be complete only if it doesn't try to sacrifice either
freedom or equality (an endless production of rights; a limitless extension of their number and their domain; but an extension, also limitless,
of the number of people who have those rights).

Or take another example: that taste for war, or for conflict. We used
to call it class struggle. Of course, I will never again say "class struggle,"
a phrase dirtied by so many evildoers. But that societies are divided
against themselves in the sense of Machiavelli; that hate rather than
love is their link, in the Freudian sense of the term; that a "free government" is a government that is "agitated," as Montesquieu would say;
and that we can't depend on the soft hand of providence to deal with
this agitation and division—all this, on the other hand, seems unques-
tionable. We do see injustice. We do see signs of what the ancients
called the unequal division of Goods and Evils. Some people, looking at
this fact, say: "Let it be, let it play itself out, it will work out fine in the
end." And other people answer, reflexively, before even thinking too

much about it: "Conflict . . . will never resolve itself peacefully . . . and of course that conflict can come in many forms. . . . You can emphasize the political, the social, or other. . . . You can—and this is the great superiority of Anglo-Saxon law—wish for conflicts to end not in rupture but in truce. . . . You can, you must, consider that it's the honorable position of politics to create, wherever radicalism, and therefore a rupture, looms, provisory, modest, revisable solutions. . . . What's not possible is changing a society without conflict. . . . You can't accept that this conflict-ridden structure be finessed, since that would be antisocial. . . . And being aware of this antisociality, recognizing the dissimilarities among humans, betting on this discord which is our destiny and which can be transformed into our opportunity: that, finally, is a good definition of the Left. . . ."

And then some reflexes come not from scenes but from events— the reflexes that become second nature when one refuses to forget any of the events I have described as shaping—through their gaps, their light, and their storms—a certain idea of the lesser evil and the most just.

I'll take the French case once again—letting the reader fill in his or her own particular examples.

The Dreyfusard reflex: not the calculation, not the reasoning, but the reflex, truly the reflex—there is no better word—which urges us, in the face of a baying crowd and a solitary person facing that baying crowd, to hear, first of all, what that single person has to say—and the reflex that resists all the voices that say, every time: "What does that one person have to do with you? Aren't there other people? Other solitary people? Other martyrs? Why does it have to be this one and not that one? Why choose him? To what does he owe this privilege, this election?" I tend to think that the voice of that lone figure always echoes all the others, as well as the universal (Dreyfus, of course; but also the kidnapped, martyred Daniel Pearl, and before him those Cuban, Soviet, Polish, Czech dissidents who were by immanent and eminent grace greater than themselves and their own individual destiny; and *after* all of them, the irregular, secessionist dissident from the Arab-Muslim world today . . .).

The Vichy reflex, or—more precisely—the anti-Vichy reflex, or—even more precisely—the antifascist reflex: this one has its source in the memory of historical fascism, in the fear of its return, and in ears tuned to the slightest hint that, just as we did under Vichy, we are about to submit to it. That was why, when Ilan Halimi was murdered in Paris—an event some people wanted to write off as just one more awful murder, just one more sleazy *banlieue* issue without political importance—I myself immediately saw an anti-Semitic murder—since when you remember fascism and Vichy, what else can you call the murder of a young Jew tortured and then killed because of the idea that he was Jewish and that Jews have money? It was the same reflex that made me sniff—at a time when others saw nothing more than some madly skirmishing blacks involved in a local tribal war—the bad odor of a mass pogrom, of a genocide, in Rwanda. And that was the reflex that, again, under other names, in other forms, and even in countries that, like the United States, have never seen actual fascism victorious, makes me smell the bad odor again: such and such a way of denouncing public figures that recalls the black hours of McCarthyism; or such and such a pointless discussion of the cases and the circumstances under which torture might seem legitimate—suddenly, again, we need a truly antifascist culture. . . .

The '68 reflex (to translate: antiauthoritarian, which means antitotalitarian, since it in some sense was at the origin of the great movement of antitotalitarian, pro-human-rights revolts in the seventies and eighties): the reflex that makes it hard for me, even today, to see much difference between a brown (Nazi), red (Stalinist), or green (Islamist) despot; the reflex that keeps me from waiting, before I condemn a dictatorship, to see what place it occupies in the geopolitical Great Game of the moment; nor, even less, if it is pro-this or anti-that or anti-anti-something else; it's what makes me see, beneath the mask of a Putin who is always, everywhere introduced as on-the-road-to-a-democracy-which-doesn't-happen-overnight-and-needs-a-bit-of-time, the beastly scowl of the murderous KGB man he has always been. It's what makes me, once again, refuse to find the least mitigating circumstance (humiliation, despair, misery, response to other acts of violence . . .) in a Sri

Lankan terrorist, a Palestinian suicide bomber, or some son of a bitch in Afghanistan who stones his own wife because, despite her burqa, she had the nerve to look at another man. Or, once again, of course, the murderers of the World Trade Center which the fake Left, once again Arundhati Roy, John Holloway, or Walden Bello, saw, here again, as the work of poor boys whose actions were "motivated by a feeling of injustice and moral outrage largely shared in the world."

And then there's the anticolonial reflex, which has to do with some of those famous issues of repentance Sarkozy brought up during his campaign. Of course, Mr. President, not everything is Europe's fault. Of course it is not responsible for the Rwandan genocide, for the massacres in Sierra Leone, or for the pillage, by their own elites, of so many African nations. And, of course, one can't eternally blame the notorious colonial "humiliation" for the criminal behavior of people like Saddam Hussein, Bashar al-Assad . . . or Gadhafi (and wasn't the "humiliation" argument, by the way, the same argument used at Munich to explain Hitler's appetite for territorial conquest as an understandable answer to the humiliating Treaty of Versailles?). But the rest? Our criminal behavior? Since when does someone else's criminality cancel out my own? If one person lies about his own shortcomings, does that excuse others from telling the truth? Doesn't the moral imperative mean that my actions do not depend on someone else's actions toward me? Doesn't true morality mean that whatever someone else does— and whatever, especially, someone else says about it—we have to take responsibility, and say so, for what we do ourselves? And finally, doesn't it mean—no matter how shocking the notion may seem, no matter how uncomfortable, or unjust, or indefensible—feeling vaguely but fundamentally guilty, in some part of oneself, for the things one hasn't done *as well*?

A BRIEF WORD about this indefensible idea of guilt for crimes one has not committed.

On this point too, humanity splits down the middle.

On one side are those who remain seated, satisfied, sure of themselves and of their place in the world; who don't question anything, and especially not the legitimacy of being what they are; who, as a consequence, are only very rarely bothered by the notion that they might be guilty of anything—and certainly not for someone else's crimes. These are exactly the people Sartre described as "scum."

On the other side are those who remember Primo Levi's "shame at being a man," who think there is something shameful, or at least humbling, in the human condition. I cannot—these people think—help but be a little uncomfortable being who I am, since I can only be that way at the expense of some other person. I've probably done nothing wrong; I may not be guilty of anything; I am well-deserving, virtuous, generous, attentive to other people, a good activist, a good citizen; but I live with the unpleasant, inevitable thought that my position, my possessions, my prosperity, the air I breathe, my confidence, my dreams, my peaceful sleep have been—just a little bit—taken from someone else.

Sartre wrote about the difference between the "scum" (locked into what he is, frozen in his place and being, justified) and the non-scum (Dostoyevsky's shy, sweet man; the man who worries about his existence, concerned, nauseated; who cannot escape the feeling that he takes up too much room in this world, and whose excess room inspires him not to pride but to remorse).

Similarly, Emmanuel Levinas's entire philosophy revolves around the distinction between the moral man (indebted to the world, a hostage to it, obliged to answer for its disorders and injustices, even when he has not caused them) and the immoral man (who, claiming to have "done nothing," simply feels innocent, wanting nothing of this "heteronomy," this "substitution," which seems to him a contradiction in terms, absurd, outrageous).

And long before, this was also the great theme of the Greeks: you didn't know you were sleeping with your mother? You didn't know that the man you were about to kill was your father? Of course not! Nobody questions that; but that innocence is meaningless from the gods' perspective; it doesn't make you any less guilty of your greater guilt—the guilt stemming from your mere existence in the world. And this is also the *other* Greek theme—of the unjust, hellish, but inevitable transmission of this guilt, itself unjust and hellish, to those who come after you: The parents have sinned? The children will be punished, since there are crimes that the gods cannot excuse: so much evil has gone into these crimes that nothing can, or ever will be able to, make up for them— there is no such thing as "innocent sons," wrote Pasolini, the most Greek of Italian writers, in that beautiful book of rebellion against the cult of youth, *Lutheran Letters.*

On this point, I am a follower of Sartre and Levinas. And even, for once, in agreement with the Greeks, who, on this point, also agree with the Bible: "The fathers have eaten a sour grape, and the children's teeth are set on edge."

I know, of course, that this wisdom can lead to extremes.

I am well aware also of the damage it can cause (and that it is not a guarantee of holiness).

Even worse, I know how a soul who truly subscribes to this notion—and who could somehow break through all the obstacles standing between him and a "substitution" that wouldn't be worthwhile unless it was universal and limitless—who could suffer every suffering, grieve every grievance, cry every tear, and pray every prayer on earth— could become a kind of monster invaded by a negativity, a blackness— Spinoza would say a depth of sad passions—that would be the death of him as surely as Nietzsche's last man, smothered by the weight of his own memories, dead because he cannot forget.

And I know, finally, that it's in this Greek light—and in the commentary, particularly, on the myth of Oedipus—that Hegel elaborated his terrible concept of objective guilt which, in the actual history of the twentieth century, condemned so many innocents on the basis of being "Hitlerian Trotskyists" or "unwitting agents of imperialism."

But I still think there's something to it.

I think that without a bit of shame, of real shame, humanistic politics will always risk turning into its opposite—and the idea of "honor in being a man" will creep into the "man with a capital M," or "the proud name of Man," or, even worse, the hard-core Stalinist notion of "man as the most precious capital."

I think, in other words, that repentance is an immediate, essential part of our conscience.

And there again, I see a good compass for orienting one's thinking and one's life.

Those who let themselves be physically captive to other people and their misfortunes belong on the Left—man, the man of the Left, is the only animal who can shed his own self to enter, without fusion or effusion, someone else's mind and heart. As Aragon said in his *Défense de l'infini,* he is the only animal who sometimes prefers to "lose his arm rather than his compassion."

Those who wash their hands of this concern, and who have no intention, under any circumstances, of taking on other people's suffering, belong on the Right—enough mortification! Enough of the bad spirit of empathy and shame that accompanies it! Enough obsessing about wanting to be one's brother's keeper, or one's neighbor's brother! Enough of these forced brotherhoods, of the "continual crucifixion" which Paul Morand, in *L'Homme pressé,* said belonged to the "Old Continent."

Pardon me for dotting the *i*'s and crossing the *t*'s: but between Aragon and Morand, those two symmetrical scoundrels, I'd still take Aragon, the Aragon reflex, even today. . . .

The thing is, of course, to bring those reflexes together.

They're useful only if they can be combined.

And it's clear enough that everything depends on how they can or can't be harmonized.

Let's imagine one of these penitents—an anticolonial liberal, say— crying out in favor of human rights (this is the sensibility of '68, which is to say antitotalitarianism): he'll be on the lookout for the slightest attack on the national sovereignty of any Third World country, but will say nothing, on the other hand, when the very bearers of that sovereignty infringe on their own people's rights.

Let's imagine the opposite: an antitotalitarian who only thinks in terms of human rights and sees the colonial question—what's left of it in people's memories, its consequences on the ground—as something from the past: the wretched are the wretched, alone responsible for their misfortunes; the West can probably help them; and so he can meddle in their business to bring them democracy, for example; but don't tell him that among the forces resisting his democracy are even older forces dating to before the society was destroyed by the colonial bulldozer—that, on the other hand, he doesn't want to hear.

Let's imagine a Dreyfusard who isn't, or isn't sufficiently, or is no longer, antifascist: in the name of an errant Dreyfusism, he would defend a writer, Renaud Camus, who, in one of his books, found there were too many Jews on French radio; or an English Holocaust denier, David Irving, imprisoned for denying the existence of the gas chambers. . . .

Let's imagine an antifascist who could forget his Dreyfusism, who considers truth relative—dependent on circumstance—and who would therefore be uninterested in a Justice that surmounts differences in place, time, and circumstances. American sectarians believed, and said, that every community has its own ethos, language, and, almost, laws; and, in the United States as in Europe, these "official" antifascists who, because they were not adequately educated by the Dreyfus Affair—because they can no longer imagine a universal crime—have no answer for Ahmadinejad, or Chávez, or the leaders of Hezbollah, when they launch their anti-Semitic diatribes.

Let's take, once again, an alumnus of '68 who's forgotten his anti-colonialist and therefore antifascist reflexes: it's forbidden to forbid; limitless freedom of expression; tired of "politically correct" habits which supposedly weigh down consciences with an intolerable censorship—and which I, myself, consider a rather healthy habit, within, of course, reasonable limits.

The Dreyfusard who isn't at all a graduate of '68, who has no idea what the antitotalitarian revolution of May '68 was: the absolute Dreyfusard, who thinks that every man, simply because he is on his own, no matter how ignominious are the things he writes, needs to be supported; this is Chomsky's preface to Robert Faurisson's book denying the existence of the gas chambers—not merely a preface but a defense as well.

The '68er who has cast off his antifascist moorings: once again, he is generally suspicious, with a relativism derived from Nietzsche or, depending on when we're talking about, Foucault; thinking that all cultures are equally worthy, that all have their special dignity; wary of that European norm called human rights that tries to block practices which might seem barbaric but which, in the places they are actually carried out, are a part of a culture with its own coherence and greatness . . . This person would therefore have nothing against stoning adulterous women in Afghanistan. Nothing against mutilating the genitals of small girls. The world is a multiplicity that cannot have its irreducible uniqueness threatened by the leveling, "neocolonial" arrogance of the West.

This is the anticolonial reflex without the reflex, memory, or culture of the antifascist, the opposite of what we've just seen: Europe blamed for everything; all crime placed on the ledger of the West; and, when the historian Olivier Pétré-Grenouilleau writes about the slave trade and dares to assign responsibility for the crime, in almost equal thirds, to Westerners—to be sure—but also to Arab merchants and to black leaders themselves, shame on the professor! Media lynching! A trial!

Anticolonialism once again, but without May '68 and its cosmopolitan dimension: that caricature of internationalism now known as "alter-globalization"; and, behind the caricature, a hatred of liberalism, a more or less disguised rejection of the European project, and all the tensions of identity and nationalism that go with that hatred.

Anticolonialism without Dreyfusism: communitarianism and, in the French *banlieues,* the renunciation of the universalism that the republican ideal nonetheless implied.

ONE COULD GO ON.

There are good and bad combinations.

Right and wrong combinations.

The Left I dream of, the Left we have to rebuild, and, for that reason, restructure—and which we can restructure only if, in the same breath, like the son of the widow of Nain hearing the "Arise!" and recovering the use of his five senses—can be rebuilt only once it rediscovers its four reflexes and teaches them to work together: the sure instinct of Dreyfusism, the good memory of antifascism, the lesson of the anticolonial struggles, and those of the antitotalitarianism that is the legacy of May '68.

Note on a Fire

A final word on the revolt in the *banlieues* that stirred France at the end of 2005—somewhat like the one that set the United States aflame forty or so years before: because this was an extreme case, but nonetheless a case, all the more eloquent because it was extreme, of what I'm trying to say here.

When those riots erupted, the first reflex of many of my friends[1] was to exclaim: They're barbarians, nothing more than barbarians: when rioters can only say how much they hate everyone else and themselves; when the leaders of the dance start off torching schools, dispensaries, ambulances, doctors' and dentists' offices, buses, libraries; when the discourse is reduced to screaming, and the scream is nothing more than the hopeless squeak of a human animal rendered incoherent by its own vandalism; when the bottom line is reduced to either the ghostly silence of those whose message goes no further than the hallucinated repetition of sinister cries of "Fuck your mother," "Fuck the police," or "I'll fuck France till she loves me"—then aren't we indeed faced with something that has always been called, literally, barbarism? And in the face of barbarism, of hordes of thugs who single out women, the old, the weak, the destitute—when we see them hooded like members of the Ku Klux Klan, manipulated either by Mafiosi or by Islamic extremists, or by both—forming, according to Pascal Bruckner, something that looks like it's mistaken itself for the first assault columns of the future French Fascist Party—when we see them happily turning their backs on what was, for previous generations, the spirit of May '68, of antifascist resistance, how can we still think that dialogue is possible? And how can we not treat these people as fascists ought to be treated—without discussion, without listening or thinking?

My own reaction was quite different.

Of course there was a whiff of barbarity.

Of course there was a dimension of savagery one would have to be blind not to see, and deaf not to hear.

Of course the battle cries of the rioters were resentment and nihilism—"Leave us alone; Let us riot in peace; We don't want new rights: we want zones where the law can't enter; We don't want a different society: we don't want any society at all; We aren't asking for another social contract: we want to tear the social contract to bits."

But after all . . .

Hasn't there always been, first of all, a bit of that in the many other riots that have shaken, and sometimes bloodied, American and French history?

Hasn't violence accompanied all those uprisings that started out full of ferocity and furor, and were smoothed over only by the historian's distant gaze?

The Paris Commune, for example . . . Do we really think that event was purely grandiose, majestic, and glowing, worthy of entering, all of a piece, the golden legend of the Republic?

And, in any case, can we be so sure that we ourselves don't bear any responsibility for the disaster?

And, as we've already discussed, does—can—someone else's obvious, overwhelming responsibility exonerate me from my own?

I'm looking at the poem Victor Hugo wrote just after insurgents burned the Tuileries Library, the same poem I gave Ségolène Royal at the beginning of her campaign.

The poet is "preaching" to one of the arsonists.

He accuses him, as we do today, of the "unheard of" crime of burning a cultural site.

He shows him that the books he burned were the "light of his soul," the "torch itself" that ought to guide him along the road to happiness and progress.

This "light" was "yours," he insists.

The book was "your liberator," your "doctor," your "guide," your "guardian."

And it was all that, all these priceless goods, these talismans, these flowers of the soul, which you've chosen to "annihilate."

But then he has the honesty to wonder about the arsonist's reaction. And what do we think he answers? "I don't know how to read . . ." Just a humble "I don't know how to read," cutting off the wise man, the prophet, the man of the Enlightenment, who firmly believes that opening a school is tantamount to closing a prison—and who is reminded that he might have taught the arsonist to love the very books he's accusing him of profaning.

This says it all.

And during those weeks, I had two reactions, one after the other, and simultaneously.

First—like Bruckner, like Finkielkraut, like Glucksmann, and for the same reasons—I was horrified by this modern arson and the screech of so much overheated hatred.

But at the same time, other reflections led me to part ways with my colleagues, reflections that recalled the same astonishment, the jolting, the moment of realization that people had when the Tuileries Library was burned in 1871—a kind of *misgiving*, in fact, that I can't describe better than by offering the following recommendations.

First of all, beware of the word "barbaric," which has a way of ratifying, consecrating, and cementing in the public mind a secession from society of a group of people that urgently needs to be reabsorbed.

Beware, generally, of all those words we throw around and which end up creating their own meanings: I probably can't help it that the "language of the *banlieues*" is a language of hatred and sometimes of war: but if I am a state minister I can avoid hurtful words and think twice before declaring—disregarding the truth of the matter—that Zied Benna and Bouna Traoré, the two young men whose death by

electrocution in Clichy-sous-Bois kicked off the firestorm, were, when
they were being chased, about to commit a burglary; I can avoid the
systematic condescending speech that I wouldn't allow myself to use
toward any other kind of Frenchman; if I am the State, I can avoid
resuscitating—while the riots are still raging, and at a point when a reinforcement of police measures would have the exact same effect as the
law of 1955—the so-called emergency law used during the Algerian
War to legalize racial profiling and which meant, instead of calming
things down, accepting that one part of the French people was at war
with France—or, even worse, that they were no more French than their
parents or grandparents, the victims of the same law in the fifties and
sixties. And if I am the permanent secretary of the most famous, prestigious, and official cultural institution in this country, I can spare us
the racist whopper uttered in an interview with Russian television: that
if the *banlieues* were sick, the problem was . . . polygamy![2]

We can even—given the word's unfortunate associations with
the medieval *lieu de ban* ("place of banishment") and with definitive
exclusions[3]—rethink the very notion of *banlieues,* using instead the term
"neighborhood" or even "tough neighborhood"—and too bad if the
difference sounds petty! Too bad if it sounds sociological! Better that
than connotations of banishment; better something overly sociological
than something that reeks of banished pariahs, the refuse of the social
contract, rubbish, ghosts, the damned. Because after all . . . arsonists are
one thing. But how useful is it to treat entire neighborhoods just as the
"dangerous classes" used to be treated? And is it useless to realize that
these arsonists live in urban areas with problems found nowhere else in
the country (a mass unemployment which, in certain areas, affects one
young person in two)?

Just once, let's look at the other side. Even though I have always
found the idea of contextualizing "great" crimes shocking, and even
repugnant—as much as I have fought, and will continue to fight, the
"excuses culture" applied to events such as 9/11, suicide attacks in
Jerusalem or Baghdad—I think, quite frankly, that in this case we're
nowhere close to that. The rioters were detestable. Their methods and
their crimes were inexcusable and *barbarous.* But this was not the March

on Rome; nor an SS parade; not even the bloody riots, once so dangerous and problematic, that the United States suffered in the 1960s. And
a democracy cannot, when confronted with a problem of this nature,
fail to reflect *as well*—calmly, coolly—about how much responsibility for
these events actually does fall to mass unemployment, to the mediocrity of decades of city politics, and to the laxity that allowed these lost
territories—these ghettos—to exist.

Instead of rolling out the professors of *banliologie* who do nothing
but repeat the same old clichés,[4] we could try to listen to the people
who actually know the areas, and who, supported by statistics, almost
immediately rejected the idea of an immigrant uprising (most of the rioters were French), with ethnic or religious inspiration (the rioters
told the imams the government cleverly dispatched to calm them down
to fuck off); or that it was led by hardened felons and serious criminals
(at the Bobigny court, the first arraignments of the car-burners showed
that the majority had no criminal record); or that it was a mass uprising
(the grand total of people involved barely reached a few hundred)—
and to try to listen to them, especially when they describe the living
conditions, and sometimes nonliving conditions, common in those
neighborhoods.

And then (final, main recommendation—though in these aseptic
times, when the very idea of a collusion, I won't say of Good and Evil,
but of Evil and Real, has become almost unthinkable, it might be the
hardest one to understand): We have to try to see what unites these
crimes with those of Victor Hugo's arsonist. . . . Because social movements do not always think like social movements. Crime, destruction,
and arson are often dimensions of what history books cover up with
the polite name of "popular insurrections." So a proper understanding
of the event—the right way to act when faced with an act that is doubtless criminal but which for the time being is mainly suicidal; the acts
of people destroying their schools, their hospitals, their lives—is also,
despite everything else, to see them as a kind of social movement. . . .

There's no question that it's a weird kind of movement. An aber-
rant, erratic, crazy movement. A caricature of a movement. A movement whose real difference with its predecessors, moreover, has less to

do with its brutality than with its inability to come up with a coherent project, a discourse, or even a wish list (isn't this crowd, aren't these rioters, part of the new age following the end of the great utopian and messianic projects—a directionless age, without illusions or hopes, an age which, everywhere, has made political honor so rare?). But a movement all the same. With all the word implies: a constitutive division, first of all, even in its most barbarous forms, of the democratic space; of the shame, second—yes: I'll repeat the word—of the shame we should feel at the thought of allowing a situation of banishment to develop over the years (it's one thing to exhort the law to be merciless with criminals who, before setting a bus on fire, spray its passengers with gasoline—it's something else entirely to forget that long before that the democratic state had an indisputable, unconditional duty, no matter what, toward those neighborhoods); third, and last, of an unformulated appeal to the law (I say unformulated, but I might almost say unallowed, since I don't care whether this appeal comes from the very people who would benefit from it: an appeal that society as a whole somehow makes to itself: an internal demand to rewrite the social contract: this is simply the state's duty).

Vichy, colonization, May '68, the Dreyfus Affair . . . Images spin through my head. And now these reflexes are like the "red and forever unjustifiable reflexes" of which Aragon spoke.

"I am irreducibly a man of the Left," he, Aragon, wrote in the first preface to his *Libertinage*—and "if that expression makes you laugh you're nothing but a buffoon."

PART TWO

THIRTY YEARS LATER

How We're Less Sanctimonious

I also said that I emerged from my conversation with the future president filled with a second feeling, one no less vivid than the first, since it was no less apparently obvious: that he wasn't necessarily wrong about the current state of the Left: not of the Left of my dreams, not some programmatic or ideal Left, but the actual Left. Why?

I wasn't thinking about the series of low blows leveled against the Socialist candidate from the beginning of the campaign, which her opponent—all's fair in politics—took full advantage of.

Nor am I thinking of the more generalized accusation leveled against the French Left: its datedness, its persistent ideological backwardness, its neurotic attachment to the old-fashioned principles of traditional socialism.

I'm not thinking of that old tune, which returns with every election, and more than ever during this one, about the Left's inability to adapt, to accept clearly and unreservedly, like all the leftist parties in the world, or at least in Europe, the constraints of a market economy to which—as, once again, everyone knows—there is no alternative.

And I'm not thinking about that because—despite what people constantly, almost universally repeat; despite what the Left itself never stops dwelling on in its fits of masochism—that problem, after all, has mostly been fixed: I no longer know many socialists who, in their souls and their consciences, still believe all those old stories of a radiant future, of a capitalism made irrelevant and destabilized by its own contradictions, of absolute pauperization, of proletarian society, of utopia. In the face of the urban riots I've just mentioned, I don't know any who still dream of a new Great Actor taking up the reins of the dying proletariat and who—nothing himself, but called upon to be everything—would regenerate a capitalism dying of exhaustion by breathing in the energy of a new Messiah. I don't know any who would dream of saying of the black insurgents in Watts, as Guy Debord did forty years ago, that "They are not the backward part of American society," but "its most advanced vanguard," the "negative on the march," "the bad side that produces the movement," helping "History" advance[1]—I think that France's official Left—just like the German Left fifty years ago, like all European leftist parties, who did so more or less gracefully, has ended up accepting capitalism as well. . . .

NOW, THIS PROBABLY hasn't been said loudly enough.

More often, it's probably not said at all, and not saying it has created a situation of incertitude, ambiguity, deep hypocrisy, schizophrenia, and profound neurosis.

So it probably wouldn't be so bad to say it, just to say it; and sooner rather than later. Without doing so the Left risks showing, for a long time to come, symptoms of the fever from which it has recovered: in being one of Europe's last leftist movements, for example, with a Communist party called the "Communist Party"—apparently unable to see, in the word "Communist," a wound, a burden, an insult to truth and honor, a burn; or in being supported by a so-called extreme or Trotskyist Left, still weighed down by this absurd, inexplicable ball and chain, which no longer can even be justified by its electoral performances; or in continuing to nourish the illusion—not electoral but nominal, almost nominalist, and in any event strangely persistent—which imagines a range of the Left, a family, a holy family.

But nobody's fooled.

The most stubborn socialist rhinoceroses know that the strategy of a united Left was no more than a meaningless ritual.

The most blind old Communist knows his Party is dying, that the only light it gives off is the light of dead stars, and that it owes its survival only to the obscure indulgence of a system that, for over a century, has been in the habit of gravitating around it, like a galaxy moving around its central star, afraid that if that star is finally put out the whole system might implode.

The Trotskyist groups themselves are no longer really groups but sects—and sects that, remarkably enough, no longer believe in their own catechism.

In a word, we are no longer living—I won't even say in the imminent expectation—in the hope of a Great Transformation, or in a time in which the words "reformism" or "social democracy" were inaudible, unspeakable: enough, when spoken, to get one dispatched to the hell of class treason or of nothingness; we're no longer in a time in which François Mitterrand felt obliged (once, at Latché, his countryside house, I was the stunned witness of this) to spend his summer vacation— besides observing butterflies, taking walks among the great trees he talked to in the same way he addressed his donkeys, or reading favorite writers such as the Cardinal de Retz or Jacques Chardonne—to spend hours, like a purge, poring over the rudiments of a new Marxist system that some post-Stalinist intellectual had forced onto him; and when, taking a page from a few others, Ségolène Royal complains about "Blairism," which ten or twenty years before had been the absolute scarecrow which could frighten off everything the Left had in the way of Robespierrist crows, no crow, unfortunately, is scared off—nor any follower of Robespierre. . . .

I MUST SAY THAT I'm not even thinking about that famous "totalitarian temptation" which was the shame of the Left and the dishonor of its intellectuals.

I'm not thinking about that long—that so very long—compromise that I denounced, in my first essays thirty years ago, with the same crimes already denounced by Camus, Arendt, Aron, Revel, Orwell, Popper, and so many others.

And I'm not thinking about that because that temptation—the totalitarian temptation in the strict sense of the term; the shameless praise of the Russian gulag or the Chinese *laogai;* the notion that revolution isn't a fancy-dress party and that because it's a revolution it's worth a few mass graves beneath the sun of Good, for the sake of the New Man; the fascination of the clean slate and the white page, which until my generation drove so many projects and desires; the profane millenarianism that was, until so recently, the religion of progressive humanity and whose principal article of faith could be summed up, in its popular version, in the famous saying "You can't make an omelet without breaking a few eggs": well, all of that, as everyone knows, isn't exactly the problem today. . . .

There may well be a few people out there who are nostalgic for the workers' paradise of Enver Hoxha's Albania.

There may be a few perverts who, in the dark recesses of their hearts, believe that there was something good about the gulag, that the people condemned by the Moscow show trials had probably done something wrong, and that the concentration camp system is the quickest road to socialism—I can hardly imagine it, but just for the sake of argument let's say they exist.

I'm convinced that the collapse of the Communist house almost everywhere has even, in certain cases, had the unexpected side effect of wiping out the traces of its crimes, the visible signs of its failure, allowing certain people to start dreaming once again of an unsullied Communism, uncompromised and happy.

Even worse: it's still true that—beyond the Left but casting their shadow on the rest of the political landscape—there are debates on the origin, and even the extent, of Communism's crimes; there are vibrant discussions about the legitimacy of comparing those crimes to the Nazis'. One can wonder about the incredible lapse, for example, of former president Jacques Chirac who, on July 16, 1999, when he came to inaugurate a "Center for Memory" in Oradour-sur-Glane, condemned, in one fell swoop, the crimes of Nazism, the sixteenth-century massacre of French Protestants on Saint Bartholomew's Day, the massacre of the Vendéens by the Jacobins during the Revolution, the Rwandan genocide, ethnic cleansing in Bosnia, Guernica, Sabra and Shatila—but found nothing to say, in the course of his long enumeration, about the crimes of Communism.[2]

But who seriously believes that that's what the Left is really about?

Who can actually claim that the French or European Left is still apologizing for the crimes of Leninism, or dreaming of reproducing them?

Where is the prominent political leader who would refuse to sign his name, even a bit halfheartedly, to the unanimous condemnation of the crimes of the Siberian gulag or those of Kim Jong Il's North Korea?

IN A WORD, we are well aware that a page has been turned with the implosion, at the end of the eighties, of the Soviet system; and that another page has been opened, for better or worse, in which the old Communist parties, their allies, and those who tried to get along with them or flatter them no longer have any place.

We know that a whole range of contemporary political discourse, a whole history of modern turmoil and posturing, a whole ideological range, had its moment in the sun but has become like a black hole swallowing up its own light and history.

We can be glad about it, or we can regret it.

We can—and I don't—think that the Left back in those days had more flair and appeal.

We can regret—and again, I don't—the Left in its salad days, with its secular saints, its titans clambering skyward, its meteors, its bloody but milky dawns, its insurrections, its fertilizing cruelties, its eagerness, its men tired of being too human and longing to be supermen; and we can say that, compared to that, without that horizon and cut off from that dimension, the Left today has an I'm-here, rebel-without-a-cause, power-to-the-little-folks side to it that is as distant from that earlier incarnation as the burning of cars in the *banlieues* in 2005 was from the grand gestures of the marmoreal proletariat of yesteryear.

Or we can (and this *is* the category I fall into) regret that this disenchantment, this secularization of dreams, this lucky casting-off of thoughts, afterthoughts, and ideals, has not accompanied all the political revisions that logically ought to have followed; and we can be astonished that this Left has remained hanging between two worlds, smoke without fire, froth without water, radical gestures but without radical words, words without meaning, leaving the twentieth century without quite entering the twenty-first—or, rather, leaving that totalitarian twentieth century only to enter another side of that same century, in which other words, other kinds of radicalism, are lurking, and which are almost worse, and which—but wait, let's not get ahead of ourselves!

This is where we are for now.

It's wrong to say that the Left feels it is still owed a revolution and is taking its time making peace with the world.

It's not true that—compared to a right wing which is still nostalgic for Vichy, for the civilizing mission of France in Algeria, or for the way things were before May 1968—the Left has learned nothing, understood nothing, and forgotten nothing of the Communist and totalitarian nightmare.

We could even say that the Left has—though once again without coming out and saying so—moved further away from its totalitarian past than the other side has from its own—or that it hasn't done enough on this account, or that it may have already done so but is now rolling back that progress as quickly as it can.

And I'm not thinking about any of that when I say that Nicolas Sarkozy was on to something when he emphasized, and mocked, the decrepit state of the Left.

A Secret Calendar of
the History of This Century

All the more so because the situation is even more complicated.

I've said that the totalitarian temptation was broken, roughly, after the fall of the Berlin Wall and the breakup of the Soviet system.

But that's not really it.

That's not only, or even essentially, what happened.

And if there was a reckoning—if the old-school totalitarian temptation is actually, and mostly, ancient history—if we've grown more lucid, thinking twice before praising the collective farms, the destruction of bourgeois thought, or the violent proletarian revolution—then that has more to do with events that antedate the fall of the Wall, which turned out to be nothing more than their natural and logical sequel—and which, if less often mentioned, give that conversion a much stronger and probably irreversible necessity, a depth, an anchorage in reality.

As I've said, if I could single out a single aspect of France's May '68, it would be its libertarianism, and therefore antiauthoritarianism, and therefore anti-Stalinism, and therefore—whether we want to admit it or not—its profound, fundamental, antitotalitarianism. Did this antitotalitarianism express itself in the language of the more ossified Left? Yes, of course. It expressed itself in the words of a Marxism whose key word was "antirevisionism" and which, we could reasonably fear, would be even stricter, more orthodox, and more radical than the Marxisms that came before it. Even worse, its more radical fringe was not afraid to sing the praises, and to be the messenger, of a dictatorship of which the least we can say is that—from the Great Leap Forward to the so-called Cultural Revolution—it was not outdone, in the terror department, by Stalinism. But ... We need to add two restrictions to this true statement. The first is that those fanatics—and I am mainly thinking of the Maoists—didn't wait twenty years, or even ten, to criticize themselves and to apologize for certain texts that were overheated, incitements to crime, or simply stupid.[1] And the second is that Maoism, since that's what we're dealing with here, was different from Stalinism: Maoism never meant supporting what was actually happening in China; it was an expression of the rejection of the only other totalitarian model that had, in the previous half-century, any historic weight, any attractive or inspirational strength, any risk of real contagion—the Soviet model. In the matter of Marxism, the "Maos" were actually cleverer than the Marxist-Leninists, "Maoism" being the vehicle, or the language, of a global revolt against all then-extant systems of authority.

THEN TO PORTUGAL. Once again, I think about Otelo de Carvalho, in the final days of a boiling summer which was also the last summer, before his decline, of the old Stalinist leader Álvaro Cunhal, telling me that the rebellious captains of the Movement of the Armed Forces had stolen his job inside the Party; and that they only had fomented this conspiracy, planned this revolution with a technique unprecedented in the history of coups d'état, by double-crossing the Left, or the Right, and, for that matter, Curzio Malaparte himself, only *so that* the Communists couldn't do it first, instead of them. I see him now, over-exuberant and happy, baroque, larger than life, a kind of uniformed Danton where I expected a Saint-Just, a commedia dell'arte actor, more than a Shakespearean Moor of Lisbon; I see him now, that famous night at Belém Palace, when—tired of my learned questions about his relationship with Vasco Gonçalves, Marx, Lenin, the

"COPCON" from the Right and the Left, Eurocommunism, Thermidor, about whether or not the revolution was frozen—he finally burst out in laughter and said, "C'mon, I don't give a damn. I'm not an intellectual. Let's roll the dice or, better, have another drinking match to settle the question": he had taken off his pea coat; unbuttoned his shirt collar to reveal his Cherubino-like neck; an officer had poured out twelve glasses of port on a table of varnished wood—while down there, on the square, the people waiting for him to appear, pope-like, at the window were chanting "the people united will never be defeated"— each of us started at a different end, the goal of the game being to drink the greatest number of glasses, bottoms up, and to get to the center of the table first, not too tottering—if he won, the Communist Party would crumble once and for all, and if he lost, the Party had gained the upper hand and the officers had failed; I hardly need to add that in that night's comedy of errors he won the game. . . . And I see him one more time, thirty-two years later, in the Lisbon restaurant where we've met up to remember those times and others—another Otelo, thin, modest, who's acquired a Pessoa-like expression, but who nonetheless explains to me—with the same smile as in the old days—that all his troubles, all his years in prison, the accusations of conspiracy against the state, of membership in an armed organization, and of terrorism that were brought against him, that all of that was nothing more than a low vengeance by the Party he had warded off, finished off, and which just had enough life left in it to attack the author of all its misfortunes. . . . The twilight of socialism. The beginning of the end of Communism. The whole old revolutionary theater shattered in only a few weeks. Still a heaven, but one stripped of its gods and exiled to a little corner of nowhere. This was the great Portuguese lesson of the last century. That is—whether we know it or not, whether that's how it's written about in the mythology of the time—Otelo's legacy.

THE EVENT THAT was Solzhenitsyn. An event that shook our generation to its core. There was André Glucksmann's *La Cuisinière et le mangeur*

d'hommes. Then Claude Lefort's book *Un homme en trop,* entirely dedicated, like *La Cuisinière,* to commenting on *The Gulag Archipelago.* One may
remember, I do remember, that famous *Apostrophes*—the most remarkable television show of the seventies—where it all began, where I arrived
with an indifference, even an innocence, that I've never recovered, miles
away from imagining that anything important could happen there.

No other modern book has ever, as far as I know, unleashed an explosion like *The Gulag Archipelago.* It was a worldwide earthquake whose
unexpected power I'd so much like the generations who didn't experience it to feel: everything we knew without believing, or believed without seeing, or saw but didn't understand: by the millions, suddenly, by
the tens of millions all across the world, we knew, believed, saw, and understood! Because Solzhenitsyn was an artist? That was my idea (the
Shakespeare of our time . . . the contemporary *Divine Comedy . . .* showing
the unshowable . . . naming the unnameable . . . forcing us to confront
evil . . . to look the horror in the face . . .). Because that work, though an
artist's, had theoretical merits that none of the books by writers like
Ciliga, Koestler, Merleau-Ponty, Istrati, and so forth had displayed (the
Archipelago didn't explain but simply said . . . simply described . . . not
taking the risk, in so doing, of making excuses and justifications . . .
lending the panorama all its intact power to outrage . . .)? Was it because the time was right? Was that all? Yeast in the dough of the age?
Dough waiting for the eyes that could make it rise? Was it because the
shock came right when history was already accelerating anyway? Probably, yes. There was surely some of that. Whatever the reasons, this was
another event. A book, to be sure. But also an event. Cut from the same
cloth as its predecessors. And one that—on the day someone sets to
writing the phenomenology of the twentieth-century European spirit,
the day that someone describes this mix of concrete history and
thought that was the secret fabric of our existences during those
decades—will occupy a place at least equal to that of other officially
"major" events. The Communist dream *dissolved* in the furnace of a
book.

—

AND THEN A FINAL episode, even less frequently mentioned but possibly the most significant of all—an episode which, in the true calendar of the age, and, in any event, in my own calendar, ought to rank alongside "great" events such as the October Revolution, the Crisis of the Thirties, Mao's Long March or, for that matter, the fall of the Berlin Wall: a fourth episode; a fourth moment of reorientation and reversal, after which we finally and permanently enter another era: Cambodia is when everything unravels and the age finally realizes what's what, the Cambodian Revolution of 1975—and the fatal blow it delivered not only to Marxism, or to the leaders of the Stalinist parties, or to the Communist dream, but to the very idea of Revolution. . . .

Let me explain.

Until Cambodia, it was commonly thought that—if all revolutions had failed, if they had produced dictatorships even worse than those they had overthrown, if they had been frozen, if they had degenerated or missed their goals—it was because they hadn't gone far enough, because they had lost their nerve, their power, their courage.

It was said that one revolution had gone wrong by trying to limit itself to simply changing the ownership of the means of production.

That another had rearranged the underlying relationships of production but had failed to address the superstructure—which was to say the political structure, the State.

That though yet another had tackled the question of the State and started to make it fade away, it hadn't dealt with those other superstructures, even more superstructural, which were ideology and knowledge, as well as their means of inscription and reproduction in individual minds.

We thought (my generation, this time, thought) that all of them, in other words, really all of them, had inevitably failed because they had fallen short of taking on these final remnants of the servitude we had learned to recognize from our perfect teachers, masters at chasing away illusions, students of limits and confines, experts in the art of recognizing the devil's many disguises.

What were these final remnants?

First, the relationships of desire in the Freudian or Lacanian sense:

oppression, violence, attacks on the body, the dark continent of sexuality and desire, death—no revolution worthy of the name would fail to address those issues too.

Second, the very structure of language in the sense of Ferdinand de Saussure, Roman Jakobson, Louis Hjelmslev: "the relationship with language is political," Barthes concluded in the famous declarations that only made the Saussurian message explicit—"Language is not a superstructure"—the world's injustices, disorders, unearned hierarchies, miseries, were all a "glossematic" reality, "political effects" of language, and what we needed to understand them, and, at the same time, to liberate ourselves from them—the thing a new Marx should produce, and which would have an instantly liberating effect, was a *Das Kapital* of linguistic science!

Third, and finally, we knew since Rousseau that humanity was inscribed in a geography that inevitably became a space dividing human beings into slaves and masters, subjects and overlords, as a result of the division of the countryside and the city, the wild zone and the policed zone, the place suited to the solitary walker versus the precincts of the Voltairean sneer. We'd known, I said, since Rousseau—we'd learned it in his *Émile* and his *Reveries* that unhappiness was the child of the city and even, perhaps, of cities; but now our knowledge had been "refreshed" by that strange event that was the Chinese Cultural Revolution; the event theorized by teachers who are a bit forgotten today but who then enjoyed immense prestige, people like Charles Bettelheim, that crypto-Althusserian economist, severe, lacking in literary talent but with a furious and glacial intelligence, and here those teachers were explaining that the great originality of that revolution, its truly "cultural" aspect, was that, through the "new kind of social organization" that was the "Popular Commune," it encircled the cities with the countryside, rearranging the very space where that opposition was situated, modifying even our perception of that space and raising, therefore, the bar higher for what we could seriously describe as revolution.[2]

Then the Cambodians arrived.

People who had, for the most part, studied in France.

Revolutionaries who, in the cases of Pol Pot or Son Sen, the future head of the armed forces of Democratic Kampuchea, had stayed in France until the middle of the fifties—or who, in the cases of Ieng Sary or Khieu Samphan, the future ministers of foreign relations and the interior, respectively, had stayed until the end of the decade.

These new revolutionaries seem to have paid attention in their classes at the Sorbonne, at the French Communist Party's Université Nouvelle, or even, in the case of Ieng Sary, at the Institut d'Études Politiques—discovering there, in those French schools, among other wonders, writings of Mao, such as his famous *On the Correct Handling of the Contradictions Among the People,* which were then starting to fire student imaginations.

And then the more brilliant of those young people, who discovered, paged through, or simply breathed in the first works of Bettelheim, Althusser, and possibly Lacan, return to their countries charged with a revolutionary project Pol Pot himself would describe as a "new experience," a "super Great Leap Forward," an "unprecedented" attempt, important "for the whole world," to "change man in the deepest way."

So what was this project exactly?

And why was it unprecedented?

As in China, it attempted to struggle against egoism, for the abolition of commerce and money, the promotion of simple souls against the experts, the privileging of manual labor over intellectual work. It manifested a desire for immediate and absolute equality.

But by chance it also opens three completely unprecedented new paths in the history of revolutions, in which it's impossible not to recognize the stamp of the radical teachings for which the Sorbonne and the École Normale Supérieure were then the world's laboratories.

Intervention, first of all, in what we have to call the regime of desire: the Chinese had tried their hand at this, but Pol Pot's regulation of marriage, his forbidding of erotic or amorous relations outside the conjugal framework, his fixation by decree of the days every year in which young people would be authorized to copulate as well as those days on which the slightest flirtation would mean death: the pretension, in other words, to regulate feelings and emotions by politics reached in Cambodia an unequaled precision and rigor.

An attempt, thereafter, for the first time in the history of revolutions, to change language itself: language as the other matrix of despotism: this is what was behind Chuon Nath's 1967 project to reform the dictionary; the idea of an Institute of the Khmer Language in the theories of Keng Vannsak, the specialist in Cambodian language and literature who was one of Pol Pot's mentors; the "action plan for higher education" promulgated in 1977 which, in terms of "action," promoted a veritable linguistic amnesia, the erasure of entire volumes of the dictionary, and the redefinition, according to the new standards, of an equivalent number of words.

And then, finally, the desire to rearrange the very structure of space, that famous division between cities and countryside that they had understood would prevent all will for emancipation as long as it lasted: let's remember those scrawny young soldiers clad in black, surrounding Phnom Penh on the morning of April 17, 1975, and announcing that the city was going to be bombed by the United States Air Force; let's remember those two million people suddenly tossed onto the roads, in a few hours, including the elderly and the infirm, drugged sick people torn from their hospital beds, young women who had just given birth, children; let's remember that crazy picture, never before seen, of a large city emptied of its inhabitants, as indeed happened in all the country's cities. All thrown to the hyenas and the pillagers.

Just to be clear, I'm not saying that all this was necessarily connected to the books these men read in France. I don't think that Pol Pot and Ieng Sary were consciously following Saussure, Lacan, Hjelmslev, or Bettelheim. But it's clear enough that they shared certain insights. It's clear enough that they shared with the French radicals an ambition to rectify mankind's very soul and desires; this need to murder language and toss it to the dogs of the new purity; this hatred of cities and everything they symbolize. And it is hard to say that there, with the Khmer Rouge, we didn't have the perfect, pure, impeccable revolution of the kind the radicals had dreamed of and which set about digging up even the secrets of souls in order to purge them of their deepest, most hidden, and thus most virulent sources of that accursed control—if it too failed, nobody can say this revolution "didn't go far enough, stopped halfway, was too timid, etc."

So what happens?

What happens with this exemplary pure revolution?

What do we see when, in the laboratory of these souls, in the landscapes emptied of the eternal source of all misfortune, we create the New Man?

An even greater misfortune. Far from liberating men, this flawless revolution treats them like dirt. Far from leading them to the paradise of a society without classes or injustices, it hunts them, purge after purge, into the hell of the all-powerful Organization which submits them to rules much more terrible and inflexible than those from which they have been liberated. Having started out to invent complete men, to strip them of their outmoded ways, and to lead them along the path to happiness, Pol Pot and his group unleash one of the greatest insanities humanity has ever known.

Not everyone believes it at first.

At first, predictably, some people deny the atrociousness of what is going on.

But when the news is verified and spread, it comes as a shock.

The whole theoretical house of cards, all its radical models, its rhetoric, its dream, dismally collapses.

Game over.

Last exit to horror.

Unless you are both deaf and blind—and of course there were a few deaf and blind people out there—you can't pretend it hasn't happened.

Unless you're scum or a blithering idiot—or both, and there were some—you can no longer blather on, as if nothing had happened, about the true-revolution-which-will-not-be-betrayed-and-which-will-not-be-hijacked-by-the-system.

That's what Michel Foucault was thinking during the conversation I mentioned earlier, when he told me that the real novelty of our time is that people finally wonder, not about the possibility, but about the desirability of revolutions.

That's what creates what we might call the Cambodia Theorem, or the Foucault Theorem, which—even if Foucault himself was the first, two years later, during Khomeini's revolution, to contradict or even betray it—was the following rule: the more radical the revolution, the bloodier; the more serious and strict the revolution, the more cataclysms it unleashes; the revolutionary utopia is, in and of itself, by necessity and not by chance, a dream that becomes a nightmare, that brings out the worst, and that transforms men into beasts.

And that, finally, was the wellspring of the school of thought in which I was involved and which, in the middle of the seventies, was called the New Philosophy.

On the New Philosophy and Its Place in Its Time

One more thing.

A last philosophical word about the "New Philosophy" before we turn, once and for all, to the disarray of the Western Left today.

Let's look at things from a different perspective.

Let's tackle this question of revolution, Communism, totalitarianism, etc., from a philosophical angle.

And let's try to tease out its underlying beliefs, here and elsewhere, in Europe and outside it, about totalitarian fervor, totalitarian zeal, and what made that fervor mentally possible—let's try to imagine what those people were thinking when, so recently, they so willingly accepted the idea that leftist, or progressive, or revolutionary, politics could empty a city of its inhabitants, liquidate entire classes of men and women, or fill concentration camps with the representatives of the old order.

In so doing, we happen upon four simple notions that have always appeared in the twentieth century's great totalitarian experiments.

I said *notions* on purpose: they're not quite theses and even less are they concepts; they're not quite articles of faith, and I don't feel like saying reflexes either; maybe, then, they're antireflexes; or prediscursive axioms; or thoughts that aren't thought but that condition other thoughts: Come on! Let's just say notions, barely formulated hypotheses, which are like the prime numbers of this totalitarian delusion.

First the Absolute. Or Good. The idea that the Good is not just an Idea, an intangible dream, a fiction, but a reality we can usher into being here and now, during our lifetimes, immediately. It doesn't matter if we don't believe in the tangible reality of the Good and the Absolute: humanity can choose only between different shades of the lesser evil, or the better; and nobody has ever seen a revolution made, or the human race upended, for the sake of a nuance. If, on the other hand, we do believe that the principal, and even only, object of politics is to help humanity give birth to the good community it bears within itself, and if we feel that this good community is no longer slumbering on the outer edges of the present community but is close by, an arm's length away, about to break out, then all bets are off. We understand the approach of the miracle worker who believes unshakably that he has the right formula and the right tools and throws himself into politics by sacrificing the imperfect, despicable, outdated community he sees before him in favor of the beautiful and good community at his fingertips; and one not only understands but *knows* the good and shining spirits (the immense majority, actually, of the progressive intelligentsia of the twentieth century) who made the same simple and apparently reasonable calculation: what does a passing evil, or transitory sufferings, or the sacrifice of a generation or two, or a police state, or camps, matter, if it's the way, the step, the means, to bring about the sovereign good?

And then there's History. More precisely, the idea that there is a vehicle called History, which leads to, searches for, and becomes the Absolute. Or the idea, even more precisely, that there is a boulevard of History, where shadow and light mingle; but that there is light at the end of the shadow, true light, a sure and necessary light, the victory of Good over Evil, of good sense over bad, of the better being over the lesser, of the Absolute, once again, above all that resists and opposes its revelation. This idea was the other source of totalitarianism and the other source, above all, of the consent given to it. Since, again, why get worked up about it? If it is really for the sake of the right meaning; if it really will guarantee a higher state of being; if we can be absolutely sure that the time to come will be happier than the one we live in now, how could we possibly refuse it? In the name of what petty calculation can we turn up our noses at it? Wouldn't we be monsters, and incorrigible fools, if, in the name of our petty happiness, of our survival, of our narrow and narrowly egotistical interests, we decided to endanger the glorious future of humanity? If we believe in History, we let it run its course. If we let it run its course, we can't fret about occasional abuses of power. And if we don't fret about occasional abuses of power, we're not too concerned by the vanquished, those castaways that the chariot of Time throws overboard along the way, the price to pay for its victorious progress.

The third notion, the third machine, which was not desirous but delirious and infected our best minds for decades, was the Dialectic. This really means the complement of historicism, perhaps even its core, or its heart, or its secret motor, and which roughly stated: there is no human misery that, seen from a certain perspective—that certain perspective being History, or rather the end of History and the arrival of the Absolute—cannot and must not be seen as the reverse of what it seems. An annunciation, then. A promise. The shadow or the notice of the end. A good that doesn't realize it's good. Happiness in disguise. The dark stain that, in a painting, makes the luminosity and the colors come out all the more brightly. Do you feel unhappy? Wrong . . . Miserable? Take another look. . . . You say to yourself: "I'm the lowest of the low. My life is worthless, not worth living"? No, no; get a grip; be a dialectician; see things from the perspective of their ends. . . . You say: "Me, I'm all right; but those convicts? Those forced laborers? Sacrificed humanity? Those Jews? Those kulaks? Those people who are being systematically starved? Those people who wear glasses? Those plotting Zionist doctors? Those poor peasants, less poor peasants, less rich peasants, those not even less rich peasants?" "Get a hold of yourself, by God; take another look! See how all those sacrificed people are paving the way to the good and perfectly advanced society. . . ." Yes, indeed. All those intellectuals who swallowed the poison of Communism and of the concentration camps; all the writers who cried over the death of Stalin; all those painters and poets who cooed that, on the day their child was born, they would name him Joseph as a sign of mourning and devotion; all the activists who failed to note that Pol Pot was shaping his New Man from the same flesh and blood as the old one; all those people thought along these lines—historicists who didn't realize that's what they were, unaware but consistent Hegelians, dialecticians.

And then, finally, the fourth hypothesis: Evil. That new idea, which actually belongs to the totalitarian ages and which is the true cornerstone upon which the Left built its three churches (of the Dialectic, History, and the Absolute)—that idea which doesn't seem like much and in principle even seems like a good idea, an excellent bit of news, a source of pride: the idea, that is, that Evil doesn't exist, only sicknesses. Because, there again, you can't argue with the logic. Either we believe in Evil—we are Judeo-Christians and we believe that there is, at the heart of the human condition, an unbreakable heart of darkness that no politics can finish off: and if that's the case, who's going to risk one of those construction sites/mass graves known as revolutions? Or we don't believe in it: we're anti-Christian, anti-Jewish, hostile to this offense to His Majesty Mankind which is the idea of original sin, and we suspect— what am I saying? we come out and say that these dim-witted theologians have understood nothing, chosen every side, made an idiotic mistake, confusing mankind's humble sicknesses with their terrible, enormous, radical Evil: and then, onward! What sickness, first of all? What microbe? What virus? Where is it, exactly? How can it be operated on? Off we go to reeducation, disease prevention, the extermination of harmful insects, the inhuman! Off we go, on the dissection table of the Doctor Mabuses of red fascism, to the nascent Nietzschean Übermensch (overman) and all the lesser men that nourish him! The last principle of totalitarianism, the last column of its invisible edifice: the idea that nothing is incurable . . .

SO WHAT WAS the New Philosophy?

What exactly was this group of thinkers launched by Maurice Clavel and led by André Glucksmann, myself, and several others at the end of the seventies?

Back then, people said: "the gulag; the denunciation, without mincing words, of the gulag; the New Philosophers are people who've had enough of acting like political hypocrites and who, when Communism commits crimes, denounces them." True enough. But there was more. And that doesn't distinguish us from the thinkers and writers, such as Gide, Koestler, Istrati, Popper, Camus—I can do without Merleau—who, before us, had unstintingly denounced the Red Terror and the gulag.

People also said: "Marxism; we used to blame Stalin and Stalinism for the gulag; the New Philosophers turn back the clock all the way to Lenin, then from Lenin to Marx himself and the entire holy family." Also true. But that wasn't all. Since the notion attributes a work begun by others, once again, to a few individuals. After all, shouldn't Aron get more credit for denouncing Stalinism? Revel for attacking Leninism? Didn't Camus give an example by denouncing Marxism, and in no uncertain terms? What about Lefort? And Castoriadis? And the infantry, behind them, of "Socialism or Barbarism"?

People also said—I myself said similar things at the time: "It's about Marxism, yes; but attacked from the Left, since there are two ways to escape Marxism; the right-wing critique that says it leads to insurrection, that it makes revolutions; and then the left-wing critique, ours, which charges it with the opposite crime, since it sees in Marxism a machine for crushing and oppressing people, for creating an ironclad order, for making revolts even rarer, for shutting off insurrections, for helping dictatorships endure, for robotizing economies, for treating people like cannon fodder." That's better. I prefer to put it that way. But it still falls short of what we were saying.

Since the truth is—I see it clearly today—that if the movement played a role; if it played a note, even a single original one, in the concert of the ideas of that time; if it was more than the flash in the pan, the media sensation, happy misunderstanding, and passing disorder that certain people claimed, and still claim, that it was, that was because—strengthened by an entire legacy and notably leaning on that so-often-denounced way of thinking that comes from 1968, and of which Foucault was the most active thinker—it was also part of a landscape of thought that infinitely surpassed it: the whole antitotalitarian movement, which denounced all four false notions, the prediscursive axioms, the prime numbers of the totalitarian delirium, and methodically took them apart.

The Absolute? Obvious. The New Philosophy was about a politics that no longer wanted to talk about creating the City of Good or the City of Ends on this earth. It dismissed any idea of a final solution to misery, disorder, or the tragedy of mankind. It thought it was better to agree on Evil than on Good, and that once we've agreed on what is Evil, we can figure out how to lessen it. And it was the choice of a politics that, in place of the ancient concern to shape the world according to a moral ideal, thought we should make the world a bit more livable for the greatest number of people, and that we would not, therefore, make concessions on the little things: life, rights here and now, human rights; and a politics, above all, that would no longer slip into the easy rhetoric of the radicals or what was called, back in the days of Stalinism, the "politics of the worst." The end of Platonism. The death of the theological-political. The victory of Epictetus and his choice of the preferable. The advantage to the sophists, and to politics conceived of as a world of indecision, indetermination, which takes into account the complexity of human affairs, the need for deliberation and compromise.

History? Also obvious. Much more than Marxism, we aimed at historicism. And, far more than historicism, at what I called, in my *Barbarism*, "the reactionary idea of progress." "What are we doing about time?" the crypto-surrealist Arthur Cravan asked, "about to leave the scene" during the famous meeting with André Gide he recounted in the July 1913 issue of *Maintenant*. "What are we doing about time?" was the same thing that Franz Rosenzweig's philosophy asked at the same time, confronting the power of a Hegelianism that had just announced that History was over and that it had given up its secret. Forty years later, after Auschwitz, the Rosenzweigian Emmanuel Levinas took up the question of "What are we doing about time?" when faced with the privilege History was assigning itself to decide what was true, just, and good; and faced with the way it had, in so doing, of fomenting not only just another dictatorship but the matrix of all dictatorships. At the time, we hadn't read Levinas. Rosenzweig's *Star of Redemption* hadn't even been translated. I myself didn't have any idea what it was about Levinas's work that was particularly Jewish. But on our own we had taken up the same question and come up with similar answers. People at the time pretended not to understand what we meant. Like the fool who looks at the finger when the wise man is pointing out the moon, or like Gide looking at his watch when Cravan asks him "What are we doing about time?," people still today can pretend that the New Philosophy was only about the gulag, Marxism, and so forth. It was basically about something else. Our first concern was purely about time. Because when we recalled that time is nothing, that time has no positive meaning, that it is not about a particular issue or a particular story, we were taking on the heart of progressivism.

And the dialectic? That Supreme Court of human misery, without appeal or recourse, which was the dialectic? Another target of the New Philosophy. Now I openly referred to Levinas. To my discovery—at first in little bits and then with increasing passion, and at the same time, by the way, when Sartre and especially Benny Lévy were discovering him too—of this great teacher, this unequaled educator, this unreserved anti-Hegelian who was the author of *Difficult Freedom*. And a whole metaphysical plan—I do mean metaphysical, since politics, at the time, was far, very far, all the way on the horizon, but a horizon that had to be redesigned, restructured, stripped of its ballast of concepts— a whole plan, I mean, in which "exit from the dialectic" was at stake and which tried to do nothing less than take up the challenge that had been launched, from the depths of night, and for almost two centuries, by those solitary men, damned men, poet-philosophers, people animated by God but who didn't believe in God, antithinkers, Batailles, Benjamins, Kierkegaards, Jews and Catholics, believers and unbelievers, godless theologians and antitheologians filled with faith: the whole brotherhood of thought that later, in my *Sartre: The Philosopher of the Twentieth Century,* I would call "Hegel's Jews" because they shared, as I do, the refusal of the idea that Hegel was the messiah that the history of philosophy had been waiting for.

And then, finally, the question of this political medicalism, this confusion of politics and medicine, which we took on with the twin tools of Foucault (*The Birth of the Clinic*) and the rudiments of theology that we had for better or worse absorbed. That was the thesis of *Barbarism with a Human Face*. As well as of the *Testament of God*. Of Laurent Dispot's *Terror Machine*. And, though he later moved away from it, this was also Philippe Muray's contribution to this moment in the history of ideas. I'm thinking in particular of his admirable *Céline*. In that book, Muray asked: how did the brilliant author of *Journey to the End of the Night* and *Death on the Installment Plan* manage to become the abject pamphleteer of the *Bagatelles pour un massacre* or the *Beaux Draps*? Relying partly on the ideas of Julia Kristeva, he answered that all that was necessary was for him to renounce his terrible but strong intuition of a humanity plunged into the darkness of its condition; all he needed was the idea, even the illumination, that the thing he had thought of as an Evil from which we could only free men by amputating a part of themselves was nothing more than a curable affectation; Céline became an anti-Semite when, replacing politics with technique, he put the question in terms of a bad germ and a good cure; he became that Nazi, that propagandist of the Final Solution, right when he remembered that before he was called Céline he was Destouches, the good doctor Destouches, the doctor of the poor, a doctor above all, an expert in curing human, all too human illnesses. New Philosophy? "Some things are Incurable. . . ."

PARDON THIS historical digression.

And pardon me, above all, for emphasizing this historical moment in which I myself was so directly involved.

The truth is that whenever I can, I try to speak of things I have lived through personally and therefore know less badly than I know other things.

And the fact is, when I look back at this short series of events; when I think back on those feverish years; when I see us there, dueling, on the podium of the Revue Parlée of the Centre Pompidou, with morons who called us fascists because we were explaining that the advantage of the Catholic concept of sin was that it kept at bay those who wanted to remodel the human race; when I see us, with André Glucksmann, during the Mexican lecture tour I've already mentioned, battling in the amphitheaters full of students calling the poor people fleeing Castro's tropical gulag on flimsily improvised rafts *gusanos,* literally "worms," and where we expressed our concerns about this word *gusano,* objecting that a worm can be crushed underfoot and that we found it a bizarre form of socialism that sought to crush its dissidents underfoot, under its jackboots, flourishing the paper bags full of human excrement that were thrown at us and that farted when they hit us; when I see Maurice Clavel—who had just discovered Lardreau and Jambet's book, with its radical questioning of what they called the "barbarous angel"— exclaiming, foaming at the mouth, gesticulating wildly, and walking with elephant-like steps down the middle of the Rue des Saints-Pères and through the cars that were honking at him: "It's the Patton offensive, it's the Patton offensive"; when I see Foucault, the dreamer; Deleuze, mocking but interested, during our long afternoon teas at the Lutétia, who earlier, when he discovered the way he was dealt with in *Barbarism with a Human Face,* counterattacked only in a vengeful article that was rather funny about the "infection" we represented. When, indeed, I look back on all that, I think that in that whole adventure there was something in it that was random, contingent, full of comical and absurd misunderstandings, agitation, useless disorder, thunderous polemics that were soon forgotten, farce—but that it nonetheless had its virtues, and that among them was that it methodically finished off the four pillars of totalitarianism.

One could take any number of other examples from other philosophical and spiritual families that participated, at the same time, in the same great movement of antitotalitarian resistance and revolt that was the dominant theme of those years.

We would get the same results if we focused on the story, for example, of the journal *Esprit* in the days of Olivier Mongin; or on the heirs of Socialisme ou Barbarie; or on the collaborators of the magazine *Tel Quel*—here I've got Philippe Sollers and Marcelin Pleynet in mind— with whom the New Philosophers cemented an alliance at the end of the seventies, an alliance that still exists, and that exists *because* it was the product not of some passing political circumstance but of shared metaphysical concerns.

Because the simple fact is there—and it touches on the entire period.

Today, I no longer see many people trying to explain that concentration camps, massacres, crimes against humanity, genocides, can, in certain circumstances, bearing in mind a certain conjuncture or a relation of powers, be historically necessary, have an almost divine legitimacy, and be part of the plan of the Absolute.

I don't hear many people say that the Chechen rebels are the salt of the earth of the Caucasus; or that the Palestinians are not only about to achieve their own state but to regenerate humanity; or that the massacres in Darfur are part of the plan of History and therefore blessed by the Gods; I don't hear—as one still did thirty years ago with regard to other bloodbaths—that the humanists who get worked up about the victims of Rwanda are simpletons who haven't read enough Hegel and who would know, if they had, that the dialectic might very well have to chop off a few heads; and neither do I hear, as one did back then, literally, forty years ago, that the Tibetans are lice, harmful insects, germs, who can be treated only by the millenary political medicine of the Chinese.

I see myself thirty-five years ago in the Bengal jungle, running after the delicate murderers who were the Indian Naxalites, ready to see them certainly not as heroes but as fully fledged political actors, a mix of activists and adventurers, the poetry of fugitives, doing the double bidding of arms and dreams; I see myself, after several days of marching through the flooded rice paddies of the Ganges Delta, meeting up with one of their leaders, the mysterious Mohammed Toha, who, like Frantz Fanon, was dying in his oxygen tent but still found the strength to explain, without much argument from me, that the deliverance of the Subcontinent, perhaps its health or its regeneration, started there, in that forest clearing where, that very morning, his forces had executed, with a Mauser bullet to the neck, a dozen "landowners": I see that, yes; I see that scene as if it were yesterday and, in a way, it was yesterday—except that it has become impossible; neither I nor any young man today as old as I was then would fall into that trap and stomach such phrases.

TIMES HAVE CHANGED.

Paradigms have moved on.

An ideological battle, the real one, has been won.

And I might say it's been won twice—or, rather, it took two victories to triumph over it.

Once in real history (Portugal, May '68, Cambodia, Solzhenitsyn), which destroyed all the old foundational myths of the totalitarian notion of progress.

And a second time in the history of ideas—New Philosophers, but not only them, who, like the bird that sees well in the night, finished off, conceptually, everything that had started to dissolve in the realm of real history.

After that, the Left kept talking nonsense, of course.

Still today, as we shall now see, it still errs, sometimes infamously.

But it's no longer the same nonsense.

These are errors of another order.

Because here's the crux of the matter, which I confusedly felt on that afternoon of January 23, 2007, but which now comes into sharper relief: once upon a time there was the Left; once upon a time there was a Left which, for more than a century, was threatened by a terrible totalitarian temptation; for the most part it's gotten rid of it; after an unremitting, decades-long combat, one which it often nearly lost, it's managed to overcome it; but everything's gone on in the ruins that combat created—or, put another way, a part of the Left got stuck in the void the first temptation left behind, and this is the part we now need to diagnose.

The Return of the Ghosts

Which one, then?

What are its symptoms? Its pillars? Its new structures?

And above all, how does this *second temptation* relate to the first—do they share common roots? Does the second one have any of the characteristics of the first? Is there a continuity, and if so which one?

I'm getting there. . . .

But first, a final, a very last detour—connected, like the first, to the presidential elections: this time, with the campaign of Ségolène Royal.

One day I'll write about it.

One day I'll explain my reasons for my vigorous, determined involvement in her campaign.

But anyway.

For now, the important thing is that Ségolène Royal seemed to me to be standing at the intersection of two contradictory forces.

The important thing is that almost every time she ended up doing the right thing, despite the two antagonistic Lefts who warred over her campaign and her speeches, almost whisking her away in the process.

There was a Left that cared about human rights and one that didn't.

A Left that thought freedom was nonnegotiable and another that was ready to sell it out.

A Left for whom being on the Left was meaningless if it didn't mean always, everywhere, taking the side of the victims, of the oppressed—and another that tied itself into knots, in the name of some ideological considerations that weren't immediately clear to me, exhorting the candidate not to let herself be carried off by some trendy feeling for victims and to distinguish clearly between good and bad oppressed people.

The same old story, as it were.

The same eternal trash I've spent my life denouncing.

But there was one detail.

One little difference—but a decisive one, one that changed everything.

There was no longer any talk of Revolution.

There was no longer any question of a future Good in whose name people had always been ready to sacrifice present generations, short-term emotions, those useless Chinese, Russian, or African dissidents.

THE ANTITOTALITARIAN revolution had left its mark; the old paradigms had been shattered; the old notion of progress no longer held water; and there was no longer the slightest sign of another world being possible, of a more radiant future, of singing tomorrows—together with a wait-and-see attitude toward human rights.

In a word, I saw in what Royal sometimes said—and especially in what certain people seemed to want her to say and which, thank God, she didn't always—a strange tone, like a low voice accompanying her campaign, a funny mix of energy and world-weariness; of the useless wheel-spinning of idle angers churning inside; of old reflexes shorn of the system that went along with them; of certain unfortunate declarations, but without the language that once programmed them and lent them their meaning; naïve and above all hopeless radical standpoints; cold fevers I observed, bursting up like bubbles on the surface of the "Royalist" discourse, some dubious little phrase about Israel or Islamism, some surreptitious quote from Viviane Forrester's *Economic Horror* or from Naomi Klein's *No Logo,* some silly charge against liberalism or against the universality of rights imposed on the whole planet, some minuscule movement away from Europe, which she immediately corrected—and I told myself, basically, the following.

I've seen a full-blown obsession with a Marxist notion of progress that didn't bother with human rights.

I've seen a totalitarian temptation that had the nerve, when it was being oppressive or blessing oppression, to claim it was doing so in the name of a superior Good.

I was seeing the burgeoning of a Left that wanted to keep on oppressing and murdering people in Darfur, to keep on muzzling Chinese dissidents and the free journalists of Russia, to keep on, meanwhile, and out of sheer habit, attacking the American-Zionist axis—but not in the name of anything in particular, not in the name of any great Good.

So what's left, when there's no more Good?

Can it just be pointless hatred? Hatred of the void, and in the void? A pure desire for revenge? Servility as a bad habit? Politics as a sad and washed-out passion; smoke from some old fire; a ghostly, futile uproar; a useless but persistent lie? Progressivism without progress? Socialism reduced to the joint ownership of resentment?

Weirder and weirder . . .

BY PAYING CLOSER attention, I understood.

All around Royal, even sometimes in her very words and in those of her nearest advisers—but even more around her—you could hear other strange words, not exactly those borrowed from the Left's old lexicon.

You could see—as when she suggested sticking the tricolor flag on the windows of every French home, without a thought of adding the European flag—certain concerns, even obsessions.

There was the "just order," the "popular juries" to keep an eye on elected officials, the talk of placing young people over the age of sixteen in "military-like institutions to teach them a trade or to carry out humanitarian work after their first act of delinquency," the fantasy of transforming society into a kind of generalized boarding school—and now there was, at the end of the rope, as soon as a difficulty appeared, the constant suggestion of referring everything to the deep wisdom of the "territories," our version of Middle America.

In the words of a man who was still then one of her closest advisers, we could read that the candidate Sarkozy was an "American neoconservative with a French passport."

We didn't hear many voices, on the other hand, resisting Sarkozy's more obnoxious statements, which therefore sailed through—about a France innocent of the Final Solution, the Algerian War, or May '68.

And then, above all, there was one character operating backstage and who I quickly learned—in the climate of amateurism around the candidate, and in the desert that grew up around her—was busy placing himself in a position of considerable influence: one character I had known in the past and whose voice, whose footsteps, and whose signature I could have picked out from a million, who was truly one of the bad spirits of the campaign: the character of Jean-Pierre Chevènement.

I remembered him as a young Socialist leader, part of that "Group of Experts" for which François Mitterrand had recruited me to counter him in 1972, after my return from Bangladesh.

I remembered him next as a state minister; he's enraged that I dared to write, in *Le Matin de Paris,* which is to say the paper that he ought to see as the official organ of the government Left, in which he is one of the leading figures, about the Vichy-like feel of the first months of the Left in power, and in particular regarding his own speeches (national socialism; France alone; praise of the little shopkeeper over great cosmopolitan capital; anti-Americanism; and—borrowing a leaf from Maurice Barrès—praise, on Armistice Day, of the earth and the dead, etc.).

I thought about everything I'd learned since about his crazed nationalism; about his frenetic anti-Americanism combined, back when there was a Soviet Union, with a simple-minded Sovietophilia; about his calls to "reestablish France" by keeping its connection to the "real country"; about his passion for authority, the army, order. His hatred of May '68, which, like Sarkozy but long before him, he'd always seen as the beginning of the "liberal, libertarian" ideals that had undermined the foundations of the Nation and plunged France into decline. Joan of Arc. Authenticity. The defense of Saddam Hussein and his so-called secularism.

I thought about all of that.

I heard the echo of all of that.

I never met him or even ran into him during all those weeks of campaigning. But old enemies are like old friends. You can feel them a long way off. The slightest signs, which nobody else pays attention to, tell you they're coming.

Chevènement wasn't Chevènement; Chevènement was much less, or much more, than Chevènement himself; Chevènement was a slip of the tongue; Chevènement was a symptom; and when I made the connection between this slip of the tongue and what I was seeing happen, at the same time, in other fields, and particularly in the scene that I knew best, the intellectual world, when I connected this symptom to others, less visible but not necessarily less eloquent, such as—to take a few random examples—the rehabilitation of Carl Schmitt by Giorgio Agamben or Étienne Balibar, Heidegger triumphing once and for all over Marx and Hegel; Régis Debray's drift toward nationalism and his critique, soon after, of the "democratic obscenity"; Alain Badiou's writings on Kosovo or Judaism; Jean Baudrillard's text about the September 11th attacks; the debates on Islam—I couldn't fail to see that a true coherence was taking shape and that this campaign was just one more outcropping of one phenomenon.

LET'S GET TO THE POINT.

This is the hypothesis of this whole book, so I might as well come out and say it.

I was thinking that this progressivism without progress, this pointless radicalism, might not have been quite as empty, nor as ill-conceived, as it seemed.

I was coming to realize that what we'd been witnessing since the collapse of the totalitarian temptation was a chemical process of combustion, distillation, and recomposition that was more complex than the metaphors of a cold fever or a mechanical lie—useless, habitual reflexes—might suggest.

I was coming to understand that it wasn't enough to say that the Left had triumphed over its first totalitarian temptation only to fall into another, one that took its place in the void it had left behind, like grass sprouting among its ruins—but that we had to add one more thing to the description: by virtue of a new, singular ruse, but one not unprecedented in the history of ideas, the most singular characteristic of this second temptation is that it no longer takes its inspiration from the Left but from the Right.

A right-wing Left, indeed.

Literally from the Right, in fact.

An oxymoronic Left, a Left that makes your head spin—a Left that, if words have any meaning at all, is sometimes more right-wing than the right wing itself.

That's the situation that people who understand that words do indeed have and keep their meanings find themselves in.

And that's the situation, in particular, of the author of this book: thirty years on, I mean exactly thirty years since a *Barbarism with a Human Face* that already had opened with an address, full of hope, to the Left ("I'm talking to the Left; I'm speaking to it because it is my family, because I speak its language and because I believe in its ethics, if not in the depth of its knowledge")—the same situation, the same configuration, as before—the settings have changed, but the struggle rages on.

PART THREE

CRITIQUE OF NEOPROGRESSIVE REASON

Liberalism Is Their Enemy

The very first symptom of this reversal, the first flagrant case where we can see its pernicious effects, is the odd fate, nowadays, of anti-liberal themes.

Of course, this is not only happening on the Left.

And I'm well aware that, for reasons having to do with its past and with the history of its national software, all of France, and Europe, and the Western World as a whole, resists a liberalism that is the object of an unprecedented condemnation: isn't the word *liberal,* for the entire political class of my country, a kind of dirty word that nobody ventures to utter without elaborate precautions? Haven't we had a president, once again Jacques Chirac, who, defining liberalism as "a perversion of the human spirit," concluded that its triumph would be "as disastrous" as the triumph of "Communism"?[1] And didn't Alexis de Tocqueville, as so often before, get to the heart of the matter when he evoked the way the French think about the relationship between the State and society—the attachment not only on the part of the party of Progress but of the conservatives themselves—to the centralizing, and strictly Jacobin model that came from the Revolution?

But at the end of the day I've decided, here, to focus on the Left.

I want to make a list of the poisons that threaten it.

And then I have to admit that, regardless of whether I focus on it, the Left is, in any case, where the malady is the farthest advanced—I have to agree that our Left, ever since its Marxist days, has issued a kind of fatwa over the word *liberalism,* and that, as it usually goes with fatwas, hasn't changed since Marxism died: from the neo-Communists, who make liberalism a near-synonym of fascism, to those leaders of the antiglobalist group ATTAC (Association for the Taxation of Financial Transactions for the Aid of Citizens) who explain, in the purest exterminating-angel style, that their "objective" is to "root out the liberal virus from people's minds so that those minds can start to function normally,"[2] to that "socialist left" that rejected the European Constitutional Treaty because of its "liberal inspiration," to that first secretary of the Party, who in principle was pro-European but who agreed that "liberalism runs against the European spirit itself,"[3] which is to say that antiliberalism has become not only a slogan but a commandment, a horizon, a program and the substitute for every program, the lowest common denominator for all branches of the family, a crusade, a hope. France is the only country in the world in which people use the word *antiliberal* in the same way they used to use the term *anticapitalist....*

I AM WELL AWARE that the liberalism we're talking about here is "economic" liberalism.

I know that we're dealing with a liberalism which Socialist leaders take care to describe, whenever they are asked about it, not as liberalism "itself" but simply "neo" or "ultra" liberalism.

And I know, above all, that most of them sincerely believe that they're making a point of this only because the others, their adversaries—the advocates of happy globalization, the apostles of profit and of the law of the economic jungle, the partisans of a society in which everything's for sale—have raised the issue.

But at the same time, who are we kidding here?

Let's leave aside the reflex, which claims to be post-Marxist, which describes the market as a terrifying biopolitical experiment using citizens as guinea pigs: besides the fact that this process has been taken down a notch since the creeping Godesberg Program our Left has had to resign itself to, the Marxist analysis, the real one, the one that stressed the "revolutionary" purpose of the market, had other attractions—and now our postmodern antiliberals are getting closer to the obscure abominations Marx attributed to the "Parisian literary bohemia" or, during his polemics with Lassalle, to "the essentially absolutist anti-liberalism" or the "royal-Prussian governmental socialism."

Let's ignore—since it would be too cruel for those beautiful minds who think they're at the vanguard of the party of intelligence—the modern analyses about the "metaphysical" meaning of money, the "sociality" of money, as Levinas put it: its "civilizing" function; the virtuous way it substitutes commerce for war, open borders for closed worlds; the rhythm of negotiation, transaction, and compromise that commerce substitutes for violence, barter, plunder, all-or-nothing, fanaticism.

Let's forget about that nice text[4] in which Jacques Derrida—from whom I will soon part ways—establishes that the "very possibility of money" and of "price," the generalized "principle of equivalence" is what, all by itself, allows the "neutralization of differences to achieve pure singularity as a dignity and a universal right"—let's forget, in that same text, the conclusion that could mediate the Pavlovized adversaries of alienation through commodities and exchange and all those who imagine that economic liberalism is a refined form of dictatorship: the "rejection of money or of its principle of indifference," the "contempt for calculation" and of "the logic of the merchant," could "connive"—here it's still my "old teacher" Jacques Derrida speaking—with "the destruction of morality and law."

Let's even forget the question of knowing if we can, philosophically or technically, separate things the way some people would have us do, dividing political liberalism from economic liberalism, Constant's liberalism from Smith's: if we can know whether they're substantially connected, part and parcel of the same package, the double pistons of the same machine for cooling the Leviathan's ardor—not coincidentally the same word: language watching a bit over people's minds and the truth of the matter; as we know, this is Montesquieu's thesis, in the *Esprit des lois,* that "without economic liberty, political liberty is endangered"—and vice versa.

Let's forget all of that.

The problem is the crazed ignorance most of these people display when they try to tell us that liberalism *is* the market, when it really is the contract. This deep idiocy causes them to repeat, to the point of dizziness, that liberalism *is* the jungle, the state of nature, humanity submitted to wild whims, whereas in fact—according to the theorists of the Manchester school, according to Adam Smith and Jeremy Bentham or Friedrich Hayek today—liberalism is precisely the attempt to master the law of the jungle, to leave the state of nature, to invent norms and rules allowing us to rise above the struggle of every man for himself.

Real liberalism has always meant, according to all its theoreticians, thinking about how law, and thus the State, can reduce the effects of concentrating income or creating monopolies, which the free market always risks engendering (doesn't Leo Strauss go so far as to say that for that very reason—because liberalism is no more than "the political doctrine whose fundamental fact is in man's natural rights as opposed to his duties"; because it lauds a State whose "mission" consists, against the free rein of all the laws of all the jungles, of "protecting and safeguarding these rights"—Hobbes is the first liberal thinker?).

Adam Smith theorized the invisible hand, of course. He still believes in a God who is no longer a watchmaker but an auctioneer, who allows supply and demand to adjust to one another. But, as for the famous pure market, unshackled and left to its own devices, which its adversaries brandish like a fan, what a joke! Rather, that's one of those fictions which political philosophy, from Plato to Rousseau, has always employed to make social realities more intelligible. And *The Wealth of Nations* was written instead to counter the very concrete spectacle of those monopolizing English businessmen who refused competition, as Smith's attempt to make them fall back into line. In any event, this is all far removed from the famous "free market." . . .

The problem, the drama, is that these morons have forgotten the lesson of Michel Foucault who, at the end of his life, in his *Leçons,* written on the very topic of liberalism,[5] established that there is a "liberal art of governing" or—which amounts to the same thing—that "liberal" is another name for a modern form of "governmentality," which he worried about, of course, and whose perverse codes and sources he tried to break down, but which he never would have allowed to say, first of all, that it was pure "laissez-faire" or an "absence of government," and which he then planned to show had had the historical merit of "breaking" with a regime of "raison d'État" which, "since the end of the sixteenth century," had justified authoritarian and cruel forms of "governmentality." The problem is that, forgetting Foucault, we fall into Bourdieu, and—this kind of fall being as interminable as it is irresistible—eventually forget Bourdieu himself, only to fall into the hands of those dwarves who call themselves his disciples.

For there is another example of this collapse.

There is the case of that other adventure of the antiliberal dialectic which has been deployed over the last few years by the followers of Bourdieu, dealing with and departing from Foucault's concept of the "episteme."

For Foucault, "episteme" was a notion that allowed us to identify the underground rules governing, in any period, the appearance of knowledge, formulations, and events in discourse (a notion perhaps derived from Heidegger but which found, in *The Order of Things* and *Archaeology of Knowledge,* an impressive descriptive and heuristic power).

Bourdieu takes this down a notch, since his "episteme" becomes the "field" and—with this idea of a "field," reputedly more "inventive" than the subjects who hold to it—comes the "cartographic" vision of "intellectual life" conceived as a program of fatal "behaviors," a tight grip of "neighborhoods," even a collection of "slots to be taken" by individuals who—even when they look different, even when they seem to be moved by a spirit of fierce competition—all submit to a group of prescriptions which really indicate their dark and profound "connivance." . . . Who was it who said of bad philosophers that they are violent people who, with no weapon at their disposal, get a hold on the world and reduce it by locking it into a system? What is certain is that we're quite far off, with this concept of "connivance," from the "basement" of "anonymous rules" that, according to Foucault, accounted both for regularities *and* for ruptures, for common structures *and* for unexpected setbacks, in short, the "epistemic simultaneities," the "rules of the constitution of objects," *but also* of the "play" which, in any given episteme, can make books, for example, "a kind of scalpel, Molotov cocktail, or underground tunnel."[6]

And then, at last, the epigones, which we find in all the lowliest followers of Bourdieu, disciples too busy looking for a "critical thought"—in which they think that "critical" means detestation or denunciation—all those hacks, with their idiotic alter-globalization mania, of the *Monde diplomatique* variety, who really seem to believe that a "hermeneutics of suspicion" means a philosophy of seeing cops, interrogators, and prosecutors in every nook and cranny of society.

Sometimes it's a theory of "networks" and of "systems of influence" in which the famous "field" becomes a vulgar machine at the "orders" of the "government," of "business groups," of "owners" of newspapers, in a word, a handful of invisible, corrupt, ill-meaning actors, "sufficiently few in number to be able to act together" and sufficiently crafty to be able to "veil their real plans." Really a strange process, of the degradation of the conceptual energy which, starting off with philosophy, making its way through sociology, and petering out in the lowest form of conspiracy theory—the obsession with the plot that was always the stock in trade of the far right and which is now becoming the creed of antiliberalism . . .

But anyway. Let's forget all that as well.

And, for the time being, let's not think about the criminal effects this kind of theoretical silliness can have when it bumps into the real world—the conclusion that could be drawn, for example, in the Third World: since liberalism is the source of all the planet's evils, local states, elites that monopolize and pillage them, government practices that meddle with their citizens and treat them like cattle, ought to be declared innocent of a misery for which the System, and the System alone, bears full responsibility.

And now let's take a serious look at these people's other big idea, which they seem to cherish above all others—that the term "liberal

state" has two different meanings, and that we need to remove its ambiguity by separating the two: taking the "good" and leaving the "bad";
keeping liberty but getting rid of liberalism; keeping—if we must—
liberalism, but only its rational core, prying away its extremist trap-
pings; as the most constructed of these characters say, in their moments
of lucidity: "Don't abandon liberalism to the antiliberals." . . .[7]

SO WE WON'T even do that.

Even that gesture, that small gesture, that tiny semantic-political
battle: the Left talks about it, but doesn't do anything about it.

The Left, which goes so far out of its way—so it claims—not to
abandon the flag or Joan of Arc to the Right; the Left, which for decades
has insisted on not letting Le Pen monopolize patriotism or the idea
of the nation; the Left, unrivaled when, for its own purposes, it tries
to retake the symbolism that would allow it (I'm still quoting here)
to face off with the enemy when it comes to an insecure electorate, taking on the debates about violence, the *banlieues,* and so forth: the Left
stays mute, as if completely dumbfounded, on this one point: faced
with a problem that at the very least is no less essential to its destiny,
the problem of giving a purer meaning to a word misused by a group
that isn't entirely on the Left but isn't, as far as we know, made up of
concentration-camp guards either—for the first time the Left has no
answer. . . .

If you think about it, this phenomenon is stunning.

Whether it's a slip of the tongue, a gap in the discourse, a theoretical distraction, a denial—call it what you will—it has terrible consequences that we have not given enough thought to.

And the memory of words being what it is (ruthless—sometimes
more so than the simple logic of facts); the unconscious of political languages working in the way we understand (behind its actors' backs);
this gesture, or rather this nongesture, can itself only have incalculable
consequences: the representatives of this trend—of this Left that has
not given the beautiful word *liberty* a hundredth of the amount of
thought they have devoted to words like *fatherland, nation,* and *security;*

those scatterbrains who haven't felt the least bit of compunction in seeing themselves dubbed or, especially, dubbing themselves, "antiliberals"—
those people, in other words, of this other "French exception," who
have never felt the need to sketch out the lines of demarcation that,
for example, the Italians inherited from Benedetto Croce,[8] dividing
"liberism" from liberalism (for Croce, "liberism" meant a corruption of
liberalism holding the free market as the supreme law of social life, not
preventing its utilitarianism from contaminating even ethics: a notion
whose latest incarnation is Silvio Berlusconi . . .), and committing, in
fact, three errors, three major mistakes: and which is the most worri-
some I can't say.

They reject, first of all, the three great revolutions—the English, the
American, and, in its early years, the French—which were explicitly liberal revolutions; which conceived of liberalism as an instrument of
struggle against absolutism; and which, thanks to liberalism, brought
down its centuries-old reign: Adieu Lafayette! Farewell to the abolition, thanks to our Constituent Assembly, of guilds, corporations, priv-
ileges, and other monopolies! Farewell to the Whigs, the disciples of
John Locke, and their fight for civil liberties! Down with those "liberals" on the other side of the Atlantic who according to our "neos" em-
body "the other America," the one they claim to love and for which
they say they're fighting but from which one word, that single word, in
fact separates them hopelessly! And long live, on the other hand, that
Iranosaurus of the worldwide antiliberal crusade! Viva Chávez, whose
antiliberal rhetoric, the Latin American bishopric itself notes, resem-
bles "that of regimes of the Nazi or Fascist type"![9]

They then throw overboard the entire popular memory, in France
and Europe, which, over the course of centuries, has never managed to
dissociate (and we've already seen that this is not the worst definition
of the Left) struggles for liberty from the fight for equality: the barri-
cades of 1830; Gavroche and Delacroix; indeed: thinking they're getting at George Soros, they manage to take down Gavroche; the first
Socialists, every last one of whom, including the utopians, described
themselves as liberals; public and private liberties against Leviathan;
the Herculean work of societies refusing, step by step, thanks to liber-

alism, to be dragged along by a state with totalitarian pretensions; the Commune, once more, making it a point of honor to guarantee, almost to the very end, the free circulation of the newspapers from Versailles in the rebellious capital; the right to organized labor invented by European liberals and then, after the Commune, while the Socialists opposed it out of fear of demobilizing the working class, engraved in the marble of the (liberal) law of 1884; not to speak of those working-class insurrections which, from Budapest (1956) to Gdansk (1980), all, and always, kept alive the spirit of the European Enlightenment, which is to say the double flame, inseparable, of a nonnegotiable demand for political rights and a nostalgia, no less negotiable, for a social situation in which conditions would be less unequal.

And as for the Enlightenment itself, as for this question of the Enlightenment which has lately been stirring up the intellectual community, here is what these "antiliberals" do with it. In the best-case scenario, they are still hashing out the old debate, which raged in Althusserian circles in the sixties, contrasting simple "liberals" like Turgot, Voltaire, or Montesquieu with "eighteenth-century materialists" such as Helvétius, d'Holbach, Du Marsais, or La Mettrie, whose works were supposed to be Marxist *avant la lettre*. But in reality, and more often than not, they distance themselves from that whole old Enlightenment scene to go right to the only scene that managed to create a real, serious, critique—without concessions or mincing words—of this liberalism that had become their main enemy: the Radical Enlightenment[10] is still, according to them, bogged down in the swamp from which they have to be extracted at all costs; Marxism itself is out of fashion and has, in front of that cursed liberalism, a far-too-nuanced attitude. So, all that is left is, for them, to rediscover what Hannah Arendt called the "Counter-Enlightenment," the tradition that leads from Burke to Herder and then to Maurras and the fascist and Nazi ideologues, good workers who had long been laboring to foil the liberal plot.

This odd reunion was achieved in several steps.

It took the form, over the years, of the many Red-Brown syntheses I'll be coming back to.

I'll only cite one particularly devastating example: a few of the leading lights of the intellectual class, in the limited but still pacesetting circle of those in the world of ideas who long for a "great" debate, just rediscovered and even heralded one of the most powerful theoreticians of the Counter-Enlightenment—or, putting it more precisely, a theoretician whose antiliberalism led him to the very worst, which is to say Nazism: Carl Schmitt.

THE STORY REALLY is extraordinary.

Since we know the story of Carl Schmitt.[11]

We know that his case is at least as awkward as Heidegger's, and even more consequential, since Schmitt actually produced some of the canonical texts justifying the anti-Jewish Nuremberg laws (among other wonders of Nazi legal studies, *The Constitution of Freedom* of 1935 and the two works from 1936 charmingly entitled *The Führer Protects the Law* and *The German Science of Law in Its Struggle Against the Jewish Spirit*).

Above all, we know the story of this great professor who defined himself, in a conversation with Ernst Niekisch, as "Roman by origin, tradition, and right":[12] in other words as a Catholic intellectual, conservative, not in the least romantic and rather hostile, as a result, to anything that might seem like a repugnant revolutionary paganism— we are perfectly aware of the logical process that nonetheless led him, ineluctably, from his methodical hatred of abstract universalism, human rights, rights and law in general, the parliamentary system, humanism, liberalism as a whole, to an unreserved and—to top it all off—unrepentant allegiance to the Nazi Party (unrepentant because, in the journal he kept after the war, published after his death under the title of *Glossarium*,[13] he was still haranguing those damned Jews who— unlike "Communists," who "can improve and change"—"always stay Jews" and, in the guise of the "assimilated Jew," still incarnate the "true enemy"; unrepentant, too, because even in 1963 he expressed as few regrets for his "foolishness" as his contemporary Heidegger, seeing Nazism as nothing more than the "ills of the modern age" and, in the Holocaust, an almost banal "war crime").[14]

It's hard to say that none of this, none of these statements which at the very least are awkward and which contaminate, from one end to the other, the system and the prose of an ideologue who certainly wasn't stupid but who also was neither Heidegger nor Hegel, nor any of those giant thinkers whose embarrassments we have to swallow because their writing is unavoidable and because without it we can only think less well and less highly—it's hard to say, I repeat, that none of these delicate statements has been enough to dampen the very strange infatuation, practically an epidemic, which has been developing over the last ten years and which has seen our antiliberal intellectuals not only reading this character but signing on to his writings.

Am I overstating it?

All you have to do is read him—the texts are there.

Althusser's disciples send our common teacher spinning in his grave when, like Étienne Balibar, they celebrate the author of *The Leviathan in the State Theory of Thomas Hobbes*[15] as the theoretician of the "state of exception" which always takes precedence over "the hegemonic order"; the contemporary philosopher who best allows us to "conceive of the constitutional order based on the state of exception"; the man who managed to "examine in an extraordinarily acute fashion the formation and the function of the modern state";[16] the guide to the perplexed for the lost Marxism.

The mind-boggling indulgence of the historic leader of the Revolutionary Communist League[17] who, in February 2006, meditated on the "eclipse of the strategic debate" which seemed to him to mark our age and returning, on this occasion, to the concept of "the dictatorship of the proletariat" and on the "state of exception" which is the "obligatory passage" which also lends itself to the "attentive reader of the polemic between Lenin and Kautsky," the theoretician who "perfectly grasped the issue" of the necessary distinction between the (bad) "dictatorship of the commissars" and the (good) "sovereign dictatorship," this master of thought who allowed the antiliberal movement to move past the "social illusion" that brought down all the antiglobalization movements of the Seattle or Porto Alegre variety—Carl Schmitt once again, always

Carl Schmitt, a Carl Schmitt who is frankly presented to us as the savior of a Left that is adrift and no longer knows what saint, or what devil, to worship.

That's how Pierre Bourdieu himself answers—without citing its author, but textually—Schmitt's definition of liberalism as the "politics of depoliticization,"[18] since having lost the good science of distinguishing between "friends and enemies" which is the major contribution of this grandee of political science (I have to say in passing that I've never understood very well why this distinction between friends and enemies was so extraordinarily important . . .) who takes from it, at least in part, his critique of the contradictions, the deadlocks, and the weaknesses of the liberal regime.

Intellectuals like Giorgio Agamben[19] once again call on Schmitt to think about the "state of exception," which is supposed to tell us, this time, the "truth of the political," the "real face" of democracies, and the real face, in any event, of American democracy post-9/11. And even more troubling, the same Agamben seeks in Schmitt's condemnation of the notion of a "just war" the tools he needs to allow the European Left to oppose Bush's adventure in Iraq. It's true that the concept of the "just war" poses problems. It is true that—because it is carried out in the name of justice and righteousness, because it morally disqualifies the enemy and tosses him into the shadows of barbarity—the "just war" can't impose limits on itself. And it's true that this is a kind of war that—unlike traditional wars in which people fought over, for example, a territory—will always be tempted to annihilate its enemy. But do we really need Schmitt to realize that? Isn't there another way to warn us against the dangers of morality in politics than to dig it out of a book, *The Nomos of the Earth,* which was also a legitimization of Hitler's expansionism? Wouldn't the antitotalitarian and therefore liberal critique of the idea of the Sovereign Good—the warning we find in Hannah Arendt or Camus against all forms of political hubris—have done just as well? At most, didn't Clausewitz's concept of the rise to extremes have everything required, and even more, for describing the madness of wars?

In the last years of Jacques Derrida's life—in *Voyous,* and then in *The*

Politics of Friendship, and then in the texts that resulted from 9/11—we saw the theoretician of decisionism's incredible stranglehold over the apostle of deconstruction—though, to be sure, with a step backward, for all purposes, though a step backward which is only all the more eloquent for that: when, in April 2003, Derrida met the founder of the "Brussels Tribunal" and its "Investigating Commission" on the "New Imperial Order" desired by the Cheneys, Rumsfelds, and other such Wolfowitzes; when he decided to grant an interview to people whose questions led one to guess, as so often with sects, that they themselves no longer have the slightest shadow of a doubt about the new line that claims there is no hope for the Churches of the radical Left except recourse to a Nazi thinker, he feels the need to warn that we "have to be very careful when discussing Carl Schmitt"—we "have to take him seriously," he insists, we certainly have to read him and take him seriously, but we have to avoid letting that "thoughtfulness" be "construed as agreement with his theses or with his past history."[20]

This is the new darling of the antiliberal movement, Slavoj Žižek.[21]

And this is Peter Sloterdijk, in his interviews with Alain Finkielkraut,[22] saying that it's time to move from the paradigm of the other (Levinas) to that of the enemy (Schmitt, once again).

In other words, a whole part of the Left, deprived of Marx, is now embracing Schmitt—seeking in the latter the reasons for thinking and acting that they can no longer find in the former.

A whole segment of the European—and notably French—intelligentsia is marching as a single man behind the strange and, the more one thinks about it, hallucinatory idea that we need a Nazi thinker to help the Left out of its gridlock.

And in the United States a whole swath of enlightened opinion feels the same way. Schmitt's influence on neoconservatives like Wolfowitz is well known. We know how well Schmitt's thought rhymes with the writings of Leo Strauss, just as it does with those of Alexandre Kojève—who claimed, at the beginning of the fifties, that Schmitt was "the only person worth seeing" in Germany. We know how, more recently, when he was cooking up his bad concept of "civilization," Samuel Huntington could not have not been thinking—just as he was of certain ideas derived from Spengler—of the notion of "Greater Space" (*Grossräum*) as it appears, among others, in *Land and Sea*. We are less aware of the deaf influence Schmitt's thought exercises on the other end of the political spectrum, on those known in the United States as "liberals"—or even, in certain cases, of the veritable war of appropriation raging between the two sides over the concept of decisionism. This is what Judith Butler is doing in her text about Guantánamo as a place of tension—very "Schmittian"—between the concepts of "naked life" and "sovereign power." Or Gopal Balakrishnan, member of the editorial committee of the *New Left Review*, penning a quite self-indulgent work called *The Enemy: An Intellectual Portrait of Carl Schmitt*[23] in which he discusses precisely Leo Strauss's interpretation of Schmitt. Or Chantal Mouffe, inviting her readers, at the opening of *The Challenge of Carl Schmitt*,[24] to "think both with and against Schmitt." Or William E. Scheuerman's insistence on the "disturbingly relevant" character, in post-9/11 America, of a *Theory of the Partisan* which has just been translated for the first time into English.[25] Or of course Ellen Kennedy, the first to promote the idea of Schmitt's influence on the theoreticians of the Frankfurt School and then on the liberalism of the American Left, inviting her readers to find in the writings of the author of *The Nomos of the Earth* the theoretic tools required for a world that is no longer intelligible in the terms and concepts of traditional liberalism.[26]

ONLY ONE GOD can save us, Heidegger used to say.

Only a Nazi can save us, this group on the Left, both American and European, echoes.

We can see this as either an enigma or a confession—or, as I do, a sign of the times.

Since this is probably very far from the Left that undermined the campaigns of Ségolène Royal or John Edwards.

I am well aware that these people have nothing but disdain for what they never call the "parliamentary left."

But this gets to the heart of the laboratories where the spirit of the age, and the politics of the future, are being distilled.

LIBERALISM IS THEIR ENEMY

And what we find brewing in this pot is a mixture of moldy radical-ism and dismal provocations, brownish aggregates which we have to believe reveal very strange attractions, a soup of warmed-over words we'd thought had long been forgotten but which in fact were only frozen: this augurs nothing good.

At the very least we are finding the old, badly made grenades from lost armies, which can explode at any moment, without warning, with a single false movement, one badly timed gesture, one miscalculation, one shock.

At the most, they are a real symptom, an early indicator of the worst thing of all—the feature of a face that might be that of the old notion of Marxist Progress if other similar characteristics join it: the first arti-cle; the first pillar; only a start: the fight goes on.

A lost army, then, or a vanguard? A last gasp or a sign of things to come? Are these really just old grenades, or is this a profound shock, a new wave, whose extent we're just now beginning to grasp?

I lean toward pessimism—but I'm getting there.

Once Upon a Time, Europe

Because there's a second symptom.

For someone of my generation, the debate on Europe—in France generally and on the Left particularly—is starting to move in a no less devastating direction.

In May 1968, I remember hundreds of thousands of young people marching through the streets of Paris chanting: "We are all German Jews."

I remember how back then it went without saying that students could—out of solidarity with another student who was attacked by a Communist-Pétainist apparatchik, Georges Marchais—feel French, naturally enough, but German at the same time: Franco-German, and therefore European.

I remember Rudi Dutschke, another leader of the far left, who got shot in the head in April 1968 in Berlin; recovered; lost his memory; got it back; and then died, once and for all, of an epileptic seizure in his bathtub. I knew him slightly. He wrote the preface, two years before his second death, to the German edition of *Barbarism with a Human Face*. Together—over the course of a leftist period in which he got far more involved than I did but from which we both emerged at the same time and for the same reasons—we participated in demonstrations in favor of Soviet and Eastern European dissidents. And I remember him in his earlier period, his leftist period—as a dissenter, to be sure; as a Council Communist; as a follower of Amadeo Bordiga; Che Guevara; as a Neo-Trotskyist; as a crypto-Maoist, whatever—and unfortunately there was plenty of choice! All we had were choices between bad teachers, bad groups! But I remember him most of all as an intellectual who could be found in any city and could speak any language. He lived in Switzerland, Italy, England, Ireland once he got kicked out of England, the Netherlands, Denmark, England once again, France. He was in touch, every time, and thirty years before the Internet, with all the like-minded people in all those capitals. Just as other people were interested in the weather or in probability theory, he tallied and retallied, sniffing out every trend, tirelessly recalculating the distance of the horizon or the bent of the time, to try to figure out what country in Europe was going to see History unleash itself and the Revolution break out. He could say the stupidest things about terrorism. He could idiotically raise his fist on the day of Holger Meins's funeral, that member of the Baader group who "committed suicide" in Stammheim prison and whose face, I'm embarrassed to say, and partly under his influence, I was stupid enough to put on the front page of *L'Imprévu,* the short-lived newspaper I'd just founded—this was in January 1975—with that other fake Frenchman, by which I mean European of French origin, Michel Butel. But like the Englishman Rousseau or the Berliner Voltaire, like Winckelmann the Italian or Beccaria the Frenchman, like Montesquieu who, before he started writing *L'Esprit des lois,* took the time to visit all of Europe; like all those whom he admired and who became, as he matured, his increasingly acknowledged teachers, he was, above all else, a citizen of Europe.

I REMEMBER THE period that began in 1978, when Sartre and Foucault received the cream of Eastern Europe's dissident crop at the Théâtre Récamier, including Milan Kundera—a period which goes through the time of *L'Invention démocratique,* in which Claude Lefort denounced the crime of seeing the two Europes, Western Europe and Central-Eastern

Europe, not only as two different areas but as two different civilizations, almost two separate universes; and culminating, five years later, with Kundera's own article "L'Europe kidnappée"[1] which made the "liberation" of that imprisoned half of Europe the most categorical, the most ardent, the most urgent of imperatives. To be on the Left—this might not have been Kundera's problem, but it was that of many of his readers—was to fight for a freedom that no longer excluded the Kremlin's enclaves. To be on the Left was, without the slightest shadow of a doubt, to think about Europe, to live for Europe, to advocate rights and liberties whose natural context was Europe. It was the Right who greeted Leonid Brezhnev at the Elysée Palace and slammed the door on Leonid Pliouchtch. It was the old Left who, as the "common program" demanded, turned up its nose when the Polish workers' movement started to emerge. But for the other Left, the new Left—the one that was shaking off old habits; the one that laughed, joked, and forgot with Kundera; the one that was wrong with Deleuze and right with Foucault—for the modern Left, for the living Left of the future, it was obvious that there was no future in Europe without Europe: Foucault once again explaining, in a memorable dialogue on Poland with the trade union leader Edmond Maire, that "what's happening over there was posing (posing once again, but for the first time in quite a long time) the problem of Europe."[2]

And I still remember—just to mention one last case—a few years later, when my friend Alain Finkielkraut started a magazine he'd baptized with the lovely name of *Messager européen,* and which is completely forgotten today: Too bad! In it we defended Václav Havel, poet and politician! We familiarized ourselves with the work of Jan Patočka as well as that of Hans-Georg Gadamer! We discovered the beautiful writings of Václav Bělohradský about America or Peter Kral's on the history of Europe! Danilo Kiš was there; and Ludvík Vaculík; and Kundera, of course; and the Pole Tadeusz Konwicki; and, in my recollection, at least at the beginning, the French writers François Furet and Elisabeth de Fontenay; it was still the real Europe; it was the Europe we still were living; it was, as Franz Werfel might have said, the Europe of

minds, of poets, of scholars; it was Europe "as a single big city," the fatherland of "libraries" sung by Valery Larbaud in the poems of Barna-
booth; it was Europe. . . .

NOW THIRTY YEARS have passed—and what's happened?

The *Messenger* is gone, oddly, silently—the only case I know of a magazine of that quality being scuttled with so little fuss. Once I tried to
learn more. I said to Finkielkraut: "You have to admit that it's strange,
that magazine you stopped just like that, without warning, without explanation." But he just shrugged. He wandered off, as he sometimes
does, into obscure explanations about disagreements with his editors
and the confusions of the time. And he left me with my hypothesis—
the worst one of all, because it touched on something that, despite the
passing years, despite our enduring friendship, despite our common
struggles, despite Israel, despite Bosnia, separated us more and more
often: times were changing; the wind was blowing another direction; in
place of the European hopes that followed the fall of the Berlin Wall, of
that new Belle Epoque that lasted (like its predecessor?) exactly three
years—which is to say, in reality, until the beginning of the siege of
Sarajevo—there came an age of disappointments, of the violent asser-
tion of national and ethnic identities, of wounded or murderous neo-
nationalisms, of national communisms, of retrieved clericalisms, and,
soon enough, of holy alliances of the old and new clergies; so that, as
people were gathering up their own thoughts and drawing the conclusions that their temperament and metaphysics led them to, my friend
had chosen to transform himself from a messenger of Europe into a
messenger of small nations, of their unknown or trampled-upon genius, of their sovereignty, which demanded reconsideration, or of their
independence, which demanded respect—thereby pushing back even
further the lovely dream of Immanuel Kant, the solitary philosopher
who, in 1784, envisioned the establishment of a "cosmopolitical state of
public security among states" to keep them from "tearing each other
apart"!

Kundera is still there, an immobile strategist and a shadowy novelist. But it is not to speak ill of him to observe his silence—annoyed? in-different? shared?—in the face of the wind of chauvinism that is today blowing over his former country, and over Slovakia, Hungary, and Poland, that beating heart of Europe where a pair of twins, the Kaczyn-ski brothers—those "cretins," said Wałesa, who himself was at least European[3]—could go about trying to demolish the entire edifice con-structed by the Schumans, the Adenauers, the Churchills, and other founding fathers of Europe! Between *Slowness* and *Immortality*, Milan Kundera has clearly removed himself from all that. He has left the ranks: not only, of course, of the delicate murderers of Europe, but of those who might be able to save it. And as for *identity* . . . I don't want to be uncivil. But it is never a good sign when a great writer devotes too much time to the question of identity. Because identity is not art. It has even less to do with culture. Nor, even more, with that very special Eu-ropean culture, whose principle is recalcitrance, rebelliousness, and even methodic hostility to anything that might resemble a fixation with identity. Goddess Europe, so quickly passing by . . . Europe, that marvelous machine for creating peace (France and Germany), democ-racy (the countries of captive Europe as well as, before them, Spain, Greece, and Portugal), prosperity (everyone), but also for un-creating, for breaking, for nipping in the bud, everything that makes a European feel he has to stay in his own narrow world, on the side of the road, pure-blooded, aligned with his line, prisoner of his origin, naturalized, nationalized . . . Who still knows that? Who, in this age of "returns" to all directions, still recalls that Europe is the opposite of an odyssey? Who, while hymns to the local (and to localities, we are once again led to believe, of which our souls are said to be simple reflections) are being sung everywhere, wants to remember that Europe is nothing if not, first of all, a spiritual insurrection against the evil demon of identity—even if that identity is European?

AND AS FOR THE official Left—as for the moderate, reasonable Left, which sincerely believes itself to be cured of its radical fascinations and which, to a certain degree, really is—the picture is only slightly more reassuring since, ten years after François Mitterrand who, until the end of his life, held that the construction of political Europe was the only worthwhile project and the best part of his legacy: that official Left is, as everyone knows, split in two.

The half of it that voted no on the constitutional referendum of May 2005 but which, instead of minimizing its no—instead of describing it as a no based on circumstances and mood—instead of saying, "We voted no, okay; but it was a no to the president at the time; the no was a provocation; we've got plenty of other things to do in life, plenty of other things to say, other battles to fight, rather than dwelling on that no"—instead turned it into the basis of a whole story, the alpha and the omega of an ideological program, a standard, a flag—how often, before and during the presidential campaign, did we hear them talk about a "no from the left," about the "no party," of the "spirit of no," even of "no-ism," with a seriousness usually reserved for great political narratives and essential points of doctrine. . . .

And another half voted yes, but (this may have been even more remarkable and more devastating) without being able—with a few exceptions—to explain what was really behind their yes. An ashamed yes. A yes for lack of anything better. And, above all, a yes not to Europe but to a France that, it was whispered, would be, thanks to Europe, even bigger, stronger, more momentous, more France; a yes that didn't dare say: "I'm voting yes because it's for Europe and Europe is an unprecedented political project, never before seen in human history; and one which means, for free nations, renouncing a part of their sovereignty in order to create a new political body based only on the rule of law, free democratic discussion, and compromise," but instead: "We have to say yes because we are French and because I'm telling you it's a good deal for the French, a good way to pull the wool over the eyes of other countries—not for less but for more power, advantages, pride, even sovereignty and influence, for the Gallic rooster." What a disaster!

THERE ARE SEVERAL explanations for this fiasco.

The first explanation is Jean-Claude Milner's,[4] which I'll sum up by saying that Europe's real problem is that it got off to a bad start, by necessity. We used to say: "Black Africa's off to a bad start." Well, that's not it! Milner is basically saying. Off to a much worse start, and far earlier, was the Europe that claimed to be building itself against Nazism and in order to make sure that Nazism never returned but which Nazism had, at the same time, unified and devastated: devastated because Nazism unified Europe; unified because Nazism devastated Europe. How can we recover from that? What reconciliation, what union, what Constitution, can mend the gap that is the absence of the six million murdered Jews? According to Milner, talk about the crisis of Europe, its problems, or even its ruin, is far too little to describe the cry of a stillborn Europe, or one born after the death of a part of itself, and which no longer knows how to live, because of this fact, except as a ghost.

There is another more recent explanation that I myself expressed—or rather screamed out, begged, sobbed, screamed out again—during those hellish months, those years, of the Bosnian War. Since Bosnia was a miniature Europe. Not just its symbol. Nor its symptom, as people sometimes said. But really Europe in miniature. Europe on a reduced scale. The very image of what Europe ought to be, when, according to its founding fathers, it would be itself. Was Europe a never-before-attempted political project? Never before seen in the history of mankind? A new body? An animal of unknown species? I did just say that. But it was only half true. Since there was Bosnia. Since there was the miracle of Bosnia that brought together its three nationalities, and even four, if we counted the nationality of those who didn't describe themselves as any of the three others. Well, that miniature was destroyed. Well, we let that image die. Europe was there, existing, living, and we let it be blown up by shells, targeted by snipers, shredded by rockets and finished off—to the thunderous applause that followed that of the explosions—by the pitiful Dayton Accords, imposed on President Izetbegović after four years of suffering and which amounted only to a brief pause. I recall the "old gentleman," first in Paris, then in Sarajevo. I see him, sad, bitter, in the uncertain glow of the first autumn without shelling. "I didn't want anything to do with it," he said, "with the alms they offered us: a Muslim nation. I dreamt of Europe. I was holding on to my little Europe. And that's what they condemned! And in Dayton they signed its death certificate!" I'm convinced that a bit of Europe died there, in Sarajevo, lost in the ashes of Dobrinja, drowned in the dark waters of the Drina, where the badly aimed shells were landing.

There is a third explanation, more general, which has to do with the unique mental laziness and weakening of the will that so quickly followed the passion of the founding fathers. Build Europe? Want Europe? Lean on it in order to expunge nations of the bad demons of chauvinism, of fixation on origins, of the obsession with motherlands, which kept popping up like weeds? That's what had to happen. That's what happened at first. And that's what stopped happening afterward, after the fall of the Berlin Wall and the arrival of the idiotic idea that History was over, that Democracy had arrived, the question of Mankind answered—so let's not talk about the question of Europe . . . Europe would happen, people told themselves. It would happen anyway. It was inevitable. Prescribed by the meaning of history, as we well knew. It was so obvious that it represented something positive for European humanity. It was so obviously obvious that more Europe was better than less—and that for no other reason it couldn't help but happen. So all we had to do was let it. All we had to do was let it come. We could go to bed. We didn't need to think about it anymore, nor really want it, and could even pretend not to want it at all. It was happening behind our backs. It said yes even when we said no. It grew rich off our poverty, strong from our slumber. One morning, it would emerge from limbo, all dressed up and armed, like the Greek goddess that it also is. . . . One day, we will realize that this wild notion—which dominated the last twenty years—cost us the idea of Europe. One day, we will realize how much damage this providentialism has done—this notion of progress, understood in the larger sense, common to the Right and the Left, of an irresistible, necessary Europe, one we could believe in as we once believed in God, or Providence, or History. Moreover, since a misfortune like that never arrives on its own, it was happening on the watch of a generation of men and women who—and I'm thinking mainly of

Jacques Chirac—for the first time since the war, were not committed Europeans. . . .

For now, a final recollection. It's a much older one, from long before the fall of the Wall, but it's a good illustration of what I'm saying. I am at the house in the Rue du Bac of the most antinationalist of all great French writers. I am with the only modern writer who, to my knowledge, ever dared to write that "the time that France has spent on the chessboard of history is nothing."[5] I am with a novelist, more rightist than anything, since he was a Gaullist, but who always thought that the Nation, in France, was a new idea, a weak idea, an accident of History, an aberration. I am with Romain Gary, author of a marvelous novel about youth called *Education européenne* and author, moreover, of several decisive pages about this anti-event which is the Jewish gap in Europe. It's May 1978. I've come to show him something I've written in *Combat*, which I'm not a little bit proud of, which I think he'll be proud of too, and which has to do with the existence or nonexistence of a common culture among all the peoples of Europe. And then, to my great surprise, like Proust throwing his slippers at the head of Emmanuel Berl, who's come to tell him that he believed in love more than in its poisons, he grows darkly angry. "It's too late, buddy!" he cries. "Much too late! You had to do it right away! With forceps! With heavy instruments! You had to charge right in, when the enemy was on the mat! Now it's over, definitely over; since we've let them return, remake themselves, put themselves back into fighting position; the nations now are charging ahead; now it's the turn of the bigots, of all their xenophobic bullshit, to do their worst; you'll see, it's over."

It's 1978. More than ten years before the fall of the Wall and the reawakening of nationalisms he foretold. And, as usual, it's a writer who sees before anyone else what's right in front of his eyes.

So those are three explanations. And they all have a bit of truth to them. But none of them, nor all of them together, will keep me from saying that there is a last explanation, and not the least of them, for the failure of the meaning of Europe—for the fact that Europe, like God according to Lacan, had become unconscious in Europe—for the increasingly oppressive feeling all real Europeans have of being exiled in their own countries and even more exiled in the fatherland of their hearts—and that comes back to the decomposition of the idea of Progress, no longer in the broader sense but in the narrower sense: this idea of historical progress in the strict meaning of the word which we've seen unravel, then put itself back together, but for the worst.

I'M NOT SAYING, of course, that there was a golden age in which the Left was spontaneously, totally, in favor of Europe.

I'm not even saying that in the past it was more in favor of it than the Right.

What I know is that it *was* in favor of it.

What I know, what I've lived through, and what I've tried to re-introduce into the debate, is that, if only for the sake of internationalism, only because of its taste for big ideas and its fear of anything that closes people in, the Left could not *not* participate in the adventure, and was therefore, on its more modern fringes, fervently in favor of Europe.

What I know is that even when Europe was still a project, the Left was the leading edge of that project, its spearhead, its avant-garde.

Today the spear is broken. The wind, with the changing times, has shifted. On the Left, the background was red; today it's gray; and some-times, when we denounce the immigrants from central Europe coming to steal the jobs of real Frenchmen, it even tends toward the brown; and the reality is that we have a frightened Left, shaky, scared of the sound of its own voice if it's made to recall its previous daring state-ments, a Left that is no longer the avant-garde of anything at all, ex-cept, perhaps, for the sake of being avant-garde, of prudence, of falling back on itself, resistance to the risk of Europe, regression.

Europe? The market. Europe? Liberalism, which it abhors. Europe? Those deregulations, de-localizations, privatizations, regulations, which it can't stand and which it fights as if for its very life. Europe? It can tell us until the end of time—or, preferably, until the next election, since time waits for no man—that it's not against Europe in and of itself but against that Europe, that Europe in particular, and that it's really fight-

ONCE UPON A TIME, EUROPE   111

ing for "another" and "different" Europe: but the reality is that Europe frightens and horrifies it.

The future, here again, will say if this whiff of defeatism is something new or old.

Historians will determine what, here, belongs to our own age and what hearkens back to other dark ages when the Left, with the Communist Party at its head, backed off of internationalism, let loose all its old fusty smells, and echoed the populist temptation which never ceased to haunt it and which in France called itself Guesdism.

That's where we are for the time being.

A second sign indicating how deep the malaise runs.

Undeniable evidence showing that we, the Left—just as when Jules Guesde triumphed over Jean Jaurès; or as at the time of the patriotic and national-republican Left of 1914; or as when Léon Blum refused to lead the French proletariat toward a confrontation, even indirectly, with the uniformed German proletariat—are the ones who are finishing off Europe.

And for someone nostalgic for the old tradition—for an old young man who lived through the European euphoria of the seventies and even the eighties, this is a source of very deep sadness.

I don't like how this Left says it's in favor of local sovereignty when it means it's anti-European.

I don't like how, when it can't think of anything better to say, it cries "Republic! Republic!"—as if someone were planning to take away its Republic.

I am not going to cry on the graves of our great Europeans—Blum once again, Jaurès, the Enlightenment thinkers—but does that mean we should let others spit on them? That, too, causes me infinite grief.

And, finally, I've already said what I think about this insistence on not abandoning the national colors to the Right—this sudden desire they all have to burst out in the "Marseillaise"—this craze for waving the flag in front of our noses in order to, as they say, attack Sarkozy on his right flank.

I don't like a Left that feints to the Right, that's the truth.

I don't like a Left that, just to make sure it's scraped the bottom of the barrel, breathlessly scrapes the same barrels the other side has made a specialty of scraping.

I don't like a Left that thinks it's left behind a "barbarism with a human face" by opening the door—or the window—that leads it to the "Idéologie française."

The Other Socialism of the Imbeciles

The third trait of the Left's failure: anti-Americanism.

I'd like to refresh the memory of my friends on the Left as to this anti-Americanism, all too often a fixed ideological star.

And I want to show them, calmly, concretely, with no polemical spirit, how this principled detestation of America—the way they've turned it into the sole object of a harassing resentment—this transformation of much of the world, and even some part of America, into a zone of disapproval in the same way Spinoza spoke of a zone of ignorance, has made them fall, once again, into the same trap.

I'M NOT TALKING ABOUT, of course, the legitimate criticism of one American president or another—of Bush the Lesser, for example, whose errors and mediocrity I, in *American Vertigo,* was not the last to denounce.

I'm not talking about the Abu Ghraib scandal, nor about Guantánamo, those regions of lawlessness, those political and juridical aberrations, which still, as I write these lines, dishonor an American democracy which elsewhere has so much vitality and virtue.

I'm not talking about my own anger when I read that an average of two people are legally killed every week on death row in Texas and elsewhere; or when I see, in a school in Virginia, the concrete result of the notion that it is every citizen's inalienable right to possess assault rifles.

No. I'm talking about that strange hatred that, across the entire planet, focuses not on what America does or doesn't do but on what it *is*.

I'm talking about that total hatred that attacks not the crimes that America, like any other nation in the world, sometimes happens to commit or to cover up: but of its being, its essence, or at least what people imagine is that essence.

And I'm talking about, in France, this anti-American religion which is like a password that is coming to unite all the neoprogressive churches: I'm talking about the way they have—in alter-globalist, pacifist, agroterrorist, Zapatista, Islamo-leftist, Sovereignist, Critical Communist, Chevènementist circles; the people from ATTAC and the members of the Cercle Saint-Just or the late Fondation Marc-Bloch; the former Reds who have now turned Green and the friends-of-nature type of Greens who have now become greens of the revolutionary jihad variety; those nostalgic for the Grand Soir no less than those reformists who want to place a radical tiger in the tank of their social criticism— I'm talking about how they all, whenever they've run out of things to say, say "it's America's fault" and turn America into a place of the damned, almost a region of Being, which is synonymous with all the crimes and sins of the human race.

Isn't America, for such people, guilty of starving the world *and* of flooding it with its commodities? Of ruining the climate *and* of pillaging the planet's resources? Isn't it guilty of fighting terrorism *and* stirring it up? Of making war on Islamism *after* having encouraged and nourished it? Of being a country without culture that is flooding the world with its culture? Of being the homeland of materialism that at the same time is the seat of a spiritual revolution that is as grotesque as it is fanatical? Of having been too late to enter the war against Hitler (Long live Pearl Harbor! Thank you, Japan!)—and, when it finally made up its mind, of using methods that could have been Hitler's (Hiroshima, the dishonor of it! The true face of the GIs, our self-proclaimed liberators, who were actually rapists, thieves, murderers—see, for example, a strange documentary recently broadcast on a public television network[1])? Is there anything, any single thing, that America has been spared, now or in the past? Didn't France, during the Civil War, manage to be the only country in the world that was both hostile to slavery (that disgrace . . . that crime . . . unworthy of a democracy, as we've told you so many times before . . .) and favorable to a Southern victory (that civilization . . . that world . . . that admirable aristocracy . . . gone with the wind . . .)? Wasn't France, once again, the only country that, in Clemenceau's words,[2] dared to think it was odd, and even a bit suspicious, that our "Yankee" allies didn't lose more men in the battles for France? And when, at last, September 11th came along, weren't there plenty of people on the Left, in France as in the rest of the world, who saw the horrifying attack either as a horrifying fraud, or at the very least the result of a horrifying arrogance?

The French listened to Arundhati Roy:[3] Bin Laden is "a dead ringer for the American president," his "interchangeable twin brother."

Noam Chomsky:[4] a planetary "fraud," the mirror image of the "racism" of the Jewish state—an "atrocity" that, in any event, didn't "reach the level" of "Clinton's bombing" of a Sudanese pharmaceutical factory that was wrongly believed to be a military objective.

The journalist Robert Fisk, on the first day of the war in Afghanistan, wrote that "we are the real war criminals."[5]

Harold Pinter, later, in his Nobel acceptance speech:[6] the only, the real problem is the two million men and women locked up in the vast "gulag" that is the American prison system.

Jean Baudrillard[7]—a great mind, in other respects—almost immediately setting the tone by explaining that it's America's "rising power," its "formidable condensation of every function by the technocratic machinery and its single-minded thinking"—in a word, the "system itself" and the way it "keeps all the cards for itself"—which "has created the conditions for this brutal retaliation."

And the battalions of beautiful souls whom we never heard squeak a word in protest against the public stoning of adulterous women in Kabul or against the numberless crimes of Saddam Hussein in Baghdad—but who, when the Americans decided to hunt down the Taliban and dethrone Saddam Hussein, rush to the streets crying "Peace in Kabul" and "Hands off Baghdad" or "Busharon murderer" . . .

That's the anti-Americanism I'm talking about.

That's the passion—because it is a passion—whose genealogy and background I want to recall.

I started to do so a quarter of a century ago, in the last pages of *L'Idéologie française*: and, in light of today's events, that's the reflection I want to build upon here.

IT ALL STARTED with Rousseau.

It all started with that unprecedented book called *The Social Contract*, whose thesis provoked—first in France and then in Europe—a thrill, a shock, almost a spiritual earthquake.

What?

All people needed was a "general will" to create a society?

All people needed was to say "We want to be joined into a society; we don't have anything in common but we've decided to join together" for such an association to exist and take effect?

Starting with a transcendental purity—an abstract and empty form, whose only principle would be the well-negotiated exchange between each member's freedom and a superior liberty guaranteed by an agreement—a true community of men and women could come about?

People might have nothing in common—nothing, neither heroes, nor great events, nor shared miseries, nor even a common place of birth—and found a nation by a simple act of understanding—by one of the purely mind-based decisions described in the *Encyclopédie*, in the same terms Rousseau used in his *Discourse on the Arts and Sciences*, as reasoning "in the silence of human passions" and of "associations"?

People are never quiet about passions and associations, grumbled the *Contract*'s outraged readers.

Counterrevolutionaries like Burke and Carlyle mocked Rousseau, saying that nobody had ever seen a society come about through such vain and artificial methods.

When, on December 26, 1815, Bonald went before the National Assembly to plead for—and obtain[8]—the abolition of the divorce law that the Assemblies of the French Revolution had voted for, he insisted that history had never known a society that was not based on this common principle, these primary and natural units, that were, for example, families.

What's all this about the "contract," Lamartine himself wondered, in issues 65 and 67 of his *Cours familier de littérature*?[9] Societies don't come about thanks to contracts! They can't be decreed! They are "instinctive." They are "inevitable."

How could you possibly imagine—thundered Maurice Barrès, once again in the National Assembly, on June 11, 1912, during a session dedicated to celebrating the bicentennial of Rousseau's birth—how could you even conceive that the national congress could wish to glorify this "false spirit," this "extravagant creature," this prince of lies and artifice? I admire "the artist," he allows. I admire "the musician." And "the man himself, that poor and crabbed virtue allied to that lyrical love of nature and solitude, I won't attack him." But as for signing up for "the social, political, and pedagogical principles of the author of the *Discourse on Inequality*, the *Social Contract*, and *Émile*"—as for celebrating the person who "established as a principle the idea that the social order is entirely artificial," and that it is "based on conventions"—as for anointing with the holy republican chrism the big bloated head of someone who preaches everyone's right to "reconstruct society at whim"—as for letting France look ridiculous by celebrating that lunatic, drunk on himself and his own correctness, one whose whole life was dedicated to chasing the pipe dream of "placing all of life on a Procrustean bed"—as for following, therefore, this false prophet in his "detrimental, and moreover powerless, rebellion which advises us to act as if we had to remake everything all over again"—I won't do that: I won't "give him so much credit."[10]

Herder too followed the lead of the French Counter-Revolutionaries; also opposed to Rousseau's bad *"Gesellschaft,"* that abstract entity issued from a contractualism that was obtuse and definitively deaf to the soul (the *"Volksseele"*) and to the spirit of the people (the *"Volksgeist"*), the good *"Gemeinschaft"* which itself was founded on a community of memory and roots—Herder too, upon hearing the name Rousseau, cried that he was refusing reality, following a figment of his imagination, something arbitrary, and pulls out his naturalistic, and already *völkisch,* revolver. . . .

I'm simplifying things, of course.

One could object that there are as many similarities as differences between Rousseau and Herder, and that Barrès and Fichte disagree more than they agree.

But that is nonetheless the reasoning of the part of the "anti-Enlightenment" that Arendt evokes in her *Origins of Totalitarianism*.

That's exactly how, over the course of two centuries, with an inexhaustible rage, the mad hatred of Rousseau and his "contractualism" has been expressed.

If we agree that the leading figures of the anti-Enlightenment share the feeling that contractualism is the apex of the "sin of pride," the "vice" in "all its splendor" (Burke[11]); the image of an illegitimate government whose prince would be "more disgraced than a valet or a laborer" (Carlyle[12]); but which, praise God, is all just a big fraud—so big, so enormous—then one thing is sure: it will remain irrelevant.

Barrès, once again, thought the *Social Contract* was "profoundly imbecilic." And Renan, in a text from 1869 reproaching Napoléon III for having ceded too much to the American myth of "equal rights for all" and of transforming his government, in so doing, into a simple "public service," without memory, without ambition, and without the ability to elicit in others that elementary political feeling known as "respect": wasn't he already talking about American "impertinence"?

Since this is where we realize that it's not just a fraud.

This is where it appears that Rousseau's construction—a utopia, a whim, a dangerous and criminal fantasy, but a fantasy nonetheless—was a bit more than that.

This is where that idea, seemingly so crazy, so devoid of meaning or future prospects, incapable of bearing any relation to the real history of a real people; that idea which nobody ever imagined would go further than the project for the Constitution of a Corsica or a Poland that themselves were figments of the imagination—here's where that flight of fancy takes shape in a place that is neither Corsica nor Poland.

Far, far away, in the New World, a real place, not a dreamland or a paper construction—where, we're told, people have come from every end of the earth, people with different skin colors, different languages, different histories and traditions, different gods, different heroes, have decided to come together, to agree on a contract and to gather in a nation—there is a country, America, where Jean-Jacques Rousseau's project, that almost unthinkable doctrine that all people needed to do was make up their minds, then say it and swear to it, in order to create a political body, left the skies and descended earthward, where it actually came to pass.

At first, nobody can believe it.

They say it's so absurd that it can't last.

It goes against the grain of things and it will necessarily fail.

They say, they repeat: it's nothing, it's ridiculous, a remake of Glaucon's "City of Swine" in the *Republic*, an experiment, a flash in the pan—it will fall just as it rose, in a cloud of dust and a burst of laughter, once reality strikes.

But here we are.

Time goes by.

The experiment has staying power.

The country Renan thought was impertinent scoffs at the serious nations.

The impossible state becomes a power, a real one, that in 1898 declares war on a large European country, Spain, and wins.

The country on paper becomes a prosperous nation as well as a political actor of the first importance which intervenes once, and then again, in the affairs of Europe: and which, during World War II, saves it.

In the darkest hours of that dark age, moreover, while a whole segment of humanity is threatened with being washed away in the flood of Hitler's hatred, that country becomes a place of hospitality and asylum unequaled anywhere else on the planet, making the mocked, condescended-to America a gigantic Noah's ark.

Even better: while, as Husserl warned us in his Prague and Vienna lectures, the idea of Europe is about to sink utterly;[13] while in Germany, from the very heart of Europe, a regime claiming to unify the continent under its leadership is busily emptying that continent of its substance, amputating the best of itself, destroying its very soul, it is once again America, that supposedly "soulless" country, drunk on "materialism" and therefore "devoid of spirit," which, in an extraordinary return, like that remainder of Israel that the biblical prophets said saved what it can from the times of catastrophe and holocaust, grabbed from the flames of nihilism the works, the books, what's left of the libraries, the remains of the values and the people who will allow, when the time is right, to reignite the flame, the other one, the unconquered lights of the Europe of Husserl and Kant.

We have to note two things, in other words.

First, all those great minds—all those German and French Romantics, all those who were opposed to the spirit of the Enlightenment and of Rousseau—were terribly wrong, and the very fact of America—the reality of this nation made of men of different origins, of blacks and whites, of Europeans and non-Europeans, of Jews, Protestants, Catholics, Indians, Asians—is the living proof of their mistake.

Second, when traditional nations engage in an apparently unstoppable process of collective suicide; when the disaster is unleashed by those nations that ended up taking most seriously the "natural" and "anti-Enlightenment" program that had been opposed to America for two centuries; when neighboring nations, with their ancient ways of knowing and doing, with their heavy jaws and their bodies so nicely rooted in the supposed soil of their antique and collective history, throw up their hands in the face of the Beast, or frankly take his side, it's the little, fragile, precarious upstart, the one we thought was so congenitally defective that it would hardly be able to walk without crutches—so you think it's going to rush to someone else's rescue!— that little upstart comes to our aid and saves us.

European anti-Americanism is born there.

From that humiliation.

Or, to put it more precisely, from a double and repeated humiliation.

First of all, more recently, from the classic resentment of the debtor toward his benefactor.

AS JULES RENARD so wittily put it: "I don't have any enemies, since I've never helped anyone."

Or as Confucius said: "What do you have against me, since I've never given you a thing?"

Or again, as Pascal Bruckner suggests,[14] a reverse Oedipus complex in which the mother (Europe, in this case) can't stop hating the child she has given birth to or, put another way, which has given himself to her under the pretext of coming to regenerate her—and which, actually, and at the end, arrives, as predicted, to save her old, crippled civilization (Europe) . . .

Europe had so mocked this new Europe, which had fled the Europe of tyrannies, planning to make a new start somewhere else, really to start all over again, keeping only the best parts and avoiding the same old mistakes!

They had so looked down on these poor fellows who, as Tocqueville tells us, had taken care, before they sailed off, to gather up a bit of that precious "democratic seed" drowned in the "old landscapes" of Europe and "strangled" by their "feudal vegetation"; and who went to "transplant" it over there, in those "virgin lands without a past" which the American lands were supposed to be; and who had always kept, in the back of their minds, the idea that one day, later on, much later on, they'd have to bring back the "first fruits" to that first Europe, which they were still attached to!

And that's what they did.

We made fun of them, but that's what they did.

They came back to old Europe not once but twice, and almost three times, because after they saved it from Nazism, they helped save it from Communism a few years later, and even today, it's beneath the American military and ideological shield that liberty blossoms.

Unforgivable!

But there's something even more unforgivable.

And we can understand nothing of French, European, and therefore world anti-Americanism—we understand nothing about its most ancient and, in a manner of speaking, nutritive forms—nothing about the matrix that still spurs it on to this very day and which we even find in its most radical Islamist forms—if we don't think about that other humiliation, even greater, and earlier, and more fundamental, and truly metaphysical, which goes against the safest principles of the French and European ideology, which counters everything that this ideology believed and predicted from the very beginning: the very possibility of the American island.

At the beginning, yes, there is America's denial of the traditional, and supposedly irreplaceable, forms of national belief.

At the beginning, there is the American challenge, by the very fact of its existence, to one of the oldest and most tenacious Western religions.

At the beginning of the beginning, there are some people who have a *certainty* that nothing can ever make them let go of (the word *nation* means nature, and therefore body, and therefore organism, and therefore race—we should never forget that Hegel doesn't even mention America in his plan for the development of the human and world spirit); who have a *nightmare* that they'd like to snap out of once and for all or, failing that, would like to be sure that it will never become more than a nightmare (Rousseau's ghost, which ever since that cursed eighteenth century has kept on disdaining them by objecting that no, not at all, he himself is sure that we can imagine nations that are not organisms and not at all founded in nature); and who see *the reality* that suddenly starts to take them by surprise and give form to their haunted notions (the existence of America is the proof that they were wrong, and that Rousseau was right to say they were wrong).

A narcissistic wound.

A devaluation, to someone else's benefit, of His Majesty the national ego.

An attack on the credit of the psychopolitical state that the old nations of Europe, France in particular, thought were eternal guarantees—a necessary trampling underfoot of a whole range of phobias, fears, and neuroses.

For the disciples of the "Idéologie française," the discovery of America was like the discoveries of Copernicus, Darwin, or psychoanalysis for those who wanted to believe that the earth was at the center of the world, man at the center of the earth, and consciousness at the center of mankind.

The discovery of America—the real one, which is to say the discovery that America is not only real (we knew that since Christopher Columbus) but possible and even necessary (that's the shattering discovery of the period that runs, let's say, from the end of the nineteenth century up through the fall of Nazism and then of Communism)—is an unprecedented ideological shock for those who thought that Europe was the center of the world, that France was the center of Europe, and that the organic and organicist model of constructing nations was the only one possible: *eppur si muove* . . . and still it moves. . . . That America has the presumption to defy the laws of the universal gravity of nations and, therefore, to work . . . That success is not a success but a failure—our failure, our defeat, a total surrender of the "Idéologie française" and of the "Anti-Enlightenment."

AFTER THAT, WE CAN take one of three different approaches.

Or three different conclusions that, for the most part, each according to their dosage, can be combined and reinforced by one another.

First, disbelief. Stupor, then disbelief. And therefore, as so often, the denial of reality. America can't work, so it doesn't. America is an aberration, and therefore a pipe dream, an optical illusion, a figment of the imagination. That's roughly Maurras's position. And that's what's behind the very strange thesis he unveils starting in 1920, in *Les trois aspects du président Wilson:*[15] the thesis that America is neurotic. . . . He says "Kantian," of course. He begins, like all anti-Americans, by taking up Barrès's vision of a Kantian, Rousseauist, unrooted America. But he immediately hits upon a new idea—one which, if you think about it, is incredibly violent—of a neurotic nation, truly neurotic, just like its president, that friendly madman, that mental case, that autistic Woodrow Wilson. A neurotic has to be taken care of. A neurotic has to be locked up. America isn't a country: it's a *lunatic asylum.*

And then comes rage. Humiliation, and therefore rage. And therefore, as expected, a limitless, unrestrained hatred—and, in certain cases, unrestrained even by the hatred that, at the same time, might be inspired by the mass graves, the camps, the archipelago of political prisoners, the tens of millions of dead in Stalin's Soviet Union. I had already shown that in *L'Idéologie française.* I had shown how, for the far right in the thirties, for the first French fascists along the lines of Georges

Valois, for all those young people who dream of helping their country keep pace with the great National Socialist revolution then regenerating Europe, the enemy is not, of course, Hitler, but it's not Stalin either—because it's Ford, *Modern Times,* the machine, *Metropolis,* robots, standardization, mixture, mingling of races once again, generalized recruitment, uniformity: America, in a word. Arnaud Dandieu and Robert Aron say it clearly enough in the book-manifesto they publish in 1931 and whose title—*Le Cancer américain*[16]—is in and of itself a whole program. Pierre Drieu La Rochelle said it in his writings of the twenties and thirties (*Genève ou Moscou, Socialisme fasciste*), in which he works out his concept of the "inner America." He will repeat it in his last texts and, in particular, in the pages of that *Journal* that was still unpublished at the time I was writing *L'Idéologie française* and in which—defeated, desperate, about to kill himself—he wrote that "Moscow will be the final Rome"; that "nothing separates him now from Communism"; and that, in any event, the only serious problem that has faced and will continue to face European civilization is not the man with the knife in his hand but the man with a dollar in his teeth.[17] *Esprit,* the "nonconformists" of *Esprit,* themselves have no doubts, along with Emmanuel Mounier, that if there is a "barbarism" that threatens the "human edifice," it is called "Americanism"; and Mounier's successor, Jean-Marie Domenach, will say it again, twenty-five years later, in a text that I hadn't seen at the time either, and in which, like Bernanos, he denounced, just before the war, a civilization "predestined from the moment of its birth to become the totalitarian civilization," and said that American society is "perhaps the most totalitarian society in the world."[18] The idea that the real danger wasn't the USSR but America, not Communism but Americanism, will return in the ideologues of the New Right of the eighties. And then, in all the neo-Nazi sects, previously mentioned, of the Nouvelle Résistance variety. Then, at last, in the National Front, whose anti-Americanism is truly fundamental to its beliefs—one example among thousands being Jean-Marie Le Pen declaring, in an interview in *La Croix,*[19] that the three thousand people killed at the World Trade Center were nothing compared to the deaths caused at the end of the Second World War by the Allied bombardments of Dresden and Marseille. . . .

And then, finally, war. Hatred, therefore war. And a war to the death, an inexpiable war, a merciless, unceasing war between two antagonistic models. Does America exist? So be it. Let's not belabor the fact. Let's instead look at things calmly. It's one existence versus another. Their society versus ours. If the "inner America" (Drieu once more) wins, that means the end of European civilization. If Europe carries the day (Heidegger), that's the end of the American triumph of technique. America, for these people, is a bit what the Jews were for Hegel. Since we know the equation, right? We know the Hegelian theory of these provisory peoples, popping up one at a time, and then fading away one at a time, on the stage of a universal History in which they are nothing but extras. And we know the problem posed, in this context, by the mysterious endurance of the Jewish people: either I, Hegel, am right, and there shouldn't be any more Jews; or there are Jews, these odd people who, for a few thousand years, have stubbornly been disproving the law that says that a people only has one moment in the sun, and then I, Hegel, am wrong. Well, America's the same thing. It's literally the same thing for the conquered Maurras who mutters, at the end of his trial, his famous "This is Dreyfus's revenge," but who could have just as well said that "This is *Wilson's* revenge." It's the same thing for the still-hopeful Heidegger who defined America as the very "site of the catastrophe," the wellspring of the "darkening of the world," one of the two jaws—the more terrible one, but which he still hopes to break—of the "metaphysical pliers" squeezing European civilization. And it was the same thing for Hitler, who never doubted that the main, radical, and, in a matter of speaking, metaphysical enemy—the one with which no truce or pact was possible— was not the Soviet Union but the United States of America.

I bring up Hitler on purpose.

And I also recall the Hegelian theorem on purpose.

Because then we will have understood that for most of the people I've already quoted—Maurras, Drieu, Valois, Bernanos, the spokesmen of the far right today—the semantic slip is permanent: they say "America" but they're thinking "Jews"; they say "American imperialism" but they're thinking "Jewish power, domination, conspiracy": antiAmericanism is a metaphor for anti-Semitism.

—

SO WHERE DOES the Left come in?

Well, there is no Left.

No room for the Left.

And by that I mean two things.

First of all, for a long time, for a very long time, the French and European Left was pro-American. Yes indeed! I can imagine the surprise of the anti-American crusaders that the progressives of today have become. But it is a simple fact of political and intellectual history. Lenin was an admirer of Fordism. Trotsky was fascinated by New York. In order to "build socialism," the Agitprop, back in the days of the New Economic Policy, wanted to add "the efficiency of American technology" to the "torrent of the Russian Revolution." Bukharin exhorted Communists to "add Americanism to Marxism." And as for Marxism itself, its two founders, Marx and Engels, never stopped—in their theoretical writings as well as in their articles, during the Civil War, for *Die Presse* and the *New York Daily Tribune*[20]—seeing the United States not only as a place where the working class was both determined and organized—not only as the place in the world where the contradictions of capitalism were about to reach a point of maturity that would make the revolutionary explosion conceivable—but as a "magnificent" country, the "most perfect example of the modern State," the place of "full political emancipation," a people, in a word, of "legendary bravery" which, during the Civil War, especially, gave "a welcome impulsion to civilization." There probably were Socialists and Communists who, starting in the thirties, played the *homo sovieticus* against the *homo americanus*. There were probably some who were taking a leaf, already, from the far-right critique of "machines" and technology. But they were a minority. And they were so convinced, above all, that the United States was the homeland of triumphant progressivism, they felt so strongly that America was a friendly country in which the ideas of equality are perfectly at home, that they expressed their doubts with a prudence, and even a respect, that the radical right never had.

Second, I want to add that when things finally turn around—when, after 1945, the Left and the far left, thanks to the Cold War, start dancing the anti-American dance; when the image of America changes from the homeland of workers' emancipation into the buttress of the anti-social reaction that it still is today—the metamorphosis happens so fast, with so little preparation, and on ground, moreover, that for so long had been so powerfully prepared by two centuries of anti-Enlightenment thinking, that these newcomers to anti-Americanism, these rookies, return, as naturally as can be, almost inevitably, to paths already trodden by the far right in the thirties. Always the same story ... Always, in the history of thought, the same ironclad law ... Humanity doesn't have that many languages available. It can, of course, change the meaning of its words. But to do that it has to want to, and, wanting to, it has to set to work. And then it would have to put the old words through a real labor of semantic, political, and above all genealogical criticism. Nothing doing. Not the shadow of an effort. As with liberalism, as in matters relating to Europe, nobody's made a start at trying to break this shameful continuity, and therefore this full-scale risk, by saying once and for all: "They are who they are; we are who we are; and this is what we are saying ourselves, when we seem to be saying what they're saying." And that's why the Left is conquered once again by this overflowing imagination that washes down its own like a sewer pouring into the sea.

Take Maurice Thorez, who, in 1948, held that American movies "literally poison the souls of our children" and would turn "our young ladies" not into true "Frenchwomen" but into the "submissive slaves of the American billionaires"[21]—a phrase that could have been lifted from *Le Cancer américain* of Aron and Dandieu.

Look at the Communist writings of the fifties about the "new Occupation" of sweet France by the "Gauleiters" of the "Amerloques" who "strangely recall" the actual Gauleiters "by their uniforms, their helmets, and very often their language"[22]—this could be Marcel Aymé in "The Sherriff's Daughter," the Vichy fable he published at the same time in *Combat*.

Look today at that editorial published in the *Monde diplomatique*[23] explaining how America, tired of dominating the world by the rough and, finally, outdated means of "genocide," "slavery," and "colonialism," has found the secret weapon for "domesticating souls," penetrating "the intimacy of our brains," even "hacking into our brains to implant ideas that are not our own"—almost exactly the words of Drieu La Rochelle and of the young people of *Réaction* denouncing "the inner America" "inside people's heads."

Or take, in the same issue of the *Monde diplomatique*—by a pen that, I am convinced, does not doubt its impeccable political correctness for a moment—the stench emerging from the denunciation[24] of the "cosmopolitan establishment of bankers and business lawyers" that dominates America, and thus the world. Maurras or, today, Le Pen, couldn't have said it better. . . .

And reading that other article[25] signed by Loïc Wacquant and Pierre Bourdieu, denouncing America's "mental colonization" of the whole planet, a double "Trojan horse"—or, better, that "two-headed" hydra which at the time was made up, in Europe, of Anthony Giddens and Tony Blair—how can one not recall the troubling resemblances with the other anti-Americanism, the only one, the real one, that of Arthur Moeller van den Bruck, inventor of the formula "Third Reich," and inventor, too, of "Amerikanertum"—which he meant to be understood "not in geographical terms but in spiritual ones," and which a follower of Bourdieu would likely translate as "Américanité"?

Régis Debray, that follower of Chevènement, likewise saw May 1968 as "the French path toward America"[26] and America itself as a mental category that has already gangrened European heads.[27]

And the same Debray, in the guise of a fable, calmly took up Drieu's ideas about the end of nations, the failure of Europe, and the irresistible triumph of that accursed Americanness.[28]

Look at the whole Left, which, almost as a single man, cheered on Michael Moore when, at the 2004 Cannes festival, he received the Palme d'Or for a film—*Fahrenheit 9/11*—that was nothing more than a variation on the old isolationist, populist, hypernationalist, and bigoted themes of the Pat Buchanans and other far-right Americans: "No dog in this fight," nothing to do, America should take care of the Americans and let the rest of the world go to hell. . . .

There is no such thing as leftist anti-Americanism.

Anti-Americanism, too, is the progressivism of the imbecile.

4.

Counterattack on the "Empire"

The little events of intellectual life sometimes have big surprises in store for us.

It's early summer, 2007.

After a visit to western Darfur in February, I have swung into action in favor of increasing financial, economic, and political pressure on the regime in Khartoum.

Alain Finkielkraut—once again—invited me on his weekly radio program to debate with the former humanitarian Rony Brauman, who had made very strange statements hinting that what needed to happen was less arresting the murderers than picking a fight with people like me, who were concerned about those murderers' impunity.

And I accepted, probably, because of Finkielkraut himself, because of the quality of the debates he organizes, and also because of my joy at finding myself in agreement with him, but also because of Brauman, who, I am well aware, disagrees with me completely on the majority of the issues that are important to me, and on this one more than ever—but I've known that for a long time; and in the middle of the eighties, when the Ethiopian dictator Mengistu was forcibly deporting whole populations, we had fought side by side; together, ten years earlier, right when I had founded Action Contre la Faim, we had jointly organized a March for Survival for Cambodia that was not dishonorable;

and, well . . . life is such that despite our differences I have kept, through the years, a kind of intellectual respect for him.

The program begins.

Alain Finkielkraut, as always, is both feverish and precise.

Brauman, whom I haven't seen in a long time, seems older, less offensive, melancholic.

And since the old radio preambles are now outdated, it's up to me to open the debate.

I START OFF by saying that Brauman's attitude is a mystery to me and that I'd like to take this occasion to understand, really understand, how a man like him can be contented with such careful considerations, so strangely indulgent of the murderers and so discouraging to public opinion, with regard to what might already be the first genocide of the twenty-first century.

Brauman looks surprised.

I see in his eyes that he's on guard, that he's suspicious.

But when he sees that I'm insisting, that I really do want to understand how a former president of Doctors Without Borders, a seasoned humanitarian who, to top it all off, has visited all of what Schopenhauer called the mysteries of sympathy—which is to say, concretely, the traps that lie in wait for the humanitarian who keeps to humanitarianism and avoids political questions—he plays along, answering, listening to my own answers, fine-tuning his own—so that a pretty good dialogue ensues, not so much about Darfur as about what exactly should be done there, and about the reasons that have kept the intellectual and political Left, and he himself, so prudently aloof.

I'm not sure, he begins, that the word *genocide* is appropriate, and I don't think, for that reason, that . . . I interrupt by saying that I'm not sure either—but who cares? In order to worry about it, do we have to wait for a massacre to reach the maximum genocidal level on the Richter scale of horrors?

I *am* sure, he continues, that the murder rate has gone down and that the crime—since there was a crime here, which we should have

responded to—was committed two or three years ago. Fine, I answer—
but here again: what do you mean by that? And what would you have
thought of a Brauman who, in 1944, would have said that because the
murder rate had declined—there weren't enough living Jews left over—
it was too late to act, punish, and defeat Germany?

Not comparable, he objects; you can't compare a situation where
you actually have pure victims of the absolute evil that was Nazism, and
Darfur, which I know well, and where splintered, often indistinguish-
able rebel groups are warring with each other, none of which is the
angel you seem to be saying they are. Fine, I now object—let's say you're
right; but you can't deny that before that breakdown, the primary responsibility lay with the government in Khartoum: and in any case who
else is there to talk to? Who else can we pressure if not President al-
Bashir? Can you imagine us, the other states, chasing after your little
groups of bandits?

Maybe, he then says, maybe: but not the Olympics, in that case; not
that idiotic idea of boycotting the Olympics in order to pressure Bei-
jing, which would then pressure Sudan . . . Except there again he
quickly backs down, because when Finkielkraut, or me, I can't remember, insists that it really is awful to have the Games under the aegis of a
regime that according to the most reliable estimates executes eight to
ten thousand people a year, tortures on a massive scale, muzzles free
speech, forbids political parties and labor unions, practices and organizes slavery, sees no objection either to child labor or to the sale of the
organs of executed prisoners, and, last but not least, still holds in its
jails several hundred survivors of the Tiananmen Square insurrection,
he mutters that yes, maybe, he's not talking about human rights—he
wouldn't find it so crazy to boycott the Olympics because of those
human rights violations—but Darfur is different.

In a word, he stumbles. Stutters. Switches arguments like horses.
Contradicts himself. Rectifies. Mumbles again. I sometimes even get
the feeling that he, more than anyone, is aware of the oddity of his position. Until, after an hour, when the moderator offers him the privilege of wrapping up, he concludes by exclaiming, sure of himself for the
first time, finding all the right words, almost happily: "This war, any-

way, is a war among the Sudanese"; he hammers on this point twice, to make sure he's been understood: "among the Sudanese"; and someone like him, opposed to the stupid intervention in Somalia, then to the infamous war in Iraq, could never accept, in Sudan, the latest whim of the Empire. . . .

The Empire . . .

The big dirty word has been spoken.

Suddenly it was clear that all the reasons he'd cited up to that point were only decoys, fake excuses, smoke in my eyes, and smoke, above all, in his own.

I was looking at a champion of human rights who was telling me, without the slightest hint of embarrassment, that he'd decided to sit out Darfur, to write it off as just another piece of our era's collateral damage, literally to wash his hands of all the blood that the "regime" of bloodletting had unleashed—and because of the following reasoning: 1. A powerful movement in public opinion was being born in the United States in favor of the persecuted, innocent victims; 2. American democracy being what it is, and public opinion having its well-known importance, the Bush administration or its successor—despite the fact that for a large country like America, Darfur has no possible economic, financial, or strategic interest—might end up getting involved and use its weight to try to stop the massacre; 3. America, unfortunately, is not only America; it's not just a democratic state that so gladly responds to the appeal of its public opinion, since it is also the capital, the command post, the nerve center, of a system of power that imposes a regime of unequal exchange on the planet, along with planned injustices and secret massacres that are just as bad as those in Darfur even if, alas, they don't enjoy the honors of the media echo chamber; 4. For that reason, we cannot follow the United States in one struggle without following it in the other; or—more precisely—to follow its lead on Darfur would be to consent to that other system; and, by losing sight of those many other areas where America is committing just as many other crimes—since we've transported, regrouped, focused on a single point every available world-historical projector—we would be all the less attentive toward those crimes; 5. That's not going to happen to me, Rony

Brauman was really saying; I am not—by letting myself be blinded by emotion, sentimental reflexes, or the illusions of what Hegel, in opposition to the "heroic character," called "everyday man"—going to fall into this vulgar trap; I am not going to let myself be mobilized by a movement that—claiming to save those last Darfuris who have escaped the massacres—is really just a diversion in the Empire's general strategy.

I'M JUST SUMMING UP, OF COURSE.

But I think I've captured the spirit of that conversation.

And I think the reader can guess where I'm going with it.

One can raise all kinds of objections to this concept of Empire.

One can—as I did in *American Vertigo*—object that it takes no account of what China is doing today in Tibet; or what the Soviet Union used to do in its satellites and what Putin's Russia is still trying to do wherever it can; or what happened under older peoples at the peak of their power, like the Turks, the Arabs, the Aztecs, the Persians, the Incas: the notion breaks down when accounting for the workings of an America whose main historical thrust has always been toward isolationism and which, unlike the great nations of old Europe, has never colonized anyone.

One can—Alexandre Adler did it very well—examine all the recent wars of the so-called Empire: What was the imperial goal in Bosnia? What was the strategic plan in the strikes on Serbia and the liberation of the Kosovo Muslims? What was the point, other than to reply to Al Qaeda's attack on New York, behind the last Afghan war of 2001? And Somalia? What empire in the world would have been able to find any interest in invading, even successfully, that disinherited, dusty strip of earth, which every strategist at the time recommended locking up and throwing away the key? Not to mention Iraq: we can't repeat often enough that if the Americans simply wanted to get their hands on its oil, there was a much easier way: not to make war on Saddam, but to strike a deal with him. . . .

Parenthetically, and just to return to the case of Darfur for a moment, one can put to rest the false information, strictly and factually false (but it matches the vision of the diabolical Empire and its legions so well that it took off immediately, without verification or discussion), that the White House was acting, in this matter, under pressure from those very reactionary, very awful, very fascinating American neofundamentalists: that was more or less true for the other war, the first one, which stopped when the Darfur massacres began and in which, for twenty years, the Islamists of the North fought the animists and Christians of the South; but as for Darfur itself—as for the massacres that were unleashed there in February 2003 and which we are dealing with today—it is willful blindness not to see, not to understand, not to want to understand the movement that started getting off the ground, after years of indifference, in which neoevangelical groups were joined by people from the Holocaust Museum in Washington, by groups of Democratic Catholics, by black organizations under the aegis of the Black Caucus, by the veterans of the struggle against apartheid, and even (though they're not my favorite people, I do not, unlike Rony Brauman, decide where to get involved based on who I chance meeting there) by a growing number of Islamic, and even Islamist, activists, particularly those connected with Farrakhan's Nation of Islam. . . .

While we're comparing empires, we could take a look at Cullen Murphy's book *Are We Rome?*,[1] which deconstructs the paradigm underlying the imperial characterization of the United States. There are many formal similarities, the author admits, between the United States and Rome. One imaginary, monumental, architectural, ever since the time of the Founding Fathers, who were haunted by the glorious model. Ignorance of the outside world, recruitment of mercenaries for the expeditionary force in Iraq, the loss of civic values and the privatization of public spaces all, unfortunately, point in the same direction. But at the same time so many traits differ: the suppression of slavery, the taste for democracy, the relation to its time and its history, and above all, the relation to its space—incorporated in the case of the Romans, abstract and almost deterritorialized in the case of the Americans.

We could go back to Antonio Negri and Michael Hardt's book *Empire*,[2] which itself overturns the paranoid and conventional vision of a world directed from a center that, by growing ever larger, by pushing its limits and its borders ever further away, by transforming itself into a supranational super-State present on every continent, will end up swallowing up the world. I do not often agree with Negri. I do not agree with his Spinozism. I do not agree with his radical nostalgias. I do not, of course, agree with his antiliberalism (though he is heartily against the connection to Schmitt . . .). But I am grateful to him for one thing—as well as, by the way, to Yann Moulier-Boutang and his friends from the magazine *Multitudes:* this description of a headless, decapitated, decapitalized empire, whose centers of sovereignty and impulses, though perhaps not everywhere, are at least multiple (States, to be sure; but also big labor, big media, corporations, opinion-shaping, international institutions) and which, even if called by the same name, even if still called "the Empire," no longer means the same as what the official anti-imperialists mean by it, making their rhetoric sound ridiculous. . . .

Finally, we could and we must realize that conspiracy-mongering, more and more openly declared as such, is what's really behind this concept of "Empire." When Lenin talked about empire it was a concept. An interpretation of reality that one could—like Rudolf Hilferding, Rosa Luxemburg, or Karl Kautsky—question or refute. It was one piece of a shrewd machinery in which the question, there again, was about the circulation of money, the enlarged reproduction of capital, the laws for value and commodities. When Chomsky, or Pinter, or Brauman takes the reins; when John Le Carré tells us, in *The Constant Gardener,* how pharmaceutical laboratories are "white collar arms dealers, who, hidden away in their offices, are organizing genocide in Africa"; when *Le Monde diplomatique* writes,[3] based on fragile at the least and sometimes frankly delirious evidence, how a company like Nestlé, flagship of the Empire, is promoting—the better to sell its products—a baby formula it knows will easily kill a million and a half infants per year; when the same *Monde diplomatique* starts talking about Synarchism, a kind of Trilateral Commission, with its Platonic ideal of invisible "sentinels" watching over the interests of the "Triad" and exercising, in so doing, a power that is as total as it is "diffuse, opaque, and almost unfathomable";[4] when, added to this myth of the Trilateral Commission sinking its fangs into the planet, the better to dominate it, comes—in the same text and in others of the same ilk—the notion of a power that is limitless because it is completely hidden from view, belonging to the Council on Foreign Relations in New York, the Aspen and Davos forums, or the Bilderberg Group; when, finally, the Iraq War, support for Israel, the idea of Turkey entering Europe—in a word, the entire foreign policy of the United States—can be explained by the secret agenda of a group of neoconservatives, who we take care, in passing, to mention, ever so gently, are mostly Jewish and have taken over the president's brain, we're on a completely different terrain. This is no longer analysis but magic. We're no longer talking about concepts; we're talking about the occult. We're showing a world whose motor is no longer class struggle, creation of value, contradictory interests, or even the passions of men, but a game involving masks and hidden motives, a taste for disguises and the desire to see through them, the return of hidden imams, doublespeak, the false-bottomed suitcases of reality. In a word, they are manufacturing new conspiracy theories worthy of those Poliakov or Taguieff described, and sharing with those the same old desire to believe that there is a world behind this world and that all the actors moving about the stage of this world—the Darfuris claiming to be the victims of genocide, the predators disguised as humanists, these human rights crusaders working on the orders of the oil companies—are just extras designed for the entertainment of the masses: the real actors, hiding their true faces, must be unmasked. You might as well be talking to Pinter, Chomsky, Bourdieu, or a neo-Trotskyist. But no. This huffing and puffing; this policeman-like approach; this obsession with manipulations, intoxications, and other disinformations; this desire to give their activists an explanation for the things that have been hidden since the disorganization of the world; this regime of coherence that is a bit too perfect, in which everything is hidden in everything else; and, on the other hand, this shadowy unity, this system of generalized correspondences: all that might be in the far background of Marxism, but I'm afraid it still brings us back to the delirium of Abbé Barruel, attributing the French Revolution to a sect of freemasons; or to that of the tsarist police, fabricating its famous fake, *The Protocols of the Elders of Zion,* which allegedly proved that the world was dominated by the Jews. Anti-Americanism was the progressivism of the imbecile: will anti-imperialism become the conspiracy-mongering of major intellectuals?

So we can do all that. For the sake of the truth, we can and must oppose all of these arguments, step by step, since "anti-imperialism" is starting, on the Left, along with anti-Americanism, to win hearts and minds. But I left the radio program that day with the terrible and suddenly perfectly blinding feeling that there is yet another answer to this idea of the Empire—perhaps the most serious, perhaps, too, the most urgent, and for me, in any case, at this point in my life, the most burning, the most consequential: "The Empire" is what makes a man like Rony Brauman blind and deaf to the tragedy of the Darfuris.

I'm talking about Brauman. But in the United States, I could, once again, mention Chomsky. Or Robert Fisk, strangely silent on this subject. Or Prexy Nesbitt, that Chicago intellectual who sees the whole matter as a shady American plot. Or the old Black Panther Bruce Dixon, who himself is not far from such notions. Or the people from the Black Agenda Report when they find reason to doubt the reliability, and especially the sincerity, of the information produced by "Save Darfur." Every time, the same hatred of the Empire produces the same disdain for the Darfuri victims. . . .

Right after the Durban conference in September 2001, I developed a structurally analogous analysis of the wrongdoings of anti-Zionism.[5]

Some of my friends—Finkielkraut, once again; Milner—would see there, in Durban, in that South African city where a meeting of NGOs was meant, once and for all, to condemn slavery, world hunger, racism, wars, but where one mainly heard the disgusting chant of "One Jew one bullet" that extremist advocates of the Palestinian cause were shouting, and which were echoed by a number of the eight thousand members of the three thousand NGOs, which were not, at least in theory, extremist organizations—some of my friends, therefore, would see the birth of an anti-Semitism in Durban, one that once again dared to be seen in the light of day.

They were right—and I'll come back to this.

That was clearly happening in Durban—and it was shameful.

But there was another shame (and I can't say if it was worse or less bad, since I don't want to have to measure the badness of different outrages: and, above all, I don't like the kind of reasoning that tries to figure out which victims were good and which were bad, whose deaths were suspicious, and which perpetrators were better than others), there was another shame—besides the fact (I say it first parenthetically, mockingly, but at the same time not entirely . . .) that it dirtied, by associating it with such ugly events, the name of a city which, in my mind, had always been associated with that of Pessoa, who spent his childhood and adolescence there—another shame, which was that after having announced a world antiracism summit to honor all the victims of all the planet's forgotten wars with a forum that, for the first time, would recognize their suffering, it afterward let things degenerate into repeatedly saying this earth has a single criminal state, the State of Israel; into insisting that only the Palestinian people could claim to have won the contest of victims; into acting, in other words, as if the entire universe was magnetized by that single unique conflict and including no other discussion of the other great questions on the program.

I immediately described the distress of the Rwandan delegation, which had so fervently hoped that justice would at last be done, and that light would finally be cast on the origins and unfolding of the genocide they had just witnessed.

I discussed in the days that followed the phone call I got in the middle of the night from my friend David Gakunzi, a Burundian citizen and pan-African human rights activist, telling me, almost in tears, that the hijacking of the conference by Palestinian organizations had only managed, once again, to further push away any awareness of the on-and-off genocide that had affected his country for the previous twenty years.

I thought about the representatives of the Dalit Indians who had come in the hope of securing a condemnation of the plight of the 260 million untouchables who were victims of the caste system; about the activists of the cause of the Roma in Eastern Europe; about the spokesmen of the native populations of Colombia and Ecuador who never get the slightest attention; about the group from Central Europe who wanted to see a passage about the wars in Chechnya and the Balkans inscribed in the final declaration; I thought about—and I still think about, every time I think about that great moment of shame, contempt, and moral failure—about all the activists for all the just causes who had arrived full of hope, persuaded that they finally had a stage upon which to express themselves, and who ended up reduced to silence by the screaming activism of those who wanted, in Durban's Kingsmead Stadium, to see a single face, that of the little boy Muhammad al-Durrah—and only wanted to hear a single slogan: "Free, free Palestine."

Well, here we were seeing the same mechanism we saw in our discussion of "Empire."

If you replace the word *America* with the word *Israel,* and put Zionism in place of imperialism (even though the two are indissolubly mixed because the people in Durban as well as, today, Rony Brauman's anti-imperalist friends—faithful in this matter to the very deep racist disdain that has always been a motor of anti-Zionism—never insult Israel without also letting it be understood, or even coming out and saying, just to beat a dead horse, that it was only the plaything, the marionette, of the United States, and never mention the crimes and misdemeanors of the United States without also referring, usually very quickly, to the even more monstrous "American-Zionist Axis" and, therefore, to the diabolical Israel), you see the same kind of vise, the same kind of trap, the same discursive structure, that underlies the concept of Empire—and for which Durban was simply the giant laboratory.

Because there again we see a world divided into good and evil.

We see a world in which the masters of the Empire, their allies, their clients, are the bad guys—and the good guys are those who resist them, with arms if possible.

We see a world in which, on the one hand, we have the United States, its English poodle, its Israeli lackey—a three-headed gorgon that commits all the sins in the world—and, on the other side, all those who, no matter what their crimes, their ideology, their treatment of their own minorities, their internal policies, their anti-Semitism and their racism, their disdain for women and homosexuals, their lack of press freedom and of any freedom whatsoever, are challenging the former.

What happens, then, when you're not a member of this anti-Empire front?

Who are you if you aren't Chávez, nor Ahmadinejad, nor Al Qaeda, nor even Fidel Castro—to whom, I mention in passing, the honor fell of wrapping up the Durban summit?

What happens to you if you think, like a Burundian Tutsi, that the fantasy of Hutu Power, and not a scheme carried out by Texas oilmen, is the source of your problems? Or, like a survivor of the extermination of the Nuba, in the most distant corner of the Sudan, that it's your unique-ness that singled you out for misfortune and explains the determination of the Islamist regime in Khartoum to get rid of you? What is your place in the world if you're Sri Lankan and caught not between the forces of the Empire and the anti-Empire but—much more simply, and, unfortu-nately, prosaically—between the Tamil Tigers and the government army in Colombo? What happens to you if you're Burmese, Tibetan, a Syrian Kurd, a Liberian? What's to become of you if the disaster you're dealing with has nothing to do with the evil of the Empire, its conspiracies, its plots—but everything to do with the corruption, for example, of a state apparatus, or of unscrupulous national elites?

Well, nothing.

You're out of luck.

No right to complain, and therefore no right to survive.

You can go put yourselves on display somewhere else, with your little local suffering that doesn't have anything to do with the great contradiction that governs the world.

You're a hundred times less important, a thousand times less inter-esting to progressive consciences, who have much less reason to fret about your particular case than about, for example, a humiliated-Muslim-who-has-resorted-to-terrorism-in-response-to-that-humiliation.

That's the problem.

That's the crime of those who think that the Empire/anti-Empire division is the greatest question of the day and that the rest, everything else, has to be subordinate to it.

That's the other great shame that appeared in Durban and that, in the years following, has only been confirmed.

I STARTED WITH DARFUR.

I'd like to finish with Bosnia and Kosovo.

I know that indifference to that drama was not, unfortunately, anyone's particular privilege.

And in the intellectual world, those who had eyes to see, ears to hear, and a pen to shout their rage and their revulsion were too few to make it possible, today, to assign all the merit or the blame to any one group.

I still think that, in the disaster that lasted so many years, in the ocean of indifference and cowardice that was, I repeat, common to everyone—in the prize list of a crime committed in common because it was covered up by almost everyone—the antiglobalists, antiliberals, and, finally, anti-imperialists nonetheless earned special distinction.

There were those who, unsure where to place the misfortunes of those European Muslims along the scale of received opinion and who didn't even understand how you could be Muslim without wearing the colors of the heroic struggle of the South against the North and against the Empire, simply said nothing and went about their business.

There was, once again, the case of the winner of the Nobel Prize in Literature, Harold Pinter, who—seeing the United States of America finally take the side of the Bosnians, and then intervene in favor of the Kosovars, then push to overthrow the president of Serbia—decided that a person so hated by his enemies could only be a friend of his and boldly joined, along with Jacques Vergès and a few others, the "International Committee for the Defense of Slobodan Milošević."

There was Noam Chomsky, that maniacal negationist who had already distinguished himself, we recall, by his support of Faurisson (that "relatively apolitical liberal"[6]), then by his revision of the history of the Cambodian tragedy (Cambodians committing genocide against other Cambodians? A genocide perpetrated inside a Communist country without being able to place the blame on the awful Americans? Irra-

tional! Therefore unreal!⁷), and who, for the same reasons, because of
the same imbecilic and terrible reasoning, undertook, in *Hegemony or
Survival: America's Quest for Global Dominance,* the book Chávez brandished
at the UN General Assembly at the end of 2006, to rewrite, pure and
simple, the history of the ethnic cleansing of Kosovo: the massacres
committed by the Serbs, he assures us, all happened after and not before the NATO air strikes; and as for the crimes committed from
before that time—as for those that it was impossible to deny had fallen
back before anyone dreamed of intervening—they were mostly caused
by the Albanian bandits of the KLA.

In the preface to the French edition of his book *The New Military Humanism: Lessons from Kosovo,* the same Chomsky issued a warning to those
in favor of Kosovo's independence, and in doing so came up with alle-
gations about post-Yugoslav Bosnia that must have made the eight
thousand dead of Srebrenica spin in their graves, along with the fifteen
thousand martyrs of Sarajevo, not to speak of all the other victims of
the three years of an ethnic cleansing carried out leisurely, with almost
perfect impunity: you're going to create another mafia state, a "haunt of
thieves and tax cheats," like Bosnia today; you're going to create another
society dominated—*sic*—by "a privileged criminal class that exercises
an enormous political influence and steals, every year, hundreds of millions of dollars in potential fiscal receipts."⁸

And then, finally, the summit was reached by the Frenchman Alain
Badiou in the two texts he dedicated to this issue, which I'd like to
focus on for a moment.

One,⁹ which appeared just when NATO was starting its air strikes
on Serbia, began by mocking the "bootlicking penpushers" and other
"people in bedroom slippers" who were insisting that their governments embark on an "airborne police operation against a stubborn little country"; denouncing the "particularly delightful verbal invention"
which was, to him, "the right to intervene," which he describes as the
right for "the powerful" to "hit weaker parties hard"; insisting, as if to
make sure he'd been perfectly well understood, that "being small and
weak does not necessarily make one good, these days," since we were
going to "hit you hard," as we had with Milošević; and to the "gallant

people" who would ask him if it would have been better to do nothing, his answer, which "certainly requires a delicate defense," was nonetheless "very clear," since "Yes, exactly" was precisely his opinion: "Nothing was more necessary than not to intervene," nothing was more essential than to "have the political presence of mind to do nothing," since "the situation in the former Yugoslavia is miserable, but that misery must be left to its local actors."

In another article, which came out a year later while the Chechen War was once again raging,[10] he expresses his surprise (about which, of course, he is not mistaken) that the international community is more indulgent with Putin than with Milošević; he notices (and he wasn't completely wrong) that a man who, like the master of the Kremlin, has "many airplanes" and who grew "rich from winning the stock market lottery" cannot be "completely evil" in the eyes of Western politicians; but adds (and this is where he starts to go off the rails) that the "grievous war against Serbia" was not, seen this way, anything more than a "planetary police operation" designed to install, "in the heart of the Balkans," not far from the "oil pipelines through the Black Sea," the "troops" and the "legionnaires" of what he only wishes to call the "voracious imperial democracy"; and, in an imaginary address issued by a representative of the "club of bombed democracies" to a Slobodan Milošević who, as those lines were being written, was still in power in Belgrade—he wraps up (and here the tone becomes not only dubious but ignoble) by saying: "If you are weak" (the "weak" person in question, just to make it clear, is no longer the murdered Kosovar but Milošević); if you "disturb the order we desire" (ethnic cleansing, massacres, 80 percent of the population of Kosovo forced to abandon its homes, the peasants of Racak killed with a shot to the neck and thrown into a ditch: all that becomes a simple "disturbance" to the imperial order!); if you're just an "archaic worker" (the Serbian militiamen, the Chetniks, the new kapos forcing the future victim of the firing squad to take off his pants so they can be sure he's really a Muslim, compared to "archaic workers"—it's like a hallucination)—then "we'll destroy you," then "we'll bury you," since for those Balkan peoples, those poor folks, those slobs who are tearing each other apart, Alain Badiou has only one recommendation: "We should stay out of their business."

—

NOT TO LAMENT, not to curse, Spinoza said—but to understand.

What I understand about this is that we are witnessing a terrible and ruthless mechanism.

You can't be a murderer *and* be an enemy of the United States—so Milošević was innocent.

You can't be a victim and be a friend of the United States—so the Kosovars (like the Bosnians and, of course, the Rwandans) are guilty.

You can't, in general, be black, yellow, or Arab; belong to the world of poor or formerly poor countries; proclaim your allegiance to the Third World; think that Castro is a hero—and be a murderer: so, long live the Hutu with the machete! Viva Chávez banning the free press and television, dreaming of a presidency-for-life and declaring that the world economy is dominated by the descendants of the people who "killed Christ"! Hurray for the righteous struggle of Ahmadinejad against his country's women!

You can't be an event without being the symptom of the single worthwhile confrontation, that of the Empire versus its opponents—so nothing happened in Kosovo, nothing in Bosnia, nothing in Rwanda; nothing in the long war in Angola; nothing in the wars in Sierra Leone and Liberia, which I don't think ever inspired a single word from Mr. Badiou; and what about the wars in Colombia? The long suffering endured by Ingrid Betancourt and the victims of the very anti-imperialist FARC—according to Mr. Badiou, we must stay out of other people's business. A failure of intelligence and of heart.

The end of political considerations, right when we were claiming to sharpen them.

These bad teachers, these antiteachers, so strangely devoted to undoing what in politics is the hardest thing of all to construct: a way to get people to worry about other people's suffering.

Optimists will recall that this idea of an empire is a poor one indeed, a shadow of its former self, the bleached-out bastard version of the "great" empire of the Marxists, and will say to themselves that it's all for the best; it might be the end of it, since once we've reached that point—once we've arrived at that state of degeneracy and entropy—once we're no longer trying to save, like those Marxists confronting Hegelianism, the "rational core" of a great body of thought, but its core of irrationality and darkness—its days are numbered, the countdown has not only begun, but the notion is on its last legs—no longer is imperialism the supreme stage of capitalism: anti-imperialism is the terminal phase of a Marxism that is finally decomposing, once and for all.

Pessimists (realists?) will say that it's not that simple unfortunately: some decompositions take a long time; some weak notions derive a potent energy from their very weakness; some are like bad cells in a body that phagocyte the good ones, killing them but taking nourishment from them—or like the cadavers that Malaparte describes in *Kaputt,* attached to the living and finally devouring them—and those people will fear that this concept of Empire has more positive power than it appears to have, more dark strength, but strength nonetheless—a real concept, a whole theory—a theorem, strictly speaking—which, together with anti-Americanism, hatred of Europe, and rejection of liberalism, might have a bright future ahead.

In any case, it's certain that this is what the concept of Empire is about.

It's certain that its only real function is to annihilate whole chapters of contemporary history, killing, one more time, millions of men and women, whose first crime was being born and whose second was dying the wrong way.

And it's certain that even if Alain Badiou, Rony Brauman, Noam Chomsky, and the rest seem, once again, to be on the fringes of the debates of the political Left, their ideological cohesion sets the pace of the whole: to carry on like this; to choose the side of the perpetrators and not of the victims; to tell the victims that they're bad victims and that their destinies don't matter to the world; to impose silence, in a word, on oppressed people who disturb the conceptual order of the world: that's what seems to be far off—*farther and farther off*—from what I would like to call the Left.

The New Anti-Semitism Will Be
Progressive—or Nothing at All

Let's look at the problem the other way around.

Let's look at the lunacy that up till now has been unquestionably beyond the criminal pale, which is not the province of the right wing or even the far right, the delirium that is fascism and Nazism.

Let's take the case of what Robert Wistrich called "the longest hatred," which—though the word only appears in 1879, coined by the German writer Wilhelm Marr—is, of course, much older than that.

Let's examine this long scream of hatred which throughout the centuries has stalked the People of the Word and which is called anti-Semitism.

EVERY HISTORIAN OF the phenomenon agrees that the story is both very simple and very complex.

They know that its core hardly varies but that the discourse that expresses it, that clothes it, changes with the times.

And they know that, if it changes, if it feels the need to evolve, it does so because it needs to stand out, to convince, to be heard by the greatest number of ears, to reach into souls and to rally them—and that is why it has to embrace the fears, the fantasies, and the rhetoric of the moment.

And so it was, during the very long period in which most people were Christian, that anti-Semitism was addressed to a Christian public in these terms: "We hate the Jews, not because they are Jews, not because they are ontologically detestable, but because they killed Christ." Shame on the deicides: St. Paul's anti-Semitism was guaranteed to generate persecution.

So it was that when secularism was in vogue and, thanks to the Enlightenment, the anticlerical movement had the ideological upper hand, a new, opposite charge was leveled at the Jews: "No, we've changed our minds; the Jews are detestable not because they killed this Christ person about whom we don't give a damn, and whom we actually even hate; if anything, their crime was having invented him and infecting the world with this bacteria, this poison, called Christianity." Enlightened anti-Semitism. Antireligious. Sometimes pagan. An anti-Semitism that says: "I've got nothing against the Jews: what I'm against is the kind of piety they invented and which reached its logical conclusion in Christianity." Voltaire, in his *Dictionnaire philosophique* and *L'Essai sur les moeurs.* D'Holbach. Eventually, Nietzsche and, especially, Schopenhauer.

Then came the triumph of nation-states. Then came the triumph of people who thought that there was no other solution for a grown-up humanity liberated from its old masters than joining together in nations. At that point a third accusation appeared, which could be summed up in the following terms: "Nobody cares whether these people killed Christ or invented him; the problem, the biggest problem, is that they're impossible; everywhere and nowhere; travelers and wanderers; cosmopolitans; fugitives; incapable of settling down or picking a side; do they belong to this nation? that one? or some third nation of which we know nothing because it exists only in their mind or, as they put it, in their Torah? If they must be hated that's the reason; if they deserve the harshest punishment it's because of their insistence on lurking, as they say, by themselves and away from other nations; if we must somehow cut them off it's because their very existence, their survival and now their perseverance in that survival, defies the law which ordains a single solution for the End of History, the solution of the

nation." Let's say that this, if we have to give a name to this kind of reasoning, this kind of anti-Semitism, which is different from its two predecessors, is what we find in Hegel's *Phenomenology of Mind.*

Then came the Industrial Revolution, the rise of capitalism and the
emerging world mercantile system—and, at the same time, in search of
a scapegoat for all the new system's collateral damage, another message:
"the banks are Jewish; capital is Jewish; America, like England, is Jewish; so let's forget about Christ, his death and his invention; let's forget
that they don't belong to any particular nation-state, however annoy-
ing that may be; if the Jews are detestable, if they must be despised and
struggled against, it's because they are the beginning of a process that
rips the poor from their homes, lashes them to new machines, slowly
murdering and humiliating them; they are the bloodsuckers of the
poor, the beating heart of the body that is crushing and suffocating
them"—this is social anti-Semitism, leftist anti-Semitism, an anti-
Semitism that culminates with the Dreyfus Affair, including the Left's
lengthy hesitation to come out on the side of a persecuted Jew.[1]

And finally there comes a fifth and final prototype, which takes
shape at the end of the nineteenth century, with new fads in biology,
the development of anthropology and modern philology, the distinction between Indo-European and Semitic languages, etc.—a paradigm
that appears when Georges Vacher de Lapouge, but also Hippolyte
Taine and Ernest Renan, produce a racial vision of human groups and
their conflicts. "The problem," they say now, "isn't any of those ancient
issues that humanity can adapt to and has, in fact, survived. The problem is race. The problem is that, in a humanity divided into races and
governed not by the struggle of classes but by the struggle of races, the
Jews represent a separate race, perhaps even an anti-race—though the
word *race* is too good to apply to them and in fact one shouldn't use
such a nice word for such a degenerate people—the problem is that this
anti-race is a toxic body whose greatest toxicity consists in the way it
interacts with other races, in order to infiltrate them, to corrupt their
lovely purity, to mongrelize them." This anti-Semitism, which for the
first time uses the language of racism, exaggerates a difference which—
unlike religious differences, which could be solved by conversion, or

unlike national dissidence, which could be solved by what the Jews of France and Germany called assimilation[2] in the nineteenth century—is indelible—this anti-Semitism is the one that starts with Vacher de Lapouge, Gobineau, and Houston Stewart Chamberlain, who inspired, in the United States, the 1924 law privileging the immigration of the "Nordic races" to the detriment of the "Semitic and Slavic races," and carries on to Hitler, making possible a once-unthinkable "Final Solution."

OF COURSE, THINGS are not so cut and dried.

The periods, first of all, overlap.

Anti-Christian anti-Semitism does not entirely replace Christian anti-Semitism.

Social anti-Semitism is in full flower when, in France and Germany, the new idea appears that the body is the signature of the soul and that Judaism is therefore a question of the body—which is to say of race—as much as of faith.

The anti-Semitism of uncertain allegiances, which accuses the Jews of not belonging to any community, or at least not to the one hosting them, does not date from the first stirrings of nationalism: it is already there among the opponents of Napoléon's convocation of the Great Sanhedrin; earlier still, in the Middle Ages; or even in Cicero, who, in his *Pro Flacco,* accuses the Jews who refused to swear on the eagles—that is, to the Roman legions—of showing nothing more than "disdain for the splendors of Roman power" and not being interested in anything but that "distant city" of Jerusalem, which they supported with "denarii" taken from "the Republic."[3]

Never, in other words, did any of these ideologies entirely take the place of its predecessors, and real anti-Semitism, the anti-Semitism that existed in people's minds, operated all the more subtly and confusedly because these notions were never clear-cut.

Nothing was too outlandish.

Every combination, every mixture, one more far-fetched than the next.

Barrès, the social anti-Semite whose fundamental charge was that Jews were the allies of high finance, still briefly notes that he can tell Dreyfus is guilty because of the shape of his nose.

The racist anti-Semite Gobineau does not hesitate, when need be, to borrow arguments from the arsenal of social anti-Semitism.

The racist Paul de Lagarde, author of *La Religion de l'avenir,* doesn't fail to mention his hatred of Christianity, that bad religion that oppresses the vigorous national-pagan religions.

Adolf Stöcker's German country squires, while accusing the Jews of creating the "laissez faire" Manchester doctrine, and when explaining the phenomenon by the double plutocratic and cosmopolitan tropism of the Synagogue, bring together national and social anti-Semitism.

Schopenhauer, himself a racist, finds it useful, in a paragraph in *Parerga und Paralipomena,*[4] to summon the "people of the Japhetic languages" to cleanse Europe of a "Jewish mythology" that spawned Christianity—practically Voltaire.

Voltaire himself, inventor of the anti-Christian anti-Semitism that ought to have swept away the old Catholic accusations as well as their terminology, allows himself in a paragraph in *L'Essai sur les moeurs et l'esprit des nations* to thunder against the people "punished by God" for having "immolated" the nations around them.[5]

Drumont, writing in his *France juive* on the day after the crash of the Union Générale bank in 1882, then considered a repository for Catholics with small accounts, attributes its difficulties to a plot on the part of Jewish banking: social anti-Semitism laced with Christianity.

Bernanos himself was fully Christian; he was probably one of the last true Christian anti-Semites in French literature, therefore indulging in fantasies of the Jews as the people of deicide—not that he neglects social anti-Semitism (take his defense of the "humble and the modest" in his book on Drumont, *La Grande Peur de bien-pensants*), racial anti-Semitism ("those strange people who talk with their hands, like monkeys"[6]), or even national anti-Semitism à la Hegel ("I have always believed, as I still do, that the obstinacy—which can so often be admirable—of the Jews in not blending entirely into their various national environments is a great misfortune for all involved"[7]).

In Detroit, the American automobile magnate Henry Ford distills—
in his weekly newspaper *The Dearborn Independent,* whose articles he will
reprint in a series of four thick volumes called *The International Jew: The
World's Foremost Problem,* and whose German translation would be quoted
from, publicly praised, and distributed by Hitler himself—an anti-
Semitism of racist inspiration, though one that also leaned on the *Protocols of the Elders of Zion;* the idea that Jews were responsible for all the
evils engendered by liberalism, syndicalism, Bolshevism, jazz; as well as
a paradoxical but real anticapitalism (except for his own, Ford, all big
companies were said to be in the hands of Jews) and even an early anti-
Zionism (born during the course of his famous pacifist cruise of December 1915, during which "two Jews" were said to have revealed to
him that the secret goal of the Great War was the creation, or not, of a
Jewish National Home), as well as, occasionally, the good old clichés of
Christian anti-Semitism.

And then there is the case of Dühring, that same Eugen Dühring
targeted by Engels in his *Anti-Dühring,* one of those forgotten men who,
like the John Lewis of Althusser's *Reply to John Lewis,* are remembered
by posterity only because they inspired a famous pamphlet—Eugen
Dühring, who was an important man in his day, author of the *Gotha Program* that inspired the social democratic turn in German socialism: social anti-Semitism (in Marxist form) thrown into his system along
with traces of racism and paganism.

From these combinations, the reality was born.

From these hybrids, concrete anti-Semitism appeared.

It all comes about as if there were a basic system setting the pace, as
it were, framing the whole and meeting every age's expectations—a system working like a gigantic magnet attracting all sorts of old broken-
down notions.

But the basic law is the one I've described.

There is no question that certain notions appear one after the next,
following trends in science or religion.

It's true that anti-Semitism is a mutating virus, a spell that regularly
loses its powers and has to rejuvenate itself, a mad raving, but one that
has to win converts and therefore must find a respectable guise so that

everyone who succumbs to it can exclaim: "We have nothing against the Jews, nothing at all; except this terrible crime they have committed, this bad deed, this nasty habit, etc." This, we can take for granted.

Anti-Semitism has a history.

SO WHERE DOES that history bring us?

There is no doubt that anti-Semitism persists.

In some ways, it is also true that it is even advancing.

And it is a fact that it is getting harder and harder, in certain areas of certain French cities, to go out wearing a yarmulke.

Except—and this is what's strange about the situation now—there is also no doubt that none of the five traditional models can explain that fact.

Let's go back over them one at a time.

The racist model has its followers, but, as Bernanos said, using a terrible but rather revealing word, it did not survive Hitlerism, which "dishonored" it.

Social anti-Semitism endures, but it has been substantially weakened, at least in its canonical form, by the knowledge—probably superficial and riddled with prejudices but an embryo of knowledge nonetheless—that people have of the mechanisms of globalization; even those who know nothing, even those who confuse everything have a harder time than they did a century ago in making the name Rothschild the emblem of the global plutocracy.

National anti-Semitism, which accused the Jews of not being rooted in any nation, still has its partisans, but its arguments have been weakened first by the birth of Israel (even if a whiff of double allegiance endures for the Jews who have chosen to remain in the Diaspora), and then by the better reputation that cosmopolitanism and cultural exchange enjoy in our day (though something of the "Idéologie française" remains in France; it is still true, in Europe and the world, that fixations on identity are the rule and their transgression the exception; still, this is also the time of doctors, pharmacists, reporters, engineers, entrepreneurs, and other tourists without borders—we are in a time of generalized border crossing which makes it tougher to portray the "Wandering Jew" as the incarnation of Evil).

Nor is Enlightenment anti-Semitism dead. And we are familiar with all the fanatical atheists and even certain secularists who can get worked up about the idea of the Jewish people who gave the world the poisoned gift of skullcaps. But the Infamous, as they put it, has finally been slain. No matter what they say, the separation of Churches and State is a fact. Or if it isn't, if secularism sometimes seems threatened, this is no longer the fault of Christians or Jews—as they well know.

And as for Christian, or Catholic, anti-Semitism itself, it is difficult to deny that it occasionally flares up again—the success, at least in the United States, of Mel Gibson's *Passion of the Christ* would be enough to show that the theme of the deicide Jew still resonates, if we needed convincing. But it would be even harder to deny that for the most part the phenomenon is on the way out and that, as Levinas predicted, Christians are even becoming the Jews' strongest allies in their twin struggle against the new anti-Semitism and in favor of a new positive attitude toward Judaism, freed from clichés about a Christianity that is the "son" of a Judaism which it will, like all sons, have to kill. Vatican II represented a step in this direction. Then came the repentance of John Paul II. Then his successor Ratzinger who, despite what is often written, continues his predecessor's line, speaking of Judaism with respect, and mentioning during his visit to Auschwitz, for example,[8] "a crime without precedents in history," speaking of a people, "the Jewish people," who, "by the simple fact of its existence," was a "witness to God"— which is why it was targeted for destruction "in its totality" to erase it "from the ranks of the nations of the earth"—who says it better?

In other words, all the old forms persist.

In France, at the beginning of the twenty-first century, one can still murder a young Jew, Ilan Halimi, in the name of outdated stereotypes.

And all of these sects surely include enough fanatics who not only will tend the flame but can even turn it deadly.

But at the same time the flame is not strong enough to whip up a crowd to a pogromist frenzy.

These arguments are not strong enough, either on their own or in more extended form, to persuade large crowds that it is just, good, or reasonable to hate and persecute the Jews.

But I am willing to bet that neither in France nor in Europe will there ever again appear a mass movement demanding the death of the Jews to shouts of "Money Jews" or "They killed Christ!" or "They invented him!" or "They're not home anywhere" or "They're a cursed race."

I am convinced that in order for such a movement to emerge, for people to feel once again the desire and, above all, the *right* to burn all the synagogues they want, to attack boys wearing yarmulkes, to harass large numbers of rabbis, to kill not just one but many Ilan Halimis—in order for anti-Semitism to be reborn on a grand scale, an entirely new discourse, another way of justifying it, must emerge.

WHICH ONE?

Now we're getting there.

The way things are in this day and age, today's religion is more and more clearly founded on the triple pillars of the cult of victimhood, the taste for memory, and the punishment of evildoers (triumphant antifascism, the love of victimhood, and the duty of memory). Anti-Semitism can only return, can only rediscover the power, the rallying capacity—I almost said the freshness—that all the preceding models once enjoyed, if supported by three new pillars.

First proposition. The Jews are no longer exploiting the wealth of nations but monopolizing that much rarer good, more immaterial but rarer: human compassion. The Holocaust industry, says one (Norman Finkelstein, with an afterword by Rony Brauman[9]) . . . When I hear the word Holocaust, says another, I turn off the television (the German Martin Walser[10]) . . . A third says: the problem with this famous "duty of memory" which you Jews keep pushing is that by occupying public space, by saturating it to the maximum, by calling all peoples to submit to the dogmas of the new piety, you hide other duties, you erase other memories, you simply make it impossible to hear the cries of other tortured peoples . . . What's left for the genocide of the American Indians?

the anti-Semitic Indian chief Russell Means asks me one day.[11] Nothing; the American Jews have taken it all; they've even taken over the very idea of genocide. What's left for the so-called first peoples who, as former president Jacques Chirac one day explained in front of his office to a small group of intellectuals who had come to speak to him about Bosnia, were the first victims of genocide? Nothing there either: humanity is humanity; it can't mourn two genocides at the same time, and too bad for the first peoples if there's only enough left over for the Holocaust. And the Palestinians? the muttering continues. Isn't the enemy of the Palestinians, even more than the Israeli army, even more than the checkpoints on the roads, even more than the Wall, the hullabaloo around the Jewish people's suffering, which stifles their own voices? Actually, says the first proposition, that's it, that's it exactly: when the world's mourning capital is redirected, rechanneled, overflowing, for children who died sixty years ago, nothing is left, not a single tear, not a single sigh, for the children dying today in Gaza. They've made off with all the sympathy for the world's victims. Doesn't meet the standard for human suffering. A display of suffering that overshadows other martyrs. This is the first new accusation leveled at the Jews. This is their first crime in the eyes of the new mob. This is the first reason to start resenting them again and, in clear conscience, in the name of the sacred concern due to all the world's dead, to start hating them again. This is an anti-Semitism justified by the battle of memories. This is the anti-Semitism based on competition between victims. This is the anti-Semitism of a certain Dieudonné, with his theory that the Jews promoted the African slave trade.

Second proposition. If only Jewish suffering was what they said it was . . . If only the Jews were these pure victims who suffered an incomparable crime . . . But you know, it's not so clear-cut. It's even frankly dubious. Because those Jews are crafty, possibly even iniquitous con artists who've pulled off the scam of the century, the biggest fraud in the history of mankind: propagandists of genius who, not content simply to monopolize all of mankind's victim capital, not content simply to suck up everything for their own profit so that there's nothing left for anybody else; not content, indeed, to swindle us, have done it all in the name of a suffering that is nothing like what they claim. Some go very far in this direction and, like Faurisson, Rassinier, Garaudy, or that Muslim preacher whom they inspired, have come out and said that the Holocaust never happened. Others, knowing that this unsustainable position quickly sinks under the weight of historical evidence, put it another way—and this is a theme that has blossomed in the Arab world: "Look, fine, it happened, but not the way you say it did; not to the extent that you claim; and there are some gray areas that, surprisingly enough, you never mention, and which cast a bit of a shadow over the pretty, pious image you want to force down our throats" (the role of the leadership of Jewish communities, the complicity of the great powers, and even, among the more perverse, a secret alliance between Hitler and the Zionists—not to mention the so-called mystery, according to a famous European filmmaker, surrounding the absence of images of the gas chambers . . .). Still others admit both the event and the story that witnesses and historians have told and retold—but they deny that anything made it particularly unique or unusual: "A massacre, absolutely; six million dead, fine; but it's all part of the long history of massacres that are the fate of humanity; so why single out this one? What strange notion assigns this one a special status? And haven't you yourself said a thousand times that one dead person is as good as another and that it's a disgrace to distinguish among the dead?" In any case, another "solid" argument. In any event, another "good" reason to condemn a people cynical enough, unscrupulous enough, to toy with the most sacred thing of all, the number and the memory of its dead. In its most extreme forms (Holocaust denial) or more measured forms (revisionism), this argument constitutes the second rail of this new anti-Semitism.

And now the third idea. What's the point? Why bother? Who or what gains by this colossal effort, this unsleeping vigilance, this desperate necessity to prevent passing time and the disappearing survivors from eroding this massive edifice, to keep the dead from burying the dead, to keep forgetfulness—ah, blessed forgetfulness which always stifles the cries of humanity—from stifling this one too? What's the point of all this hysteria, of this whole strategy, these historians, these gatherings of historians, of this intellectual and political mobilization never before seen for any other event, these scientific commissions, these Gayssot laws, these laws in general, come on, let's say the word, this plot—the word doesn't sound so great, as we well know! but that's what we're dealing with here! nothing less than a plot, and a damned good one, too, to persuade the whole planet of something that's no more than a lie, or a half-lie, or a quarter-lie, or an exaggeration, or at the very least, a thesis, come on! let's call it a thesis, the thesis of the uniqueness of a Holocaust that isn't unique except for those who want to buy it. Well, the answer is simple enough. It's blinding. And for the new anti-Semites, for those who are looking for any good reason to reprove this cursed people, there can be no doubt. The goal is Israel. Zionism is the secret agenda. All that energy, all that intelligence, all those means, that immodestly insisted-upon duty of memory, has no other goal than to support a cause, and a basically indefensible one at that, which is the Jewish State. Let's just say a State. But what a State! Stolen from the beginning. Perpetuated thereafter by crime, occupation, violence, and lies. A fascist State. A racist State. The worst State—that was the theme of Durban—on the face of the earth. We have nothing against Jews, the new anti-Semite protests, as always. What we're against is people who traffic in their own memory (Holocaust deniers) and push out the memories of others (competition among victims) for the sole purpose of legitimizing an illegitimate state (third cornerstone of the system—its anti-Zionist stone).

IF ONE CAN STOMACH IT, it's easy enough to answer all these propositions.

One might recall that no Zionist, ever, saw the Holocaust as the foundation of Israel.

One might, as I have done countless times (but sometimes you're just too exhausted, fatigue takes over, or disgust—what's the point? for how long? can you make people listen to reason when they're determined not to?), explain that this fascist, Nazi state founded on apartheid is the only democratic state in the region and that, by the standards of any region, it is often an exemplary democracy.

You could send the hard-core deniers to Raul Hilberg or Claude Lanzmann. And you could take the time, with those who wonder, sometimes in good faith, about the uniqueness of the Holocaust, you could take the time to explain that this uniqueness has nothing to do with body count but with a whole range of characteristics that, strange as it may seem, coincide nowhere else in all the crimes human memory recalls. The industrialization of death is one such: the gas chamber. The irrationality, the absolute madness of the project, is the second: the Turks had the feeling, well founded or not, and mostly, of course, unfounded,[12] that they were killing, in the Armenians, a fifth column that was weakening them in their war against the Russians—there was no point in killing the Jews; none of the Nazis took the trouble to claim that there was any point to it at all; and such was the irrationality, I almost said gratuitousness, of the process that when, by chance, the need to exterminate coincided with another imperative that actually did have a point, when, in the last months of the war, when all the railways had been bombed by the Allies, the Nazis could choose between letting through a train full of fresh troops for the eastern front or a trainload of Jews bound to be transformed into Polish smoke in Auschwitz, it was the second train that had priority, since nothing was more absurd or more urgent, crazier or more vital, than killing the greatest number of Jews. And the third characteristic that, finally, makes the Holocaust unique: the project of killing the Jews down to the last one, to wipe out any trace of them on this earth where they had made the mistake of being born, to proceed to an extermination that left no survivors. A Cambodian could, theoretically at least, flee Cambodia; a Tutsi could flee Rwanda, and outside Rwanda, at least ideally, would be out of range of the machetes; the Armenians who managed to escape the forces of the Young Turk government were only rarely chased all the way to Paris, Budapest, Rome, or Warsaw; not to mention the Palestinians who, so we are told, are the new Jews of this new genocidal people that is the Jewish people—not only Israel, but the entire international community, would happily pay not only for them not to die, or even to gather in camps, but to set themselves up in Jordan or anywhere else in the Arab world. (That is obviously not the solution; I myself have always been in favor of a partition into two states, which would mean an Israeli state *and* a Palestinian state; but let us agree that this is far from being genocide! We can agree that a young man in Ramallah cannot be compared to the children of the Vilna or Warsaw ghettos who knew that the world itself was an ambush, a mousetrap, a slaughterhouse, a dead end.)

One could recall, at last, that the idea that compassion is a finite good which people need to fight over, the idea of pity as a kind of disputed golden fleece, strangely fails to take into account how humanity actually works. One could go into detail. One could go through every one of these genocides, even every major massacre, committed in the last few years. Far from smothering all other memories, far from an obsession with Jewish martyrdom that blinds us to other sufferings as a cloud of ink makes them invisible, exactly the opposite has happened—the Holocaust works like a radar, Walter Benjamin reportedly said like a fire alarm, a powerful machine, in any case, for stirring consciousness. This is the case of the Rwandan genocide that nobody in Europe saw coming—except a handful of intellectuals and journalists who, precisely because they were thinking of the Holocaust, instantly smelled its distinctive odor. This is the case of Bosnia, which the entire world ignored (everyone was guilty, they were all fascists, obscure Balkan tribes, which only a Milošević, like Tito before him, could possibly set straight)—except, there too, a few intellectuals, often the same ones, sometimes others, whose only advantage, whose only small talent or privilege, was obviously not their daring, or even their extra insight, but the fact that, once again because of the Holocaust, they had a measure of what could happen, a measure of inhumanity, which allowed them to identify the ill augurs when they saw them coming. This was also the case of Darfur, where we saw the emergence of an odious polemic claiming that all that uproar, all these attacks against the Islamist regime in Khartoum, were organized by the Jews, yes, yes, the Jews, a B'nai B'rith here, a Jewish Congress there, and every time, didn't their evil agenda find friendly ears in the most prestigious media outlets? The polemic made me indignant, of course; all the more so because among the organizations brought together by Urgence Darfour were Christian, secular, Masonic, Muslim organizations; but at the same time . . . part of me still knew that I wasn't wrong and that once again, it was men and women who remembered the Holocaust who were on the front lines of this mobilization. . . .

So we can do all of that.

So we can fight it every inch of the way, as I think we must.

Unfortunately, I don't think that will have any more effect than (back in their day) the libraries full of works showing that the whole "race" question was nonsense; that the Jews were good citizens who respected the laws of whatever nation they resided in; that there were poor Jews; that it was the Romans who killed Jesus; that the Jewish people aren't the "father" but the brothers of the Christian people.

I'm afraid we already have the three necessary propositions, in perfect harmony with the mood of the age and the good conscience of progressivism—three propositions which, each separately and, even more, all together, create a powerful argument, almost a moral atomic bomb.

Since if, truly, the idea gained favor that Jews are a villainous people who stifle the voices of other peoples, who play with their own people's martyrdom, and who do it all just to support a fascist State, wouldn't it be logical, normal, to hate them, just a little? And wouldn't the idea of sparing them, of closing our eyes, of indulging a bit their own claims to be victims, itself become suspicious and even reprehensible?

We're not there yet.

The three propositions have not yet come together.

But let's make no mistake.

This is the threat.

Anti-Semitism, if it returns, will do so in this form and no other.

We can track it down past its original masks and through its out-of-date discourses.

The truth is that anti-Semitism will recycle, as usual, little bits and pieces. But for the most part it will be a union of Holocaust denial, anti-Zionism, and competition among victims—or it will be nothing at all. It will either have the same progressive, antifascist overtones, sympathetic to all the problems about which what is usually called the Left has made a career of caring—or it will have failed.

A FINAL WORD.

Or rather two.

It's commonly thought that this resurgence of anti-Semitism is, in the Western world, a solely European affair, and, in Europe, an almost exclusively French matter.

Not to mention the journalists who, in the United States, inquire with concern about the return of an illness that is mainly the shame of my own country.

Unfortunately, things are not so simple.

I won't get into the case of England, recently mentioned in an article in *The Washington Post*[13] written by the British Labour MP Denis MacShane: "Hatred of Jews," he says, has become "a mood and a tone" as widespread in England, at the "dinner parties of modish London," as in the "universities" or among the "liberal media elite"—and this in a climate in which "the old anti-Semitism and anti-Zionism have morphed into something more dangerous."

Neither will I delve into the obvious resurgence, once again in Britain, of the old Christian anti-Semitism we witnessed when, in February 2006, the Synod of the Anglican Church voted by an overwhelming majority to boycott the American firm Caterpillar—as well as the mass dumping of that company's shares that the Synod owned—because of the allegation that their bulldozers were being used by the Israeli army to destroy Palestinian houses suspected of harboring terrorists.

I won't discuss the case, in the United States, of the ex-president Jimmy Carter, who never misses a chance to make way for a hatred that, in Europe and certainly in France, would immediately be seen for what it is. Consider his April 2008 journey to Damascus, when he gave unquestioning moral support to the leadership of Hamas, and consider *Palestine: Peace, Not Apartheid,* which appeared in 2006, in which he charges Israel with having unleashed the Six-Day War; in which he says that Israel was the only party responsible for the failure of the Oslo peace process; and in which he presents the creation of the Palestinian Liberation Organization, in 1964, as a response to the seizure of the waters of the Sea of Galilee by an Israel hell-bent on irrigating the sands of its Negev by any means possible. . . .

BECAUSE IF WHAT I've just said is true, and if we go back over each of the three propositions that together make up the atmosphere of the renascent evil, it's not clear at all that the New World is better immunized against them than the Old.

Competition among victims. The United States entered the arena at the beginning of the nineties, with the publication, by the Nation of Islam, of *The Secret Relationship Between Blacks and Jews,* an extremely violent book that unleashed a chain reaction in all the departments of African American Studies in American universities and broke the historical alliance of the Jewish and the black communities. It claimed that Jews were behind the slave trade. Its thesis was that the Jews are to thank for a black holocaust whose cruelty surpassed the one they themselves would later fall prey to. It concluded that the Jews, in a symbolic theft, wrongly, and with an unsurpassable brazenness, took over all the symbolic capital that today belongs to the victim. It's all there.[14]

Holocaust denial. Of course, with the publication in 1950 of *Le Mensonge d'Ulysse* by Paul Rassinier, France had a head start on the rest of the world. But it's also true that the publication in 1961 of David Hoggan's *The Forced War* and then, in 1976, of Arthur Butz's *The Hoax of the Twentieth Century,* meant that the United States was not far behind. The themes are the same. It's like an academy of infamy whose members give each other pointers. With one other head start: the creation, in 1978, in Los Angeles, of the Institute for Historical Review, and, the next year, of the *Journal of Historical Review,* which claims to be the sect's central organ—as in fact it is. (The Institute published Richard Harwood's *Did Six Million Really Die?* and was behind the 2001 denial conference in Beirut, and it also laid the groundwork for Ahmadinejad's December 2006 Holocaust Conference in Teheran. . . .)

And as for anti-Zionism, the real deal, dressed in the most re-spectable clothing, all the harder to rebut because it takes on the man-tle of the victim: is it wrong to point out to our American friends that one of its most pernicious varieties is hatching on their own ground? I have in mind that article by Adam Shatz, former editor of the cultural pages of *The Nation*, explaining[15] that "Israel shapes and even defines the foreign policy views of a small group of American liberals," notably those associated with Michael Walzer's *Dissent* magazine and appearing, for this reason, as the Trojan Horse of the very pernicious Jewish lobby for the American Left: the fact that the Iraq War, supposed to be "the" big project, at the time, of the lobby, had been disapproved of, and even vigorously opposed, by almost all of the staff of *Dissent* makes no differ-ence to Shatz, who is carried away by his passion. I am thinking of the text by Stephen Walt and John Mearsheimer, respectively professor at the Kennedy School at Harvard and professor of political science at the University of Chicago, which appeared in March 2006—in the middle of the Iraqi depression, therefore—accusing American diplomacy of letting itself be taken over by a Jewish lobby that was as extreme as it was unscrupulous:[16] I am not sure that a book like this, whose central theme was almost explicitly that of Jewish warmongering, and which took up the old arguments of Charles Lindbergh, the America Firsters, and the far-right isolationists of the beginning of the 1940s, would even have been publishable in France under the Gayssot law. . . . And I am thinking of a tiny event, almost ignored by the press but immensely powerful symbolically: a declaration by Cindy Sheehan, America's an-tiwar mother, the mother of all the mothers whose children had been killed in Iraq and who had to be shown respect because the anti-Bush climate demanded it; I am thinking of the terrible thing she said, which accused the Jewish state of the worst crime a state can be accused of:[17] "My son joined the army to protect America, not Israel"; she had had enough of these "lies," these "treasons," "which we mothers know well are for the sole profit of Israel"—Jewish state, sacrificial idol: the inno-cent flesh of American children burnt before the altar of Israel; once again, it's all there. . . .

So it's possible that America, faced with this kind of slander, has weapons that Europe, not to mention the Muslim world, lacks.

But the idea that it's protected, that the synthesis is impossible there, that it's a sanctuary where the three-headed beast has already been slain—that's less certain, and that's what might make me the most pessimistic.

AND NOW FOR my very last remark—just to avoid misunderstandings.

Does everything that I've just said mean that I think, like Pierre-André Taguieff, for example, that antifascism has had its day, since it was in the name of antifascism that the Jewish state was Nazified in Durban?[18]

Does the fact that in the United States, as in France, the neo–anti-Semites borrow the worst of their arguments from the arsenal of the struggle against racism mean that I agree with Alain Finkielkraut that antiracism is the new Stalinism, that it has become the language of anti-Semitism, and that we ought not only to break with it but to criticize its very foundations?

Does the way that the Dieudonnés, the Nation of Islam types, or even Tariq Ramadan's Muslim Brotherhood use their own grievances as a way to throw back at the Jews the accusation that their use of memory is crazy or just idiotic, because all they do is repeat: "I remember, therefore I am . . . I am, therefore I remember"—does that mean we should neglect or condemn the duty of memory so dear to Primo Levi?

I don't believe that.

I believe, in a word, exactly the opposite.

And, perhaps because I have a hard time accepting the worst, perhaps because this memory of antifascism is my own and that, as I said at the very beginning of this book, I couldn't abandon it without leaving behind a part of myself, perhaps also because the Jews did not come into the world just to fight anti-Semitism and have that determine their entire ethical and political worldview, I don't feel in the least intimidated by these kidnappings or reversing of meanings, these symbolic takeovers.

I feel no less committed to the antifascist memory of André Mal-raux than when I was twenty, when I left for my Red India, which min-gled in my mind in Spain.

I feel no less engaged by the legacy of Primo Levi than when I was thirty, when I spoke of my joy, in front of the Memorial of the Un-known Jewish Martyr, in the Rue Geoffroy-L'Asnier in Paris, at seeing a new generation take up the flame of memory in order to hand it off, later on, to the next.

And I am just as dead-set on that other duty to join the two com-bats, against anti-Semitism and racism—no more or less than when I was forty and joined a small group of young people who had decided that from now on we would raise the same SOS when either a Jew or an Arab was attacked.

The only thing I am saying is that it will be harder, murkier, than it's been.

The only thing I understand is that it will be the scene, every time, of another struggle, which will go beyond it, and in which, unfortu-nately, we also have to engage.

The only novelty, these days, is that if more than ever I feel most at home on the Left, that's also where I have to be most on the lookout for, await, and, obviously, take apart my most intimate enemy: a Tariq Ramadan, for example, skilled at doublespeak, who, in his preachings, the speeches that are not meant for outside ears, the esoteric part of his teachings and his message, doesn't take too much care to cover the crudest anti-Semitic or Islamist declarations, but, when he's speaking to Tony Blair or people like Gordon Brown, when he's talking to the mass media, when he's playing the moderate Muslim trying to calm the passions of his community, when he infiltrates that League for Secular Education, when he joins up with the far-left Swiss socialist Jean Ziegler, talks like a pure antiracist, like the friendliest advocate of the duty to memory in the Primo Levi vein.

I know it well.

It's devastating but not tragic.

Problematic, but not decisive.

And surely not a reason, in any event, to step aside for the rabble.

6.

Fascislamism

I'm more and more convinced that a Left that rides the coattails of antifascism in order to denounce Europe, Empire, America, Liberty, and, finally, the Jews, has only a very vague idea of what it's talking about.

And to prove this, as a final proof of this, I'd like to examine its positions on that other front of the ideological battle, the question of Islamism: by which I mean its clear and principled alliance, in extreme cases, with the representatives, inside and outside of Europe, of radical Islamism; I mean, in the absence of a formal alliance, that aspect of the ideology for which most excuses are made, benefiting, implicitly or explicitly, the nebulous doctrine that ranges from Al Qaeda to the extremist elements of the Palestinian community; I mean, in any case, the way the Left treats Islamism with the indulgence that tradition demands for the humble and the ill-fated—all things which, for a man of my generation, make up one of the strangest, most unexpected, and most devastating phenomena of our age.

LET'S TURN BACK the clock one last time.

We weren't angels, of course.

And we said enough stupid things—by "we" I mean the contemporaries of the "first" totalitarian temptation, the Red generation, the Communist generation—not to try to claim today that we were always paragons of clear thinking.

But it does seem to me that, at least on the matter of fascism, we were less simpleminded and, above all, less ignorant than these half-wits going around, in the United States and Europe, preaching their theory of Islamism as the religion of the poor, the wronged, and the cursed.

We knew that the two Ba'ath parties, for example, were socialist in name only, no more or less so than the national-socialist parties that inspired their founders.

We knew that one, the Syrian version, had its origins in the Hisb-el-qaumi-el-suri, in other words the social-nationalist party of Anton Sa'ada, based on the Nazi model, which had adopted a swastika upon a black and white background as its banner and whose early leaders themselves, when the time comes for them to write their reminiscences, never fail to draw the direct link with Hitlerism: "We admired the Nazis; we were immersed in Nazi literature and its books; everyone who lived in Damascus back then saw this Arab inclination toward Nazism."[1]

And we knew that the other Ba'ath party, in Iraq, counted, among other founding fathers, the group of pro-Nazi officers who took power in Baghdad in 1941, before the English got rid of them, along with the Greek Orthodox Michel Aflak, who probably converted to Islam and never hid his admiration for the European far right in general, and for Hitler in particular—not to mention the legions of these founding fathers' admirers who, in the sixties and seventies, were mostly recruited among the cells of neofascist groups, nostalgic for the brown years, who found in Saddam Hussein everything they had dreamed of.

This is all to say that never, in those days, would we have had the slightest patience for the heirs of either of those regimes; that between us and a Mustapha Tlass—that revisionist general and local publisher of the *Protocols of the Elders of Zion,* who is still today the strongman of Syria—there was an abyss that no charm offensive could have bridged; and that I can't imagine us, faced with something like the Iraq War, coming up with the idea—widespread, today, in the pro-"sovereignty," Chevènement-inspired groups, for example—of the good-secular-regime-taken-down-by-the-evil-Empire.

We knew that the Muslim Brotherhood movement, born in Egypt in 1928, was itself a fascist movement; an Arab fascist movement, to be sure, but a fascist movement nonetheless; a full-fledged fascist movement; the local version—and why wouldn't such movements have appeared?—of the worldwide movement inaugurated by the European fascisms, whose triumph they greeted in 1933 by inventing Arab-Muslim origins for Hitler—a house in Tanta, in the Nile Delta, that was supposedly his mother's birthplace.

We knew that Hassan al-Banna, its founder, was an admirer of the Nazi regime. We knew that he had placed the secret part of his organization at the service of the Reich and its spies during the war. We knew that his love of death and martyrdom, his raging anti-Semitism, his cult of the Leader, were at least partly taken from that same source—just as his enemy brother Nasser had done, the man who, as everyone then knew, had had *Mein Kampf* translated into Arabic; who hadn't hesitated to recruit Goebbels's former right-hand man Johann von Leers as an adviser to his minister of information; and who, in 1964, had managed to state that "during the Second World War, our sympathies were with the Germans."[2]

This is all to say that we never, it seems to me, would have taken at face value the apparent moderation of the Brotherhood's most media-friendly representative in Europe; never would have hobnobbed with a man capable of embracing the Sudanese Hassan al-Turabi, and of saying of his grandfather, al-Banna, that his "involvement" still inspires "respect" and "admiration" in him, and of coming out in favor of a "moratorium"—*sic:* he really does say "moratorium" and never "abolition"—on stoning women to death. Never would Tariq Ramadan, since that's who we're talking about here,[3] have been granted the honor of a podium like the one he was given in Paris in November 2003, at the European Social Forum—that, only a few days after he'd circulated a "list" of Jewish intellectuals who he felt were too often seen in the French media.[4]

We were pro-Palestinian, to be sure.

We were in favor of the creation of a Palestinian state alongside Israel.

But there was a part of the Palestinian cause that most of us found unacceptable: its anti-Semitism.

I don't remember precisely what we knew about the intellectual biography of the leading lights of the cause. And I couldn't swear that back then I was fully aware of the texts[5] in which Haj Amin al-Husseini, Grand Mufti of Jerusalem, Yasser Arafat's uncle and the spiritual father of the majority of the leaders of the Fatah, tells, without embarrassment, about his arrival in Berlin at the end of the thirties; about his friendship with Himmler; about the conversation in which he announces to Ribbentrop that "the Arabs" are "ready to cooperate with Germany with all their hearts"; about his "historic" meeting with Hitler; about the deal in which, in exchange for the Nazis' support in eradicating the nascent Jewish State, he promised to take the initiative in forming a vast "Fascist-type Arab state"; or about his visit to Auschwitz, after which he wrote: "I'll go peacefully to my grave knowing that five million Jews have been exterminated."[6] But what I do know is that, perhaps because the events were then still closer, perhaps because founding fathers were still there, perhaps . . . perhaps . . . what I do know for sure is that we still had some reflexes, and when that hatred became visible to the naked eye in the organizations that embraced al-Husseini, when his legacy was embraced by people for whom he remained, until his death and beyond, the true master thinker, when, in other words, commands from Fatah killed eleven Israeli athletes during the Munich Olympics, a shiver of horror went through everyone who had anything to do with the Left. For Benny Lévy, leader of the Proletarian Left, that was the trigger for the dissolution of his organization, with the consent of his comrades. What leader of the radical Left would do the same today? Where is the Besancenot or the ATTAC ideologue, where is the spokesman for the reigning followers of Bourdieu, Dieudonné, Chomsky, etc., who has—I won't even say protested—simply reacted to the anti-Semitic declarations of Hamas and Hezbollah? Why did former president Jimmy Carter, author of

Palestine: Peace, Not Apartheid, not react either? Why haven't we heard any of them, ever, tell us what they think of Iranian president Ahmadinejad's repeated declarations that the annihilation of Israel was his dream, his project, and one of the reasons, moreover, that made him want atomic weapons? And why, when a José Bové goes to Ramallah, does he renounce his principled pacifism in order to add to the hatred and add fuel to the fire ablaze in people's spirits? In April 2002, he saw nothing but "raids," "internment camps," and "watchtowers" on his visit to Israel. To tell about his journey, he chooses Tariq Ramadan's Internet site, where he discusses "murders," "civilians assassinated in cold blood," "ambulances" targeted "willfully" by "such violent aggressions" that "all they carry are the dead," and a Jewish soldiery that comes to take "the dying" out of "their hospital beds" to "send them to their deaths." And on television, he repeats a calumny of the far right to discuss the anti-Semitic attacks that have just taken place in Paris: the crime could only have been committed by those who "profit from it"— which is to say . . . Mossad![7]

In other words, we were Marxists, Leninists, Marxist-Leninists— we weren't Islamoprogressives.

We might not have been able to spot a Red fascist—but we were never wrong about Brown fascists.

And the fact is that, on this matter of Islamism, and, more particularly, on the German-Islamist pact during World War II about which so little is said today—even though it had, and has, no less impact than the Nazi-Soviet pact—a whole body of knowledge existed, and has mysteriously been lost.

I HAVE TO EMPHASIZE THIS.

This knowledge has to have been lost since nobody—among the good people who a few months before had been taunting the prime minister, Lionel Jospin, for denouncing the extremism of Hezbollah, whose only program has become to kill as many Jews as possible—had anything to say when, on October 22, 2002, Hezbollah's leader, Hassan Nasrallah, told the Lebanese paper *Daily Star* that "if all the Jews come to Israel, they'll make our job easier, and will keep us from having to go hunt them down all over the world."[8]

This knowledge has to have been lost so that nobody, on the Left or the far left, could be particularly shocked by the other great anti-Israeli organization—the one supposed to express the frustrations and the despair engendered by the "American-Zionist Axis" and which, in reality, was founded by another Arab Nazi, Abdullah Azzam, who moreover was Osama Bin Laden's philosophical guru—it has to have been lost for nobody to lift a finger when Hamas, in January 2006, takes power with a charter expressly borrowing, sometimes to the letter, the terms of the *Protocols of the Elders of Zion*: not only does nobody lift a finger but one eminence, an Elder, former president Jimmy Carter, speaking at the eighth annual Human Rights Forum in Ireland in June 2007, says out loud what the neoprogressive International thinks to itself, offering his blessing to this valiant "resistance" organization, denouncing the Western tendency to support, against it, President Mahmoud Abbas, and, without a word of reproach for a political program that hearkens back to the glory days of the Ku Klux Klan, describes the American refusal to accord full recognition to its electoral victory as "criminal."[9]

The whole antifascist legacy has to be erased from the memory of progressivism for the young leader of the Ligue Communiste Révolutionnaire, Olivier Besancenot, to meet, in London, in the context of a vast project that supposedly will hasten the "birth of a new European Left," such dubious people as George Galloway or Salma Yaqoob.[10] George Galloway is the MP kicked out of his party after founding "Respect," that movement, close to Iraq as well as the Muslim Brotherhood, whose real pillar, alongside its "socialism" and "syndicalism," was "the Muslims who have been radicalized by the wars in Afghanistan, Palestine, and Iraq" (in other words the most hardened Islamists, the most frenetic followers of Bin Laden, the future suicide bombers of the London Tube).[11] And, as for Salma Yaqoob, another member of the national council of "Respect," she's made a specialty of justifying the wearing of the veil and, thus, of the inequality and oppression of women in the name of the fight against "capitalism," "consumerism,"

the "power of big business and advertising," and "liberal globalization."[12]

Antifascism must really have become a dead letter in order, when
this whole issue began fifteen years ago in Algeria, for "consciences on
the Left" to have been able—in the face of that horror, of eviscerated
women and mutilated babies, of local human rights activists urging us
not only to rush to their aid but to defend, alongside them, the principles that were supposed to be our own—to hesitate, mumble, ask
pointless questions ("Who's killing whom?"), come up with dubious
hypotheses ("And what if they were soldiers disguised as Islamists trying to discredit Islam?"), to do everything, really everything, except denounce the crime, point to the guilty parties, and clearly ask what the
Islamic Salvation Front and the Armed Islamic Group were responsible for (though the same people, at the same time, often in the same
newspapers, were inflexibly harsh toward the slightest infringement of
human rights in the other large Maghreb state—the one that was, by
the way, the only part of the former "French Empire" whose sovereign,
when the Vichy laws were promulgated in October 1940, invited the
colonial administration to "provide 150 supplementary yellow stars for
the members of the royal family"—I am speaking of the Moroccan Mohammed V, a real, committed antifascist, savior of the two hundred
thousand Jews in his country and, for that reason, one of the Righteous
Among the Nations).

Not only the far left but the Left itself has to have lost both its
memory and its reflexes in order—fifteen years later, when the role
models for the Algerian Salafists decide to ratchet things up, moving to
the stage of industrialized death ("the death industry" was one of al-
Banna's slogans) and to crash planes into the Twin Towers of New
York—for us still to wonder about their ideology, their motivations,
and the part played in these motives by despair, frustration, defiance, or
a response to some previous violence—even though we know straight
from the horse's mouth, or from the mouths of those friends who, like
Shahid Nickels, hung out with him from 1998 to 2000 in Hamburg,
that someone like Mohammed Atta was another Nazi whose "Weltan-
schauung" was "based"—in the words of his roommate—"on National

Socialism" and on the simple idea that "the Jews" have as their "only goal" the "domination of the world."[13]

The Left has to have lost its moorings to allow shouts of "Death to the Jews" in a protest called principally by the Movement Against Racism and for Friendship Between Peoples in October 2001. For the Great Mosque of Paris's lawsuit against Philippe Val and the satirical newspaper *Charlie Hebdo* demanding the reintroduction of censorship. For a death sentence issued against Professor Robert Redeker by an Islamist television preacher, Tariq Ramadan's mentor, who until then had mainly distinguished himself with fatwas approving suicide attacks against civilians. For all that not to have stirred an emotion, a protest movement, a revolt, at least comparable to that which greeted the American war in Iraq. Instead, Redeker was all but accused, by the Right *and* by the Left, by the depraved authorities responsible for the fatwa *but also* by those who should have been the unconditional advocates of liberty of thought and free speech, of being an egomaniac, a huckster who had fatwa'd himself and who, if he ended up murdered, really had only himself to thank. . . .

The worst of the Vichy spirit has to have come back in order for a Socialist leader, Pascal Boniface, to calmly suggest dropping the Jewish vote in order to cement an alliance with a more numerous Muslim electorate, and for him not to be instantly expelled from the Party—as will soon happen (though here too they've taken their time) to his comrade, the deputy mayor of Montpellier, Georges Frêche, who had the nerve to call Algerian soldiers loyal to the French "subhuman." And the Left has to be completely crazy for *Le Monde diplomatique,* during a discussion by its director with "Brother Tariq," to associate itself with the anti-Semitic Dieudonné and the conspiracy-monger Thierry Meyssan in order to announce, in a single advertisement, the showing of a film ("Friday, March 4, 2005, 11 o'clock, Cinéma L'Entrepôt"— *sic . . .*), *État de guerre,* which highlighted Meyssan's wild revisionist imaginings.[14]

The Right really has to have taken over the Left for us—like the people of Nineveh, no longer able to tell right from left—to accept, in the name of tolerance, that women in the middle of Amsterdam can be caged by a burqa; or that another woman, the Somali-Dutch parliamentarian Ayaan Hirsi Ali—because she has dared protest that, and to criticize not only Islamism but Islam itself—can be kicked out of her Party, and threatened with the loss of her Dutch citizenship[15]—without seeing the Left, not only Dutch but European and particularly French, rushing to her aid and crying in one voice: "We won't accept fascism."

LET'S LOOK AT THE problem from another perspective.

What should a modern, open, responsible, and above all nonfascist Left do about the rising green tide of Islamism?

Three things which, alas, as I am writing these lines, seem tragically foreign to its program.

The first would be to limit the obsessive references to Israel in this debate.

Yes, when a progressive thinker today debates Islamism, he always starts by saying: "Israel, Israel's fault; nothing would have happened without that damned Israel, thorn in the Arab flesh, permanent source of humiliation, a foreign body in a land that is not and never was its own." Well, this is a false proposition. It is literally false, given the antiquity of the Jewish presence in the land of Palestine. But more than anything else it's shameful, unworthy of a man of the Left, because it implies that the Jewish people are dirty, impure, and that their mere presence in a place is enough to pollute it—it is, properly speaking, unworthy, because one *already* has to be inspired by the most obtuse racism to accept the idea that a minuscule Jewish presence, on a tiny percentage of Arab land, and on an even smaller percentage of the land that supposedly makes up the Ummah, presents a problem to believers; it is, it ought to be, on the face of it, unacceptable, because the logical reasoning, the reasoning of a normal, classic antifascist, one not taken over by anti-Semitic prejudice, would be to think, or at least try to imagine, that for that region of the world the emergence of a modern, prosperous, technology-oriented place might also be an opportunity. . . .

Or: "Israel is a mistake; Israel is a crime, since it's a crime to make the Arabs pay for a European crime that they had nothing to do with."

This proposition is false. Literally false. Without getting into meta-physical considerations about the universality of the crime against humanity; without entering the debate about the question of whether we can know, in a crime of such magnitude, if all of humanity is wounded and therefore concerned, what we know about Arab Nazism contradicts this. Reading the writings of the Mufti, one can no longer say that the Holocaust was a European crime of which the Arabs are innocent. One can no longer say that the Arab world is paying for a crime it had nothing to do with when we discover, in the archives of the high commander of the German army, that "only the funds placed at the disposition of the Grand Mufti of Jerusalem by Germany" allowed him to organize his little Kristallnacht in Palestine. And one can no longer make this claim or sustain this argument when one has read the book by two renowned researchers that just came out in Germany establishing, after many years of inquiry, especially in the military archives of Freiburg, two absolutely decisive facts.[16] First, that Arab anti-Semitism was not, as is always said, a circumstantial anti-Semitism, mainly linked to English support for the nascent Israeli state, which the Arabs therefore saw as a colonial creation: Germany, says the Grand Mufti in a statement the authors discovered, is "the only country in the world that has not merely fought the Jews at home but have declared war on the entirety of world Jewry; in this war against world Jewry, the Arabs feel profoundly connected to Germany"—one could hardly put it better! And second, that there was, stationed in Athens, under the orders of the Obersturmbannführer Walther Rauff, the very same man who refined and then developed the use of gas trucks at Auschwitz, a special intervention force, the Einsatzgruppe Ägypten, intended to reach Palestine and liquidate the 500,000 European Jews who had already taken refuge in the Yishuv in the event Rommel won the battle of the desert: this was an Arab unit, and it was al-Husseini who, there again, in his conversations with Eichmann, had put the final touches on the intervention plan, which should indicate his full and entire participation in the Final Solution; and only Montgomery's victory at El Alamein stymied the project for extermination. One man knew that. And his greatness was in taking responsibility for it. His name was Anwar el-

Sadat. He was a lieutenant in the very same Afrika Korps. He, like Nasser, was one of the young spies the Muslim Brotherhood infiltrated into the Wehrmacht. But above all, above all, he was the man who, by going to the Knesset on a morning in November 1977 and proposing peace to Israel in the name of his people and the Arab world, implicitly recognized Arab responsibility in the Holocaust.

And then there's that other old favorite that nobody should have to listen to any longer, and which is common to most Western foreign ministries: Israel is the key, the core, the center that dealing with terrorism depends on. This notion, too, is false. Dubious, first of all. It's got a whiff of the thirties, of those who, like Céline, already saw the Jews as an awkward people whose refusal to let themselves be liquidated put Europe into a "fine mess," working like a real "school of cadavers" of the war that was about to arrive and was the last straw, the detail, the "trifle," that made possible the immense massacre promised by that war—and therefore the notion is dubious. But above all, and once again, it's false. Literally and textually false. Because this time all we have to do is open our eyes. All we have to do, as I have done, is spend a bit of time in the Afghan or Pakistani madrassas which are the real academies of jihadist crime, the true holding tanks of its recruits, and its real centers of command.[17] Nobody there is talking about Israel. Nobody's worried about Palestine. This supposedly decisive Palestine is nothing more than a geographic reference, a very uncertain place name, a signifier at most. If one had to name a real place that those people are a bit concerned with; if there is a holy land that these nihilists, these lovers of nothingness and death, sometimes dream of liberating, then it's not Palestine but Kashmir. In other words, the creation of a Palestinian state would, demonstrably, have almost no effect on this issue. We can calculate that we could remove the so-called cancer of the Israeli-Palestinian conflict without demobilizing a single soldier of the jihad. . . .

I'm not saying, of course, that the Israeli-Palestinian question isn't an issue of the first importance.

Nor that the creation of a Palestinian state isn't, for the Palestinians as well as for the Jewish state itself, an urgent matter.

I'm only saying that in this case Israel is what the historians of science of Georges Canguilhem's generation called an epistemological obstacle.

And I have to conclude that—in order to remove this obstacle, in order for a bit of understanding to break through the thickness of prejudice, in order for us to see a bit more clearly into the dark abyss that is the question of Islamist terrorism—we have to start off by breaking the spell that restricts progressive thinking: for a moment, we have to forget about Israel.

The second thing that a real Left should do is to convince itself that its most effective tool against Islamism is not the concept of tolerance, as it believes and constantly repeats, but the concept of secular society.

We remember what Claudel said about tolerance: that's why we have brothels.

We remember Pasolini's showing that because it presupposes a lack of agreement and a transgression of that lack of agreement, tolerance is in fact "the refined form of condemnation."

We remember less Robert-Paul Wolff, Barrington Moore, Jr., and Herbert Marcuse's *Repressive Tolerance,* published in 1969,[18] which showed that we tolerate only things very far removed from ourselves, so far that they almost inspire disgust: Marcuse demonstrated that when we say tolerance we mean the limit of tolerance, beyond which the tolerable can no longer be tolerable and deserves, in fact, to be rejected. . . .

And above all, above all, it is more and more obvious that it's in the name of tolerance, which is to say in the name of the right to express any belief whatsoever, that European progressivism has, for the last ten or twenty years, developed the worst possible reflexes: tolerating the discomfort of the Moroccan who killed Theo van Gogh in Amsterdam; tolerating the pain of the Muslims offended by Redeker's article and demanding laws or guidelines that would have prevented *Le Figaro* from publishing it; tolerating, from Damascus to Gaza, and from Tehran to Lagos, protests involving burning flags, sacking embassies, killing Christians, and marching behind banners reading "Get ready for the real Holocaust," to object to the publication of caricatures in a newspaper; tolerating the anger against Benedict XVI, the hatred aimed at

Ayaan Hirsi Ali, the effigies of Salman Rushdie burned in the middle of London; tolerating . . . ; tolerating . . . ; the field of tolerance is infinite, and it's once again in the name of tolerance, in the name of our comprehension of the humiliation of Muslims and of their suffering, that after the case of the Danish cartoons, a large French company authorized its supermarkets to put up signs, in certain Arab countries, to announce that its aisles were free of Danish products. . . .

Secular society is something else.

It takes issue with tolerance, first of all, in that it doesn't treat all beliefs without distinction and distinguishes between those which call for murder (and which do not deserve toleration) and those which do not (and which not only deserve toleration but have to be tolerated).

Second, it differs in that—with respect to the latter group of beliefs, those not involving the possibility of calling for murder—it not only tolerates them (along with all the disdain, distance, and hauteur the word implies) but respects them (along with all the real, and therefore concrete, and therefore technical, consideration for everything they require in order to express themselves with full freedom—mosques, for example).

It differs, third, in refusing to choose among these respectfully treated beliefs, and is forbidden to favor one above another. Tolerance, once again, tolerates. It has its preferences and, according to its whims, can change them. It can decide that it has tolerated too much, given too much, and change its mind. Or it can decide that it hasn't tolerated enough, hasn't given enough, and change its mind once again. That danger does not exist in a secular society. Respect is an unchanging principle. It is not a matter of mood but one of structure. And its structure consists—as for the Dutch churches of the seventeenth century or the American churches of the eighteenth—of establishing a principle of equal distance between these beliefs and the center of power. In a secular state, no one religion will ever be allowed to win out against another. The secular regime, and not the principle of tolerance, allows Muslims to be treated equally.

But watch out! It differs, fourth, and as a consequence, by the very fact that, in keeping all those beliefs at an equal distance from political power, it also has to keep political power equally removed from those beliefs. Tolerance *tolerates* that one group demands such and such a special right. The secular state does not tolerate or understand that. And that is why, when the political authorities are wrapped up in the wrong done to one community by the representation of its prophet with a bomb on his head instead of a turban, the secular regime answers: "We see that you're upset; your faith is doubtless seriously wounded by such a representation; but that wound has no place in public debate; the lawmaker therefore has nothing to do with it; that's how democracy works."

For the secular society differs—fifth point—from tolerance in that it tells believers, outraged or not, that their beliefs have nothing to do with politics. The secular principle places religion on one side and politics on another. But where tolerance accepts a link between the two (to put it another way, tolerance is the last avatar of what was traditionally known as the theological-political), secular society insists there is no link between the two (it cuts the knot of the theological-political; it carries through Spinoza's gesture; it states that religious beliefs about how men ought to be connected to one another have nothing to do with the way the social contract will actually operate).[19] Where the tolerant State will always lend an ear to the believer who, for example, wants to see it apologize for the wrong a free, independent newspaper committed against him, the secular state will invest the same energy in saying: "No to your demands, if they involve defining the relationship between the state and the press, and therefore the social contract," just as it would also say: "Yes to your statements, and yes to the means they require for being heard, on the assumption that they are addressed to the souls and the private consciences of individuals."

Tolerance brings about autos-da-fé. The secular society brings books into dialogue, all books, beginning with holy books.

Tolerance constructs this legal and moral monstrosity, this crime against the spirit, which is the idea that Islamophobia is a form of racism (Since when is Islam a race? What logic says that attacking books is racism?). A secular society defends the right to blasphemy as much as, on the other hand, it defends my right, or my reader's right, to file a lawsuit against the deputies of the National Assembly who have recently been trying, in the land of Voltaire, to reestablish the laws against blasphemy that were taken off the books in 1791.[20]

Tolerance is the idea that belief has every right. The secular society establishes the (full, complete) right to these beliefs, and also the right (no less full, no less complete) to that other belief, which is disbelief.

Tolerance means that my freedom of opinion stops where someone else's freedom of opinion begins (which means that we can say only things that are already agreed upon and understood); secular society means not freedom of opinion but freedom of thought (including about beliefs whose dogmas I do not share; even against propositions— like cutting off that apostate woman writer's hand—that I reserve the right to opine are barbarous).

Tolerance grants all power to communities, and says it's too bad for Robert Redeker. In a secular society, human rights come first: too bad for the radical Islamist who wants to censor or kill Redeker.

Tolerance, as we now see, could be the cemetery of democracies, while secular concepts are their crucible.

But the third task, the third urgency—and, ultimately, the main task—is to see Islamism for what it is and, for that reason, to substitute for the mistaken concept of fundamentalism the correct notion of Islamofascism, or, better, of Fascislamism.

Why is the concept of fundamentalism mistaken?

Because it leads one to believe that the crimes of radical Islamism come from a literal interpretation of the Koran.

But that is not true, for example, in the case of the veil, which was never an absolute obligation of Muslim women before the violent Iranian Revolution of 1979: the Tradition demands only that women "let down upon them their over-garments; this will be more proper, that they may be known, and thus they will not be given trouble" (33:59); that they "cast down their looks and guard their private parts and do not display their ornaments except what appears thereof" (24:31); or even, as for that great imam during the Golden Age of Baghdad, in the ninth century, not to wear the hijab at all because "the Lord" only "recommended it to the wives of the Prophet" and that "any Muslim woman who veils her face would mistakenly look like one of them" and would therefore deserve "the whip."[21]

It isn't true in the matter of the caricatures of Mohammed, for which all the fanatics' bad faith, intoxication, and power of intimidation was required—along with, unfortunately, our own cowardliness— to turn a real but measured iconoclasm (certainly not more radical than the one found in the Jewish prophets, or in Plato) into an ironclad prescription that the artists of *Jylland-Posten* supposedly grievously profaned: we have representations of Mohammed, says, for example, my friend Abdelwahab Meddeb;[22] we have representations of his nighttime journey to Jerusalem, in which his face can clearly be seen; we have manuscripts such as that *Jami al-Tawarikh: A Monumental History of the World*, written by Rashid al-Din, conserved at the University of Edinburgh, which shows him with profoundly human traits: not to mention the case of those two Swiss ethnologists, Pierre and Micheline Centlivres, who brought back from Iran posters showing the young Prophet—a tad ambiguous, with an effeminate turban, his head slightly tilted, his shoulder half-revealed, with a gracious smile—that have been openly sold in the streets of Tehran since the end of the 1980s. . . .[23]

And it's even less true, of course, of that belligerent jihadism which—with its cult of martyrdom and death, its calls to suicide, its kitschy postmodern descriptions of a paradise in which dozens of virgins await the murderers of Jews and Crusaders—has only the most distant relationship with the background, the basis, the foundation, of that beautiful effort to restore the soul that the Koran called "Jihad."

I'm not denying that the Koran also contains a temptation toward violence.

I'm not denying that one of the big differences between Islam and other revealed religions is that one was formed in exile and the other in persecution, whereas Islam immediately appeared as a state religion, a religion of conquest, led by a religious chief who was also a warlord.

And it is clear that the Arab-Muslim world would have nothing to lose by rereading, reexamining, and, in the real sense of the word, criticizing the pages of its holy book that recall this origin—it would have everything to gain by reencountering the "Sirah" popularized by those two consciences of the Muslim world who wrote under the pseudonym Mahmoud Hussein;[24] by continuing the debate that raged during Islam's first four centuries about whether the Word was created (and therefore historical, subject to interpretation, revision, rereading) or uncreated (and therefore eternal, impeccable: and whoever touched it therefore subject to capital punishment); moreover, I'm convinced that no better service can be rendered than, in these matters, to borrow a page from the practices of the Jews—yes, I said Jews—the Jews of the extraordinary school of reading that the Jewish world called the Talmud and which is based upon the idea of a created word, living, open, inexhaustible, whose full revelation can be attained only by the multiplicity of commentaries, exegeses, glosses. (Isn't this the word with many meanings that Levinas was referring to when he spoke of "the folded wings of the spirit" and which ultimately protected Judaism from the fundamentalist temptation? Isn't that play on words, which he also said was a "struggle with the angel," what preserved it from that idolatry of dogma or from the Idea that is the ultimate source of the totalitarianisms? And wouldn't the invention of a Muslim Talmud, which is to say the relationship with a Word whose final meaning no commentator could claim to have discovered, have the same effect, which is to say a colossal effect, in that region of the spirit and the world?)

Still, I insist that reducing the radical Islamist phenomenon to a matter of literalism is nonetheless wrong.

And again, for the reasons I've already mentioned (the veil, representations of the Prophet, the very definition of Jihad), the concept of fundamentalism is mistaken.

Why, then, is the idea of Fascislamism the right one?

First of all because it is correct. Yes, simply correct. Which is to say it takes full account of the real genealogy of a whole crowd of people who themselves tell us (the Muslim Brotherhood) or who make perfectly clear (Hezbollah, Hamas) how much their mythology of pure blood, their taste for suicide missions, their hatred of the West, their phobia of a Jewish plot aiming at world domination, their detestation of America and of freedom, comes from European fascist ideologues.[25] So this is a given.

The first question to ask about any given declaration is which context, or contexts, lends it not only its source but its highest degree of intelligibility. Well, in the case of these "Islamist" declarations—in the case of these discursive formations that call for basing the Ummah on the elimination of Jews and Crusaders—in the case of these Palestinian schoolbooks that still mention, at the beginning of the twenty-first century, the First Zionist Congress as the occasion on which "a group of confidential resolutions were adopted" better known "under the name of the *Protocols of the Elders of Zion*," which "were revealed" to the world by Serge Nilus and "translated into Arabic by Muhammad Khalifa al-Tunisi"[26]—there are two contexts. One slighter one, which only slightly explains things: the Koranic context (dhimmitude, all right; Sharia, all right; but what on earth does the Koran have to do with the case of those *Protocols of the Elders of Zion* which we know were introduced into the Arab world in the middle of the 1920s by Christian translators and propagandists?). And one larger one, which largely accounts for it: the context of the European fascisms, in the way the Ba'athists, Nasserites, and followers of al-Husseini channeled and Arabized their message (what we know as radical Islamism was not born in the sixties but in the thirties; it is not the contemporary of the Third World movement but of the global movement to finish off democratic "decadence" and called, once again, fascism). Fascislamism is the concept that explains this larger context. Fascislamism is a solid concept because it refers to this larger scheme in which—when al-Banna's assault columns parade through the streets of Cairo—they are echoing and responding to Mussolini's torches and Hitler's brownshirts. Fascislamism might even be—who knows?—the concept Paul Claudel was *already* thinking of when, in his journal, on May 21, 1935, in one of those flashes of insight whose secret is known only to great writers, he wrote: "Hitler's speech; a kind of Islamism is being created at the center of Europe. . . ."[27]

Also because, as a result, this concept does what the Left, as I understand the word, ought never to fail to do: see history where some people see only destinies; inject politics into areas some would have us believe deal only with fixed forms, essences, of the uncreated word, throughout all eternity; do justice to human rights, even if that means the right to do wrong, to take mistaken positions, to kill things off out of one's own free will and not because a constitutional or religious law demands it; recognize, at last, the other freedom, the opposite one, which belongs to all readers of the Koran who have not opted for Fascislamism but for a moderate, peaceful Islam. Bush, too, speaks of Fascislamism? That's true. But first of all, there were a few of us who were talking about it back when Mr. Bush's reputation had not crossed the borders of Texas. Second, we shouldn't forget what Spinoza said: Just because a fool, in the middle of the day, says "it's daytime" doesn't mean he's wrong and that it's the middle of the night. And third, my problem is less dissociating myself from Bush than it is finding the idea that will let me dissociate the righteous Naguib Mahfouz from the Nazi Michel Aflak; the Arabs who fought for Free France from those who were rooting for a German victory; those, finally (since they too existed), who were killed by the Nazis from those who, like al-Husseini, returned, dazzled, from their visits to Treblinka or Auschwitz—my problem is dissociating Ahmad Shah Massoud from his murderers; Muslim Algerian women from their persecutors; my friends in Sarajevo from their fathers or grandparents who, in 1944, signed up for the Muslim divisions of the Waffen SS led, once again, by al-Husseini. All are Muslims. All have the Koran in common. The real line that separates them is therefore not a religious one but a political one. Fascislamism makes sure they are divided. Fascislamism is a good concept because it's the only one that lets us say that there is not one Islam but several, or at least two—the one that tolerates fascism and the one that keeps its distance.

Here again, here more than ever, we are desperately seeking an antifascist Left. . . .

The New Struggle of the Universals

And now for the last symptom: the issue of the Universal.

Which is to say the unprecedented crisis in which the question of the Universal—in the wake of everything else, as a finishing touch and common denominator to this disavowal of Europe, anti-Americanism and the morbid fixation on Empire, this recurrence of anti-Semitism, this refusal to understand the truth about Fascislamism—has found itself.

To be sure, it's not the first crisis—nor, I'll bet, will it be the last—of the old, beautiful idea of human universality.

There was the Romantic crisis, a direct reaction to the Enlightenment: universality doesn't exist; the only thing that does, said Herder, are individual cultures, each bearing witness to the progress and the appearance of God among men.

In reaction to this region of the Enlightenment continent that was Kantianism and its attempt to discover universally applicable principles of morality, there was the great Hegelian offensive: *Moralität!* The only serious basis, not only of morality but of politics, was *Sittlichkeit,* ethnicity, the conditions that the world Spirit made for every people's path toward the Absolute.

There was Kierkegaard answering Hegel's own argument, since he saw in this dialectic of the Absolute—in this odyssey of a Spirit devoted to imposing itself, not today, to be sure, but tomorrow, the day after tomorrow—an even more subtle form of stamping out uniqueness: *Moralität* or *Sittlichkeit,* what's the difference, Kierkegaard thunders! For painful subjectivity, for my irreplaceable and irreducible self, what's the difference between one person's immediate Universal and someone else's deferred Universal? In both cases, the same murderous generality suffocates me, crushes me. . . .

There was Nietzsche, of course, whose "perspectivism," whose conception of philosophy as the "art of transfiguration" and of the "hammer," the "main theme of the body," the theory of the "will to power" as a "transvaluation" of all values, was another way to shatter the concept, for him too poor, too oversimplifying, of Kant's and Hegel's Universality: "Could the culminating point, the final point, of the universal process, coincide with his own Berlin existence?"—childish, ridiculous, he suggests.

Rosenzweig, from the trenches of Macedonia, where he conceives and writes *The Star of Redemption,* amid the blood and the horror of the battles he witnessed, sees the true face of a humanity supposed, again according to the universalists, to have discovered itself spontaneously, to have affirmed God's goodness and justice in the face of the existence of evil, to be enshrouded by the divine halo of the fully achieved Presence: it was nothing more than savage states! Nations thrown against each other in combats whose violence exceeded anything ever before seen! Poor wretches, faceless and nameless, thrown into carnage, tossed into bloodbaths: that's who we are in this age of the Universal! What an idea . . .

Nazism, of course, and the crisis of a universalism to which it opposes paganism and its *"völkisch"* beliefs.

Marxism, which was another way—in the name, this time, of the "class position" of the subject, of his "interests" in relation to his own "alienation"—of rejecting a still-too-easy, lazy Universal, which wanted to treat subjects identically despite their structural differences.

Nietzsche once again: or, to put it more precisely, his return, under the guise of Michel Foucault, who called the ancient art of the hammer "genealogy," a genealogical hammering that will finally finish off these poor, empty generalizations tradition placed under the name of the Universal.

SO WE'VE GONE through all these crises.

Throughout the last centuries, the Universal has never ceased to be attacked on every front, from every side.

And there have been, naturally enough, different styles of attack, sometimes simply using homonyms or saying the same thing in different ways, or even the other way around—and nothing would be more absurd than lumping together the Hegelian critique of Kant, Kierkegaard's critique of Hegel, and Rosenzweig's critique of both Kant and Hegel.

But I do hear what's being said and written today about, for example, the American war in Iraq.

I see, in part because of this war, in the United States as well as in Europe, the exhaustion, or even the discredit, of this magnificent principle—magnificent because, to borrow a word from Kant, *cosmopolitan,* and whose establishment I had taken to be one of the victories of our generation's struggles—the principle of limitless responsibility toward others that a doctor named Bernard Kouchner baptized the "duty to intervene."

On the Right as well as on the Left—but here again, aren't we in one of those areas in which that distinction itself becomes muddied and absurd?—I see a general movement of retreat, of moving away from the duty of caring for others, even of questioning what we no longer want to call the ideology of human rights—"Such Western arrogance! Such unbearable ethnocentrism! Where do you get the right to impose rules on a bunch of people who've never asked for them and, above all, never even thought of them?"

Everywhere, indeed, we see the powerful return of the old "differentialist" doctrines—based on the idea that humanity is divided up into little sections, separated from other parts of itself, and that we have to give up the idea of imposing the same idea of justice and law, the same conception of democracy and its regime, the same regime of development and survival—all the way to Alain Badiou's "Stay out of their business" . . . all the way to "Stop imposing your norms, let others be and exist according to their own values and norms," which is the common denominator in all these retreats. . . .

And, observing and hearing all this, observing it in the reflected light of past reconsiderations, hearing it with a slightly philosophical ear, it's hard for me not to think that this is a crisis that, perhaps because it was preceded by all these others, perhaps because it randomly synthesizes and extracts from old arguments—not in detail, just taking whatever goes best with the needs of the moment (at one point someone borrows from Herder's characterology of nations; someone else from a sub-Marxism arguing against formal rights and liberties; another, from a popularized Nietzsche, suggesting that there are as many ways to evaluate something as there are cultures; yet another, in terms that a follower of Rosenzweig could almost recognize, describes the process of the leveling of the planet by the flattening universalism of the big states)—I can't help but think, therefore, that we're faced with a disarray that is exceptionally serious, perhaps also in part because we are emerging from a time that valued internationalism, care for others, and dreams of emancipation.

Alongside the classic thinkers, a new discourse is emerging.

In a chaos of references that are simultaneously contradictory and slyly complementary, a full-fledged argument is returning.

And that's the argument that, in conclusion, I'd like to address point by point.

THE FIRST ARGUMENT: the principles of democracy, of human rights, of respect for individuals, etc., are Judeo-Christian principles and therefore Western, anchored in the Western tradition and thus inapplicable to the rest of the planet.

This is obviously absurd. Purely and simply absurd. Since as far as we know, Judeo-Christian does not mean Western. And if it's true that these principles really are of Jewish and Christian origin, if it's true that the notion of the autonomy of the subject—the right of a body not to be tortured, of a soul not to be enslaved: the construction of a public space, in a word, founded on this double right and allowing its full exercise, really can be conceived only with the help of the Judeo-Christian concept of the "person" (a creature of God, made in His image and, for that reason, inviolable)—it's obviously untrue, on the other hand, that neither this concept itself nor the conditions required for creating it emerge from the West.

Is the Sinai Desert in the West?

Are Golgotha, the Mount of Olives, Nazareth in the West?

Are Moses, Jesus, the prophets, the apostles—all those voices that together produced the new, unprecedented, earthshaking idea of the "creatured" subject—Western?

Of course not. They're from nowhere and from everywhere. From that placeless place that is the true place where ideas are born. But if we have to name a place, we'd have to say that they are from the East, from the Near East, the true cradle of their birth and which—just to make sure of their paternity, just to underline it once again, as if it really wanted to put its stamp on the world—then gave, in the person of Mohammed, yet another comrade, a younger brother, to those older prophets—and a brother whose message is no less favorable than that of the former to the idea of a subject sanctified by his native kinship with the Lord of Heaven.

So one has to be remarkably schizophrenic, with a dash of revisionist and suicidal madness along with a deep self-loathing, to tear apart, as certain current inhabitants of that region of the world are doing, that part of their history, to forget it, to be ashamed of it, though it is a glorious history, and to explain to their audiences that that's a tradition, an authority, a debt, they don't want to have anything to do with.

You'll excuse the slightly robust simplicity of my reasoning.

But the triumph, from Cairo to Jericho, from Baghdad to Damascus and Beirut, of the Christian commandment of love and the Jewish forbidding of murder; the victory, following that, of that body of political precepts that we call democratic and even secular, but which did not become possible without the two holy books that came before them, and then the third (the Koran) which, in principle, emerges from them, and which is infinitely better (do we even have to say it?) than the bloody caricature that the extremists have tried to turn it into, would be, compared to that denigration, to that madness, a first step toward health.

Imposed by force? No. To the contrary. Returned to sender. An act of truth.

THE SECOND ARGUMENT. "You're playing with words. Because the commandments to love thy neighbor and thou shalt not kill do indeed apply to everyone, but these are only the distant, very distant, origins of democratic principles. But what about the rules that are much closer by and from which democratic principles actually have been taken? What about the discursive and then political formations that appeared with John Locke and his *Two Treatises on Government*? Aren't those the products of Europe? Can you deny that habeas corpus, the parliamentary form of government, the separation of powers, or even secularism itself are the results of a conceptual elaboration that has nothing to do with the history of religions and everything to do with the history of ideological struggles in England and France in the seventeenth and eighteenth centuries? And if we recognized their origin and date of birth instead of denying it, what would be the point of universalizing them?"

Of course, that's undeniable.

Things are surely a bit more complicated. For one can object that the theory of the two truths, twin sisters, which were, according to the Muslim Averroës, philosophical truth and theological truth, was an early sketch of the concept of secularism. Or that there was a time in which, while the Catholic Church let the Inquisition dishonor its whole great heritage of rationality and wisdom, it was in the Arab lands, thanks to Arab copyists, translators, and philosophers, that Greek learning survived, and thus the fate of modern reason. Or even that the encounter between Islam and the Greek logos—the way the former translated and brought over the spirit of the latter—was not foreign to the construction of that space of being and thinking that we today know as the West. But anyway. It's clear enough that for the most part those principles developed in Europe. And it's undeniable that the democratic idea in its most modern form, the wager—since it is a wager—on defining humans in such a way that we can not only assign them rights but claim that those rights are universal, inalienable, identical for everyone, is basically a European creation.

But so what? Since when does an idea's origin become its destiny? Who says that ideas are chained to the soil where they are born? Isn't it the very nature of ideas to move, to migrate, to shed their origins, to become abstract? Isn't that what the entire history of sciences and philosophy is about, the whole history of religion? And why shouldn't the ideas elaborated by Grotius or Rousseau or the concept of natural law travel in the other direction, back toward the source of, for example, Arab mathematics, or the belief in a single God?

Some ideas are greater than their bearers.

Some categories of understanding infinitely transcend—we've seen it, I'll say once again, in the biblical Orient better than anywhere else—the circumstances of their birth.

Human rights are one such case.

Being born where they were born didn't keep them from spreading across the rest of Europe; and then to that new Europe being invented in America; and then to the lands Europe colonized, by those nationalists inspired by Enlightenment ideals who used them as a weapon against their oppressors—and I don't see why their origins ought to keep them, today, from taking root in those non-European countries where neoprogressivism is trying to block their path.

Ideas, too, have no borders.

European or not, the idea that an adulterous woman shouldn't be stoned to death or burned alive is an idea worth universalizing.

THIRD ARGUMENT.

"Fine. But can't you see that that line of reasoning, the idea that the Enlightenment left its native soil to go take root in exotic and distant lands, was exactly the idea of the Spanish conquistadores at the dawn of humanity's first genocide? And the goal of those French émigrés, in Algeria for example, who wanted to convert savage peoples to the secular religion of John Locke and Diderot? Isn't that, in other words, the quintessence of the whole colonial project?"

I don't believe that either.

I even believe, to a certain extent, the opposite.

And I've had enough of the conventional wisdom that says that colonization was a product of the Enlightenment and the colonizers' desire to spread their universalist, humanist message overseas.

It's doubtful enough in the case of French colonization. Detailed studies are needed. Case by case. We'd have to go back carefully to all the literature, both military and legal, that accompanied the process. We'd also have to think about that strange practice that, at least until the Exposition Universelle of 1931, involved setting up human zoos. When zoos are involved, it means that we think we're dealing with monkeys, not humans. When one group of people biologizes another— when we create this hybrid creature, half-man, half-beast, human but only just, already something of a beast, a wild animal or a little domestic animal, but an animal nonetheless, almost always an animal—we've left the world of civilization and entered that of domestication. For the public, in Paris, we talk about civilization and Enlightenment. Nobody bothers with that useless literature on the ground in Africa. It's so much easier to biologize it. And that's why Sartre's intuition was so accurate, in his preface to Frantz Fanon's *Wretched of the Earth:* that the colonist's main fantasy was a zoological one.

With respect to the genocide of the Indians, on the other hand, the work has been done. It exists. And it established, beyond the shadow of a doubt, that universalism is not on the side of the conquerors but that of their adversaries. Who are those adversaries? The Dominicans Francisco de Vittorio and Bartolomé de Las Casas. They have an argument. A single one. They have a thesis that they base their argument on, a full-fledged product of the great polemic raging at the University of Salamanca and others. One or multiple origins? One human family or several? All really sons of Adam, or only metaphorically? And if all people are sons of Adam, then where did these other men come from, where did this "new arrival" come from, the one upon whose forehead, the Bible tells us, God placed a "sign" after the murder of Abel, to keep him from "hitting" Cain? These questions stirred the whole period. So this "new arrival," the idea that there were other men besides Cain and Abel though the Bible had just told us they were the first man's only sons: that might prove that there's another source, another bloodline, a second human family—and for those who wanted to exterminate the Indians, that would be the best possible news, since it would remove the main obstacle to that extermination. On the other hand, for Vittorio and Las Casas, denying the existence of that "new arrival," refusing to countenance the existence of a real "second bloodline," was a theological, and thus political, matter of the first importance: we don't even want to entertain the thought, they say, of these pointless discussions; we reject out of hand any notion that, even when coming out of a prestigious university, might allow the slightest possibility that it is permissible, without sin, to dispossess, torture, or kill men who resemble us but who are not our brothers; and it's in the name of that decision, in the name of the idea that humanity is a single family, in the name of the resulting universalism, that we oppose colonialism.

Universalism is anticolonialism.

Universalism is anti-imperialism.

A failure of the Universal, of the impossibility or the refusal to envisage the profound unity of the human race, leads to imperialist or colonial massacres; a reinforcement of the Universal, a reinforcement of the idea that all people issue from the same source, are children of the same father, and therefore belong to the same brotherhood, makes us resist them.

FOURTH ARGUMENT.

"Las Casas, okay. Those humanist priests and monks, with their pure motives, fine. But history isn't made by feelings. It's made by civilizations. And thus by laws. Since there are laws, real laws, that watch over the birth, death, and transformation of civilizations. They're already grouped together. Collections of them. The first law of civilizations is that they are relatively homogenous and coherent groups. And the second law is that these groups have a particular place, or an underlying location, that nourishes them, gives them their substance and their health, or the lack of it. English democracy, for example, *is* the Civil War, the Glorious Revolution, the House of Commons, the Tudor Rose, St. George, Westminster, Big Ben. Athenian democracy *is* the laws of Solon, Pericles, the reforms of Cleisthenes, a certain kind of mathematics, an idea of the barbarian versus the native, a conception of space, a way of thinking about time. Take away the former's symbols and foundational events; remove the imagination that nourished the outstanding figures of the latter, and you're hacking at a plant, starving a body, removing an organ and claiming that it can then live on by itself—it's an unnatural act of violence."

Answer: not all groups are bodies.

Not all bodies are organisms, and even less are they homogenous organisms.

And a civilization is exactly something mobile, heterogeneous, open to change—permanently being modified by a whole series of encounters, accidents, and imaginary, real, or symbolic shocks.

Spengler believed that civilizations are like living bodies, or like plants. And from this belief he concluded, first, that there are as many systems of morality as there are of civilization; second, that nobody is free to choose his morality, which is imposed upon the individual like a climate, or a destiny. Is that what we want? That determinism, that enslavement to our roots: is that what we wish for human beings? And how, starting from there, from the sacrosanct principle of respecting identities of unchanging purity, can we fail to respect the idea that impure people—apostates, in other words, who move from one identity to another—ought to be put to death?

Today it's Huntington who believes that cultures are heterogeneous, discontinuous, impermeable, incommunicable. And the corollary of that belief, here too, is that cultures are prisons, so the only way for them to meet is as one block against another, in confrontation, in

warfare. Is that what we want? How can the so-called leftist differentialists, who are talking only about the "dialogue between cultures," fail
to see that in saying this they are advocating a clash of civilizations, not
a dialogue? How can the alter-globalists and other "neo-Greens"—
those partisans of a superstitious respect for differences that should by
no means be touched—fail to understand that they are simply setting
the stage for future wars—much more surely than the Dr. Strangeloves
at the American State Department?

I wouldn't have agreed with Spengler yesterday.

I don't agree with Huntington today.

Or, to put it more precisely, I'll do whatever is in my power to keep
either of them from turning out to be right.

And that's why I'm pleading to detach human rights from their
original soil; to replant them in the soils of civilizations that might not
necessarily have thought of them: a detachment-replanting that is not
a transplant but a journey, a journey that is the first step toward a real
dialogue between cultures, a dialogue worthy of the name.

FIFTH ARGUMENT.

"Look at the problem the other way around. Not where it's coming
from but where it's headed. No longer the soil from which human rights
have been taken, but the places where they're meant to be transplanted.
That soil is fragile. It might not be homogeneous, impermeable, etc., but
it's fragile. Inject one new thing into it. Uproot something else. You're
messing with its whole ecology and disrupting its balance. Anyway, you
talk about structures. You mention the structuralism of your youth.
Why don't you do that here? Why don't you carry your structuralism
through to its conclusion? A civilization is a whole. More than the
sum of its parts, probably. But still made up of those parts. If you don't
like it, you can slice off this or that funerary practice or sexual rite. In
the name of human rights, because you think it seems barbaric, you
eliminate the tradition of abandoning sick people to die in the depths
of the forests. And you discover that that practice was more essential

than you thought and that your precious human rights are destroying everything—like those strains of cholera, typhus, or influenza that wiped out 90 percent of the pre-Columbian world. . . ."

The truth, first of all, is that I don't like organicism in this case any more than I do in any other.

The idea that cultures are as inevitable as climates or soils is, for me, no less hateful when it warns us against the devastating effects that the abolition of the burqa or the outlawing of the genital mutilation of young girls might have on a local culture than when it's telling us that human rights expire once they are removed from the places that bred them.

And, more than anything else, this image is not only hateful, it is mistaken—and we know, we Westerners, from having gone through it ourselves, how and why it is mistaken.

Let's look at the question of blasphemy, such a burning issue in the Islamic world. We, too, after all, have had our laws forbidding blasphemy. We've also had a Salman Rushdie: the Chevalier de la Barre, who, though he didn't even write books, was hit by a kind of fatwa for the simple reason that he hadn't saluted during a procession, and ended up tortured and decapitated. We, too, like the Islamists of Karachi and Tehran, have thought, like those religious authorities who today decree that the caricatured image of their Prophet in a Danish newspaper is an intolerable offense, that this was a matter of saving our souls, preserving the strength of our nation and the identity of the Catholic, Apostolic, and Roman Church. Did France vanish once it changed its mind? Did Voltaire, who defended la Barre, dig Europe's grave? And why can't something that works in one place not work in another? Why not imagine a world, still this world, but in which there would never be another Chevalier de la Barre? Why not join with those Muslims who imagine an Islam in all its greatness, but returned to its mosques and no longer having the power to demand the heads of those who choose either not to believe, or to change their beliefs, or even to mock the very idea of belief?[1]

Or the question of capital punishment. Also essential, the "culturalists" tell us, to the legal structure of this or that non-Western civilization. Prescribed, in such ancient texts, and with such an abundance of detail, that it could not be abolished without wiping out a whole store of wisdom. And I'm not talking about the United States, where still today, at the beginning of the twenty-first century, plenty of people still say that the sovereign right to take the life of the author of inhuman crimes is part of a providential plan, and that to give it up in the name of human rights would endanger our very idea of humanity. That's exactly what was said—it seems like yesterday—in Europe. And even worse things were said in Europe, since all of speculative philosophy saw capital punishment as the key to the entire penal system, the mainstay of the state machine, an act that recognized the humanity of the murderer (Hegel), who was honored by the application to himself of the same means he had used on someone else (Kant). Today capital punishment has been abolished. There—in France—where it took so long to be abolished, the demands of public opinion, a courageous president, and a determined minister of justice were needed to make it happen. So the politician was right and the great philosophers were wrong. Neither the West, nor philosophy, nor France, fell to pieces when the "keystone" was shattered. Another proof that the whole can survive the removal of one of its parts. Proof that societies are not soils and that politics is no more a subset of ecology than it is of clinical medicine. And another lesson for all those odd progressives who, by mixing everything up, end up confusing morality with legal and social conformism.

We can love a civilization and try to make it even more habitable, more breathable, for its inhabitants: that's the positive lesson from Europe.

We can respect a culture and still try to reform it by insisting on the minimum right of a man or a woman not to be tortured: that's what the West has done—and in the name of what prejudice would we prevent others from doing the same?

To argue for the Universal is to argue against different weights and measures: one set that allows certain people the right to History and condemns the rest to live in immobile societies, outside of History and Time.

———

ARGUMENT NUMBER SIX. "It's got nothing to do with that. You can't compare the two. How can you even dare compare a prosperous, solid, formerly colonizing society, which can allow itself any number of mutilations or amputations, to one that's fragile, already vulnerable, and sometimes broken, because of its former colonizers?"

I'm aware of this, thank you very much.

I don't have the slightest doubt about the damage and the calamities colonial savagery meted out.

But that's exactly the reason.

We should have worried about that beforehand.

Beforehand?

Beforehand.

Worry about it?

Yes, of course: worry that the West is *already* bringing trouble to those former colonies, and that the universalism that the relativists denounce, the democratic inspiration that they want to see only as rape and violence, might be the remedy.

Let's go over it one more time.

The West's relationship to the rest of the world is not a single one, but two, maybe three, and even four different histories.

First, it's the history of that brutal, merciless, naked subjection that was the colonial conquest: everyone agrees about that; in any case, I would agree with my differentialist counterpart on this matter, and neither of us would deny that Europe committed a violence against non-European societies.

Second, there's the story of anticolonialism, which, I repeat, borrowed from Europe the great principles of enlightened nationalism, turned them back upon Europe, and used them to defeat it.

But there is a third history here—one that is, if I may say so, the opposite of the above—which is the history of those other non-European movements like the Muslim Brotherhood or the Cambodian Khmer Rouge, which we've already encountered many times over the course of this work: they too sincerely believed they were struggling against Europe; they even thought they were the only ones who had declared total, radical war on it, since they not only attacked its armies, its police, its civil servants, but the way it thought and its very thought itself: except we know that by so doing they were, at least in part, borrowing a page from another kind of Europe, the part that gave us fascism; we know, we've seen, that there—in proportions that, to be sure, are still yet to be determined—there was another European poison, distilled in European laboratories, transported by couriers—which is to say ideologues—who themselves were often Europeans; and we know, finally, that the poison is still there, more or less true to its original formula—we know that it's there, in Islam but not only there, with Ahmadinejad but also with Chávez, in that poor South Asia ravaged by Tamil terrorism just as in every part of the world where hatred of liberty, law, intellectuals, ideas in general, and the idea of democracy in particular is taking such a toll.

So what is Europe doing about it?

Are we more shocked by the immense violence that the Khmer Rouge killers, educated at the Sorbonne, commit against their society—or that of the democrats, also educated at the Sorbonne, who are trying to heal the wounds opened by the Khmer Rouge?

Are we more worried about the destabilizing effects of an overly brutal infusion of human rights—or about the effects, destructive in another way, of the massive, high-dosage infusions of pure fascism that are the Arab, Hindu, Khmer, and other fundamentalisms?

And isn't it troubling to see that the same people who travel the world repeating that "Too much democracy can kill" don't seem bothered to walk hand-in-hand with people who—in the name of the same reasoning, in the name of a dogma that holds hatred of democracy as an article of faith—are inoculating these fragile, vulnerable, broken societies with a daily, mortal dose of authoritarianism, totalitarianism, or obsession with identity?

Europe is colonialism.

But it's also that form of anticolonialism that has taken the face of these indigenous fascisms.

And that's why, weighing them against one another—the aftermath of colonialism against the ravages of a certain anticolonialism, against those who tell us that colonization was an act of civilization and against the other venom distilled by the differentialists—I think that we have the urgent task of writing yet another page in the history of Europe's relations with outside societies: not about poisons but about remedies— democracy, indeed; human rights; and access to the Universal.

"IT'S ABSOLUTELY EXTRAORDINARY! It's always Europe! When the Third World is being pillaged, it's Europe. When the Third World is liberated, it's Europe. And if we're forced to choose between these two Europes, we have to find a third one. . . . But tell me (seventh and final argument): is it really so extraordinary, is Europe really so superior, that the world has no choice, in any circumstance, except between Europe and Europe? And can't you imagine that between these two Europes there might be a third solution, one that's not European, one that simply involves all the world's cultures?"

You won't find me saying that European culture is "superior": first of all because I don't believe in the notion that a culture, whatever it may be, can be said to be superior to another; and then because even if the notion does have some meaning, even if we are going to risk establishing that kind of classification, there's one culture that seems to have blown its chance of coming out on top—and that's the culture that produced Auschwitz, invented the Gulag, contributed to creating the dirty poison of the Khmer Rouge, etc.—which is to say Europe.

You won't find me denying that non-European civilizations have produced wonders, and whole worlds, that it would be disastrous to ignore, and even more disastrous to crush beneath the wheel of a lazy, brutal, eradicating Universal: when one has early on acquired a taste for traveling and explorations; when one has spent one's life at every latitude, observing and sometimes tempted to share ways of life that are not one's own; when one was brought up on Artaud, Segalen, and, of course, Lévi-Strauss, one is vaccinated against that kind of arrogance, as far removed as it is possible to be from the ethnocentric temptation and educated, I believe, to be curious and respectful.

If only morons and racists believe in the myth of one culture's superiority over another, only imbeciles, or bastards, deny that cultures can talk to one another, exchange and transmit to one another a bit of the best they have to offer—in a word, to judge and evaluate one another: if one has something better, an admirable rite, habit, or practice, why wouldn't another want to borrow it?

What I am saying and repeating is that, if it's simply unthinkable to say that one model is entirely superior to all others, nothing is preventing us, on the other hand, from recalling that certain ideas, simply ideas, are superior to other ideas: habeas corpus, for example, or recognizing the right of a body not to be guillotined or mutilated: and the superiority of this right, in the West or anywhere else, over the right a society gives itself to guillotine or mutilate.

What I'm saying, once again, is that one can respect a society, preserve its customs and traditions, while still being hostile, profoundly hostile, to its "orientation" toward a model that is not its own and that would disfigure it by removing its most precious characteristics—and to think that in that model there is nonetheless one characteristic, or a series of characteristics, that deserve to be borrowed precisely because they would allow the original society, without losing either its identity or its soul, to become even better, more livable: yes to rights; to the practice of liberty; to the primacy of the subject, of all subjects, over the laws of societies: women's faces, for example, finally released from prison.

And what I'm saying is, finally, that there is a truly abject way to begin with respect for people's integrity and identity and to end up allowing them only to identify with their own misery and the integrity of their suffering—and that we need to replace the idea that cultures are really nothing but concerted scourges that ought to be left to die of their own diseases with a real dialogue of cultures, in which one would basically say to another: in Europe, you can drop all the customs you no longer need, but drop the radicalism as well; drop the fascisms that are doing you as much harm as they once did to us; drop those deadly ideologies that partly belong to us as well and that are the worst of our legacy, and take the Enlightenment instead! Take freedom of conscience! Take Voltaire! And for our part we'll take Averroës, Massoud, the palaver tree, and the practice of a fraternity that you've kept alive far better than we have.

A FINAL WORD.

I've said that we can't reject everything in the modern critiques of the idea of universality.

And having recalled this basic position; and having, to a certain extent, reemphasized the importance of the Universal of human rights, I'm not saying that we can't question, elaborate, and enrich the ways in which that Universal is expressed or explained: not only do I not deny that—not only do I believe that every cultural or social expression deserves, as an ontological privilege, to be submitted to the good work of criticism—but I think that the Enlightenment categories, the very ways we understand them, the very idea of democracy and human rights, would themselves have nothing to lose by being submitted to a genealogical evaluation.

We might end up thinking they were too Greek, for example, and want to dump their more obscure aspects.

We might find them too Roman: we might think they risk veering off into that other imperialism, the only one that matters metaphysically, of submitting the world to technology.

We might regret that universalism, as we understand it, might have gone over to the "neither Jewish nor Greek" side of St. Paul, having forgotten, along the way, the taste for individuality once found in both Jewish and Greek thought.

At that point, like Levinas, we might want to reintroduce those Jewish voices, that prophetic spirit, that was drowned out by the Greeks and the Romans as well as by St. Paul.

Like him, we might want to say that twenty-five centuries of metaphysics have impoverished that concept at the same time as they were constructing it—and we could, by leaning on the Jews, try to remedy that impoverishment.

We could try to elaborate the concept and what we understand of it:

in order to convince people of the legitimacy of the commandment not to kill, to make sure they remember that they are not mere bunches of matter at the disposition of someone else's covetousness or cruelty, to give them the right to blaspheme, to apostasy, to unbelief—do we need, for that, to unify every way of life, to flatten every landscape?

We could examine the way universalism, and its extensions, work: a more difficult Universal; one that's more demanding; a Universal that would act not by extension but by intention and under tension; a Universal that works more by influence than by incorporation; magnetizing societies instead of dreaming of dominating them; a Universal that would still be called Universal, that would still speak the Greek, Roman, and Catholic language of the Universal, but that would differ by substituting, in place of the old logic of conversion, or even of persuasion, the biblical logic of the Remainder, and the example given by the Remainder, which I once illustrated in a fragment of my *Testament of God,* which itself was commenting on the page from the *Tractatus Theologico-Politicus* in which Spinoza opposes prophetic speech to the apostolic word.[2]

We could, finally, ask that other question, the real final question, and probably the most difficult one of all, which is the question of the foundation of this reestablished Universal: In whose name, at the end of the day? Human universality, fine; humanity as a family, okay; the solidarity of the weak, all right; but family implies fraternity; fraternity means, in some way, paternity; and so what is a Universal doing which, in claiming that "God is dead," would purposely skip over the question of the Father? What kind of universalism—even an agnostic one, even an atheistic one—wouldn't ask, here as elsewhere, the theological, and therefore political, question of the "testament of God"?

That's a task for philosophers, one we won't be done with even when we've defeated the temptation to differentialism.

But we've still got to defeat it.

To begin with, we've still got to arrest that disorientation.

That was the point of these pages.

The rest will follow.

Epilogue

So.

Here we are.

After having lurked all around this "cadaver,"* we might wonder if, in order to light the lantern of a Left that is still in search of itself, we really had to go through all of that, those debates, those detours, that dispute about the Universal, those excursions through Islam and the Empire, the genealogy of anti-Americanism, the return to Bosnia, that emergence of an anti-Semitism that luckily is still up in the air, Darfur, those forgotten wars, those encounters with Evil that were either avoided or, disastrously, kept all too well.

And I can hear the well-meaning progressive, who wants to freshen up the decrepit old Left, to restructure it, exclaiming: "What do I care about this quarrel with the differentialists, what do I care about your Badious, Bourdieus, Baudrillards, Chomskys, or Pinters—what do I have to do with these groups of lunatics who can't make up their minds about September 11 or the virtues of revolutionary Islamism, what's the point of these old sages, these Dr. Mabuses and Strangeloves, busily trying to rehabilitate an old Nazi but who aren't, as far as I know, in charge of anything?"

---

* The author alludes to the original title of the book, *Ce Grand Cadavre à la Renverse,* which means "the backward-falling corpse," a quote from Jean-Paul Sartre, describing the Left of his time. —Publisher's note.

He'd be wrong.

First, because even when they're not in charge of anything, ideas are what, for better or worse, drive, and allow us to change, the world.

But also because they drive it according to a logic in which the complexity of ideas, their apparent marginality—or the marginality, especially, of their proponents—have no impact on the damage they can cause.

People thought the same thing about that little group of Russian agitators exiled to the shores of Lake Zurich.

Or about that little group hanging out in the back rooms of Munich beer houses, grouped around a talkative man who dressed like a bum and who gathered together a strange mixture of national-Bolsheviks, conservative revolutionaries, right-wing Leninists, and far-left war veterans.

Or again, a century and a half earlier, in an abandoned convent in Paris, about those lawyers, notary clerks, members of provincial academies, and former seminarians who didn't seem to be doing much more than getting involved in complex rivalries and derisory excommunications.

Not to mention those other cliques, even further back, religious ones, whose colossal importance very few people managed to perceive: didn't John of Damascus, for example, holed up in a monastery spending the remainder of his life noting down the spiritual curiosities of his day, still believe that Islam was just another Christian heresy, a century after its birth?

Well, all of a sudden, every time, we find ourselves witnessing the seizure of the Winter Palace, Adolf Hitler's taking power, Louis Capet's beheading, or the third monotheistic revolution.

In a flash, thanks to a mechanism that despite the passing decades and even centuries remains mysterious, we find ourselves faced with a gigantic event which very soon starts to change the course of world history.

It starts with a group, a sect, and, within that sect, a local aberration, the tiniest little novelty, which at first no one imagines will ever go past the stage of accident, or of a freak abnormality, or both—and which, thanks to a quick reinforcement, because of a strange but irresistible attraction, soon affects all of world history.

Well, this isn't comparable.

And I don't think that either Europe or America is on the verge of such earth-shattering events.

But I am seeing this agitation.

I'm seeing this swarm of ideas whose leading actors do not always consciously realize they are expressing them.

I'm bearing in mind what happens in the ideological dens where the concepts of liberalism, the idea of Europe, the politics of human rights, or the dream of an all-embracing concept of humanity are being methodically crushed.

And yes: I do think that we should never underestimate, either in France or anywhere else, the importance of this kind of fabrication—I think that some ideas, even when cultivated behind closed doors, almost in greenhouses, are like tools or levers whose dark workings are no less important than the platforms of leading parties.

I wanted to draw the cartography of this darkness.

I've tried to describe the laboratories where this evil is being fermented.

Even though I know that—if only because of the fascination they exert, if only because of the prestige radical positions continue to enjoy in my country, or, finally, if only because of the vehicles and the bridges that link them to "mainstream" politics—those laboratories never stay simple laboratories for long. . . .

THE MAIN QUESTION, if I had to sum it up in a word, is obviously the question of atheism.

The great adventure of atheism, as Sartre said.

That "cruel and long-term adventure" which, he boasted in *Words,* he had "followed all the way through."

That immense adventure, he insisted in *Gide vivant,* the most immense, the most beautiful, but also the most difficult and risky of all human adventures.

He was right about the matter of religious history, as his other contemporary, Georges Bataille, never stopped insisting, after him; and as all those events (Islamism, etc.) having to do with the interminable death of God still do to this day.

He was right as far as feelings go—which was already the thesis of

Marcel Proust, the author, whom he could hardly stand, of *In Search of Lost Time* (as Emmanuel Berl, attacked with slippers for the crime of excess amorous credulity, had already learned at his own expense, in the scene previously quoted).

He was right about literature and art, as an entire post-Duchamp aesthetic attests: the works it has produced, as well as its stalemates, are all affected by the silence of God.

But he was even more right about politics, where it is perhaps hardest of all to get rid not only of old beliefs, but of the belief in belief.

And that's what we see, once again, in the adventures of this idea of Progress, which has finally had to let go of its old credos; which has clearly stopped worshipping the idols that were History, Revolution, the Good Society, the Absolute; which knows, once and for all, that there is no world beyond this one, and no society beyond this one; but which has had so much trouble recovering from that blow—and, above all, such a hard time in facing the consequences, all the consequences, of its disbelief, and the movement that produced it!

The sequence is unavoidable.

It started off with great fanfare.

It doesn't exactly believe in heaven but it does believe in the heaven of ideas, which amounts to the same thing.

It lives for two centuries, or maybe three, on this asset.

It creates books, gospels, and, borrowing a page from these gospels, dispatches societies toward the terrestrial Jerusalem.

And then the idea melts away.

Then the other heaven, that of the totalitarianisms, comes crashing down.

And instead of drawing its conclusions, instead of going all the way to the end, as Gide and Sartre did, accompanying the agony and death of this God who did not save us, instead of either trimming their sails or seeing in that empty heaven a source of liberty and an invitation to invent and to think for themselves—people came up with a savage belief system, cobbled together a heaven out of bits and pieces, hung on, as we've seen throughout this book, to every available remaining value.

If the Left is in crisis, it's not, as people sometimes say, because it refuses to bury the other world once and for all, but because it has, because it was forced to: and because it finds that obligation insufferable.

If progressivism eventually, once more, starts to flirt with evil—and if it's already starting to turn its back on that Dreyfusard, antitotalitarian, antifascist tradition that was its greatest honor and that is still its only reason for existing—it will be because it can no longer stand the idea of an empty heaven and the twilight of its idols.

And if, on the other hand, it doesn't—if it resists this new evil—if, after having resisted the first totalitarian temptation which was, roughly put, Communism, it also manages to resist the new one, which I have described in this book and which feeds off the remains of the old one, it will be because it has been taught a methodical atheism.

A Left that is true to its best reflexes.

A Left that is the logical result of its great guiding events; of its foundational, luminous images; in a word of what, at the very beginning of this book, I called its pantheon.

But a Left that will, therefore, have no other pantheon besides that one.

No other heaven, ever again.

No more uncreated truths, of any kind.

No ideas that offer a full-fledged solution for what it ought to do.

A Left that will get used to the idea, once and for all, that there's no more room for building castles in the air, and that only builds its plans on the disorders of the world, its injustices, its misery—and this is precisely the theological, which is to say the philosophical, foundation of the politics of the lesser evil—and, therefore, of the better.

We have to imagine happy atheists.

We have to make an antiwager that we can win not by betting on the existence but on the nonexistence of God.

That's the price of democracy.

And the alternative, the only one, is the devil and his legions of murderous angels.

THE OTHER NAME of this atheism may be melancholy.

Not sadness, of course.

And even less the indifference and tepidity of a person who no longer does anything because he no longer hopes for anything.

But the initiative, to the contrary, the Prometheanism of one who—precisely because he has no other hopes; precisely because heaven is empty and because he knows he has nowhere else to turn; precisely because the world has nobody but him, now, to light it a bit—is going to take up that practice, which after all is rather improbable, which is the child of human abandonment, and which is called politics.

That was the motto of William of Orange: "One need not hope in order to undertake, nor succeed in order to persevere."

That was at the very heart of the great biblical wisdom that anchors, if not on God's silence, then at least on the rarity of His word, the necessity for a laborious, tireless, efficient morality.

And that's the beautiful and strange invention of those Polish rabbis from the end of the eighteenth century and the beginning of the nineteenth century who—in reaction to Hassidism and its excessive reenchantment of the world, in response to this epidemic of fervor and of frenzy that, under its influence, was taking over Europe and dangerously firing up souls—proposed, as did Rabbi Hayim Volozyn, himself a disciple of the Gaon of Vilna, the theory[1] of a God who, of course, created the world; who wanted to do so and who therefore created it; but who, after having done so, his need satisfied, then "concealed his transcendence" and "withdrew"—leaving his creatures the responsibility to retain, or not, the pieces of this universe that he left to them. If men failed to take up the task, the world would fall to pieces. If they took the path of study and prayer, if they inhabited the fiery letters of the Book of Books, if they spoke the right words and carried out the required gestures, and if, therefore, they took care to keep the world from falling apart—then they would manage to prevent that *decreation.*

That is how, all things considered, I reached politics.

That is how, in any event, it seems to me that politics ought to be thought of in the democratic age.

And if I had one piece of advice, just one, for all those people I hear saying they want to renovate this and rebuild that, if I had one contribution to bring to those projects of re-foundation that seem to be the leading issue of the day, it would be just that: think about the lesson of William of Orange on the one hand and that of the Gaon of Vilna, and his disciple Rabbi Hayim Volozyn, on the other.

First lesson. The empty heaven. Or, if it's not empty yet, if idols remain, then the good Nietzschean hammer, the beau geste of the celestial road-mender, smashing the remaining stars in the firmament of Politics.

Second lesson. The mourning period. Which is to say pain, but without nostalgia. Or nostalgia, but without the hope of return. No more odyssey. Farewell to Ithaca. Regret, yes, probably—yet the regret of nothing, a complete focus on the future.

And then a third, and final, lesson. Action. Even activism. In the proper sense of the term, the *poetry,* whose Greek etymology means the act of "doing." A poetry which becomes the opposite of the lyrical illusion: demanding and precarious, difficult and prosaic—all the more burning because shorn of the pretense of transcendence.

This is the melancholy Left of Camus, when he forgets "the exile of Helen" and returns from Tipasa once and for all: the great Camus, pessimistic and joyous, a skeptic but still a fighter—the Camus who affirms with the same energy that neither the kingdom of Grace nor that of Justice is or will be in this world—but the soft upheaval of whose urgency we can still hear, if we pay attention.

This is Sartre—but the other one, the one whom I tried, in my *Sartre: The Philosopher of the Twentieth Century,*[2] to remove both from his humanist crust and from the dead end where he had been led by the mental turmoil of fellow-traveling—this is the Sartre who wrote a *Nausea* that might have been called *Melancholia;* the Sartre, also dark, pessimistic, tragic, who, in his *Saint Genet, Actor and Martyr,* couldn't get enough of quoting St. John of the Cross's theory of Evil and Sin and who, between Hegel and Schelling, between the apostle of the dialectic and the theoretician of an "antagonism" founded "in the nature of the thing itself," always, when he wrote serious philosophy, unhesitatingly chose Schelling; and the Sartre who, whenever he wrote serious works on politics, whenever he dirtied his hands—as he did under the Occupation, during the age of "Socialism and Liberty"—in order to come up with concrete projects to reform French society for the postwar period, did so with a modesty, a precision, and even a formalism, that were worthy of his brother-enemy, Albert Camus.

This is Jean Moulin, that profane Christ, that icon. At the beginning of this book, in my gallery of snapshots, I could have included his strong soul and—on the famous photograph on his identification card that has become a republican emblem—the firm gaze, the felt hat worn like a crest, the scarf eternally tied around his bruised throat. I am so haunted by those images that I could have mentioned the last railway car, the final agonies, the man who wanted to die before he spoke under torture and who finally died because he never spoke. But at the very end of this book, I'd like to imagine another role, another character, halfway between what he was and what he would have been if he had survived: a great prefect; a peerless strategist and tactician for unifying the different currents in a free France; for the non-Communist Left; for resistance rather than revolution; for knowing that the Liberation wouldn't be a cakewalk; for his championing of political atheism; for his curious blend of epic and prose, of grandeur and humility—a lay saint during the storm; a faithful helper of the state in times of peace.

Or this is Pierre Mendès-France, that other figure of a Left that knew how to resist the worst seductions—once again humble, once again truthful; seeing power as a burden; almost completely lacking the desire for power; holding that nothing is so sure that it cannot be subjected to the free and difficult consideration of the subjects of the law—I like the idea that he, along with Moulin, was one of those rare people who, during the time of the Popular Front, was against nonintervention in Spain; I like that he was one of the even rarer individuals who, over the course of the twentieth century, was on the right side of all the four great tests (pro-Dreyfus, anti-Vichy, etc.); and, finally, I like that the first time I saw him, in Delhi, in November 1971, he was coming from Bangladesh, right as I was about to go there.

The melancholy Left versus the lyrical Left: the choice, after all, is clear—if we set our minds to it, we won't want for writings or role models.

Notes

PART ONE. WHAT'S LEFT OF THE LEFT
CHAPTER 1. AND UPON THIS RUIN . . .

1. February 15, 2007, interview with Claude Askolovitch.
2. Michel Foucault, "Non au sexe roi," interview with Bernard-Henri Lévy, *Le Nouvel Observateur*, March 12, 1977.
3. Nick Cohen, *What's Left? How Liberals Lost Their Way*, Fourth Estate, 2007.

CHAPTER 2. PRIMAL SCENES

1. Paul Nizan, *Aden, Arabie*, Cahiers Libres No. 8, Maspero, 1960, p. 16.

CHAPTER 3. MY PRIMAL SCENES

1. Quoted by Alexis Lacroix, in *Le Socialisme des imbeciles*, La Table Ronde, 2004.
2. Jean-Pierre Chevènement, "Cessons d'avoir honte," *Le Nouvel Observateur*, October 25, 2001.
3. Speech in Caen, March 9, 2007. Speech in Nice, March 30, 2007.
4. Caen speech; Nice speech, March 30, 2007; Toulon speech, January 7, 2007; Letter to the CLANR (Comité de liaison des associations nationales de rapatriés) quoted in *Le Monde* on April 21, 2007.
5. Among others, his speech in Bercy, April 29, 2007.
6. Speech in Montpellier, May 4, 2007.

CHAPTER 5. NOTE ON A FIRE

1. Pascal Bruckner, *La Tyrannie de la pénitence*, Grasset, 2006. Similarly: André Glucksmann, "Les feux de la haine," *Le Monde*, November 26, 2005. Alain

Finkielkraut, "J'assume," *Le Monde,* November 26, 2005. Robert Redeker, "Le nihilisme culturel imprègne les émeutes banlieusardes," *Le Figaro,* November 28, 2005.

2. Hélène Carrère d'Encausse, declaration quoted, among others, by Laurent Joffrin, "Les néo-réacs," *Le Nouvel Observateur,* November 29, 2005.
3. Alain Bauer, *Le Nouvel Observateur,* May 24, 2006.
4. Yann Moulier-Boutang, "Les vieux habits neufs de la République, en défense d'émeutiers prétendument insignifiants," *Multitudes,* no. 23, 2005.

PART TWO. THIRTY YEARS LATER
CHAPTER 1. HOW WE'RE LESS SANCTIMONIOUS

I. Guy Debord, "Le déclin et la chute de l'économie spectaculaire-marchande," *Internationale Situationniste,* no. 10.
2. Cited by Jean-François Revel, *La Grande Parade,* Plon, 2000, p. 126.

CHAPTER 2. A SECRET CALENDAR OF THE HISTORY OF THIS CENTURY

I. For example—though, in this case, it took thirty years—André Glucksmann, "Mes années maoïstes me font toujours honte," collected by Marie-Laure Germon and Yves Lacroix, *Le Figaro,* September 9, 2006.
2. Charles Bettelheim, *Révolution culturelle et organisation culturelle en Chine,* Petite Collection Maspero, 1973.

PART THREE. CRITIQUE OF NEOPROGRESSIVE REASON
CHAPTER 1. LIBERALISM IS THEIR ENEMY

I. *Le Figaro,* March 16, 2005.
2. Bernard Cassen, conversation, July 31, 2002, with Marcos Ancelovici, quoted in *Raisons Politiques,* no. 16, April 2004, "L'antilibéralisme."
3. May 9, 2004, declaration made before an assembly of Socialist Party officials launching the European campaign.
4. Jacques Derrida, "Du 'sans-prix' au 'juste prix' de la transaction," in Roger-Pol Droit, *Comment penser l'argent,* pp. 398–399.
5. Michel Foucault, *Dits et écrits II,* Quarto-Gallimard, 1994, pp. 818–824, mainly (Lesson of January 24, 1979).
6. Michel Foucault, "Sur la sellette," interview with Jean-Louis Ezine, *Les Nouvelles Littéraires,* March 17, 1975, reprinted in *Dits et écrits I,* ibid., pp. 1588–1593.
7. Philippe Corcuff, *Politis,* interview with Olivier Doubre, January 24, 2007.
8. *Liberismo e liberalismo,* reprinted in Benedetto Croce, *L'Histoire comme pensée et comme action,* Droz, 1968.
9. Declaration to the Agence France-Presse by Msgr. Baltazar Porras, bishop of

Mérida, former president of the Venezuelan bishops, quoted by Henri Tincq in *Le Monde,* July 20, 2007.

10. Jonathan I. Israel, *Radical Enlightenment,* 2005.

11. David Cumin, *Carl Schmitt: biographie politique et intellectuelle,* Cerf, 2005. And above all Yves-Charles Zarka, who started off the whole debate, "Carl Schmitt philosophe," *Le Monde,* December 6, 2002. *Un detail nazi dans la pensée de Carl Schmitt,* PUF, 2005. And the two issues (no. 6, April 2001; no. 14, April 2003) of the magazine *Cités,* of which he is the editor.

12. Alain de Benoist, "Carl Schmitt et les sagouins," *Eléments,* no. 110, September 2003.

13. September 25, 1947. Quoted in *Cités,* no. 17, 2004.

14. Quoted in Evelyne Pieiller, "La raison et l'apocalypse," *Le Monde diplomatique,* August 2006.

15. Étienne Balibar, "Le Hobbes de Schmitt, le Schmitt de Hobbes," preface to Carl Schmitt, *Le Léviathan dans la doctrine de l'État de Thomas Hobbes,* Le Seuil, 2002.

16. Étienne Balibar, interview with Michael Löwy and Razmig Keucheyan, *ContreTemps,* reprinted in *Solidarités,* no. 30, July 2, 2003.

17. Daniel Bensaïd, "Sur le retour de la question politico-stratégique," September 10, 2006, semi-marx.free.fr.

18. Quoted by Jean-Claude Monod, in an interview with Eric Aeschimann, *Libération,* February 17, 2007.

19. Giorgio Agamben, *L'État d'exception,* Le Seuil, 2003.

20. Jacques Derrida, interview with Lieven de Cauter, February 19, 2004, www.brusselstribunal.org.

21. Slavoj Žižek, contribution to Chantal Mouffe, *The Challenge of Carl Schmitt,* Verso, 1999.

22. Alain Finkielkraut and Peter Sloterdijk, *Les Battements du monde,* Fayard, 2003.

23. Verso, 2000.

24. Verso, May 1999.

25. "Carl Schmitt and the Road to Abu Ghraib," *Constellations,* vol. 13, no. 1, 2006.

26. Ellen Kennedy, "Carl Schmitt und die 'Frankfurter Schule,' Deutsche Liberalismuskritik im 20. Jahrhundert," *Geschichte und Gesellschaft,* 12, 1986, pp. 380–419.

CHAPTER 2. ONCE UPON A TIME, EUROPE

1. Milan Kundera, "L'Europe kidnappée ou la tragédie de l'Europe centrale," *Le Débat,* no. 27, 1983.

2. Michel Foucault, "La Pologne, et après?" *Le Débat,* no. 25, May 1983, reprinted in *Dits et ecrits II,* Quarto-Gallimard, 1994, p. 1317.

3. "Le seul regret de Lech Walesa," *Le Figaro,* July 28, 2007.

4. Jean-Claude Milner, *Les Penchants criminels de l'Europe démocratique,* Verdier, 2003.

5. Quoted by Paul Audi, *Je me suis toujours été un autre,* Christian Bourgois, 2007.

CHAPTER 3. THE OTHER SOCIALISM OF THE IMBECILES

1. France 3, March 24, 2006, *La face cachée des libérateurs,* a documentary by Alain Moreau and Patrick Cabouat.

2. Georges Clemenceau, *Grandeurs et misères d'une victoire,* Plon, 1930.

3. Arundhati Roy, *Le Monde,* October 14–15, 2001.

4. Noam Chomsky, "Sur les bombardements du 11 septembre," *Counterpunch,* September 12, 2001.

5. Robert Fisk, *The Independent,* November 29, 2001.

6. February 15, 2007.

7. Jean Baudrillard, "L'Esprit du terrorisme," *Le Monde,* November 2, 2001.

8. The law of May 8, 1816, known as the "Loi Bonald," abolished divorce, which would not be reestablished until the "Loi Naquet" of July 27, 1884.

9. Alphonse de Lamartine, *Cours familiers de littérature,* M. Petit edition, Raphaèle-Les-Arles, 1959.

10. Maurice Barrès, *Mes Cahiers,* volume IX.

11. *Réfléxions sur la Révolution en France,* reissued by Hachette Pluriel, 1989, quoted in Zeev Sternhell, *Les anti-Lumières,* Fayard, 2006.

12. Zeev Sternhell, ibid., p. 83.

13. Quoted by Jorge Semprun, "Que signifie pour moi être européen," *El País,* reprinted in *Courrier International,* December 12, 2002.

14. *La Tyrannie de la pénitence.*

15. Charles Maurras, *Les trois aspects du président Wilson: la neutralité, l'intervention, l'armistice,* Nouvelle Librairie Nationale, 1920.

16. Robert Aron and Arnaud Dandieu, *Le Cancer américain,* Paris, Rieder, 1931.

17. Pierre Drieu La Rochelle, *Journal 1939–1945,* Gallimard, 1992.

18. Georges Bernanos, "Révolution et liberté," quoted in Philippe Roger, *L'Ennemi américain,* Le Seuil, coll. Points, p. 511. Jean-Marie Domenach, "Les diplodocus et les fourmis," *Esprit,* March 1959, p. 512.

19. *La Croix,* February 22, 2007.

20. Quoted by Philippe Roger, *L'Ennemi américain,* p. 301.

21. Quoted by Gérard Blain, "Le poison américain," *Le Monde,* September 19, 1981.

22. Pierre Rigoulot, *L'anti-américanisme,* Robert Laffont, 2004, p. 152.

23. Ignacio Ramonet, "Un délicieux despotisme," *Le Monde diplomatique,* May 2000.

24. Yves Dezalay and Bryant Garth, "L'impérialisme de la vertu," ibid.

25. Pierre Bourdieu and Loïc Wacquant, "La nouvelle vulgate planétaire," ibid.

26. Régis Debray, *Modeste contribution aux discours et ceremonies officielles du dixième anniversaire,* Maspero, 1978, p. 39.

27. Régis Debray, *Contretemps,* Gallimard, 1992.

28. Régis Debray, *L'Édit de Caracalla ou Plaidoyer pour les États unis d'Occident,* Fayard, 2002.

CHAPTER 4. COUNTERATTACK ON THE "EMPIRE"

1. Cullen Murphy, *Are We Rome? The Fall of an Empire and the Fate of America,* Houghton Mifflin, 2007.

2. Antonio Negri and Michael Hardt, *Empire,* éd. Exiles, 2000.

3. "Ces biberons qui tuent," *Le Monde diplomatique,* December 1997.

4. Olivier Boiral, *Le Monde diplomatique,* November 2003.

5. *Refléxions sur la guerre, le Mal, et la fin de l'histoire,* Grasset, 2001, last chapter.

6. Noam Chomsky, "Quelques commentaires élémentaires sur le droit à la liberté d'expression," the preface to Robert Faurisson, *Mémoire en defense contre ceux qui m'accusent de falsifier l'histoire,* La Vieille Taupe, 1980.

7. Noam Chomsky and Edward S. Herman, *Économie politique des droits de l'homme,* Hallier, 1981.

8. Édition Page Deux, Lausanne.

9. Alain Badiou, "La Sainte-Alliance et ses serviteurs," *Le Monde,* May 20, 1999.

10. Alain Badiou, "L'arrogance impériale dans ses oeuvres," *Le Monde,* March 25, 2000.

CHAPTER 5. THE NEW ANTI-SEMITISM WILL BE PROGRESSIVE—OR NOTHING AT ALL

1. Alexis Lacroix, *Le Socialisme des imbeciles,* La Table Ronde, 2004.

2. Jean-Claude Milner, *Le Juif du savoir,* Grasset, 2006.

3. Cited by Bernard Lazare, *L'antisémitisme, son histoire et ses causes, II, L'antijudaïsme dans l'Antiquité,* Léon Chaillet, 1894.

4. Volume II, chap. XII, p. 312, Leipzig, 1874.

5. Volume I, pp. 158–159.

6. Georges Bernanos, *Le chemin de la croix des âmes,* Gallimard, p. 421.

7. Letter of June 10, 1944, in *Combat pour la liberté, correspondence inédite, 1934–1938,* Plon, 1971, p. 546.

8. In *Le Monde,* May 30, 2006.

9. Norman G. Finkelstein, *The Holocaust Industry: Reflections on the Exploitation of Jewish Suffering,* Verso, 2000.

10. October 11, 1998; speech on the occasion of receiving the Peace Prize of the German Book Trade, in St. Paul's Church in Frankfurt; the future author of *Death of a Critic* also denounced the "instrumentalization of the Holocaust" and suggested "turning the page of Auschwitz."

11. *American Vertigo,* Grasset, 2006.

12. Bernard-Henri Lévy, "Réponse aux négationnistes du genocide arménien," *Les Nouvelles d'Arménie,* March 2007, no. 128, summary of a speech given on January 17, 2007, at the Palais de la Mutualité in Paris.

13. *The Washington Post,* September 4, 2007, quoted in Mitchell Cohen, "Anti-Semitism and the Left That Doesn't Learn," *Dissent,* Fall 2007.

14. François-Xavier Fauvelle-Aymar, "Les juifs, la traite des esclaves et l'histoire des États-Unis," *Sources,* no. 12, October 2002.

15. *Nation,* September 23, 2002.

16. *Le Monde,* March 24, 2006.

17. This statement was made on *Nightline* (ABC) by Cindy Sheehan on March 15, 2005.

18. Pierre-André Taguieff, *Les contre-réactionnaires; le progressisme entre illusion et imposture,* Denoël, 2007.

CHAPTER 6. FASCISLAMISM

1. Statement by Sami al-Joundi, one of the founders of the party: from laveritemaintenant.org and Arie Stav, *Nativ,* November 1995.

2. Statement made to the *Deutsche National Zeitung,* May 1, 1964; reprinted today, with other such, in Marsi Feki, "Le Malaise égyptien," in *A l'Ombre de l'islam,* with Moïse Rahmani and Lucien Oulahbib, Brussels, 2005.

3. Caroline Fourest, *Frère Tariq: Discours, stratégie, et method de Tariq Ramadan,* Grasset, 2004; see, notably, the extract placed online by *ProChoix,* January 31, 2005.

4. Paul Berman's article on Ramadan: "Who's Afraid of Tariq Ramadan," *The New Republic,* June 4, 2007.

5. The memoirs of Haj Amin al-Husseini are today available in a complete Syrian edition, published in Damascus in 1999, by Al-Ahali, with the title of *Muthakarat Al Haj Muhammad Amin Al-Husayni* (edited by Abdul Karim Al-Omar). Already then, however, the substance of them was known in the Nuremberg trial, according to the witness Dieter Wisliceny, Adolf Eichmann's adjutant ("The Mufti was also one of the initiators of the systematic extermination of European Jewry by the Germans and had been the permanent collaborator and adviser of Eichmann and Himmler in the execution of this plan . . . He was one of Eichmann's best friends and had constantly incited him to accelerate the extermination measures."); and during the Eichmann trial of 1961 ("It has been proved to us that the Mufti, too, aimed at the implementation of the 'Final Solution,' viz., the extermination of European Jewry, and there is no doubt that, had Hitler succeeded in conquering Palestine, the Jewish population of Palestine as well would have been subject to

total extermination, with the support of the Mufti."). Hannah Arendt, *Eich-mann in Jerusalem,* 1963; David Ben Gurion, *Ben Gurion Looks Back in Talks with Moshe Pearlman,* Schocken Books, 1965; Moshe Pearlman, *Mufti of Jerusalem,* Victor Gollancz, 1947; Joseph Schechtmann, *The Mufti and the Führer: The Rise and Fall of Haj Amin al-Husseini,* Thomas Yoseloff, 1965.

6. Quoted in the Simon Wiesenthal Report: *Gross Mufti, Grossagent des Asche,* 1947, available at the Musée du Martyr Juif, Paris.

7. *Libération,* April 3, 2002; Oumma.com, interview with Fatiha Kaoukès, placed online April 24, 2002.

8. Badih Chayban, "Nasrallah alleges 'Christian Zionist' plot," *The Daily Star,* October 23, 2002.

9. *International Herald Tribune,* June 19, 2007.

10. Claude Askolovitch, "Les gauchistes d'Allah," *Le Nouvel Observateur,* October 20, 2004.

11. John Rees, national secretary, "Where Now for Respect," brochure, 2004.

12. "Hijab: a woman's right to choose," FSE, October 16, 2004, London, www.naar.org.uk.

13. Matthias Künzel, "Islamisme et Nazisme, une explication," quoted in Omer Bartov, *New Republic,* January 29, 2004.

14. As per *ProChoix News,* March 10, 2005; other showings, across France, often in the presence of Dieudonné and Thierry Meyssan, sometimes in associa-tion with "Les amis du Monde diplomatique" or the local representatives of ATTAC, are listed on the site www.clap36.net.

15. Caroline Fourest, "Un scandale pour l'Europe: Ayaan Hirsi Ali menace de perdre la nationalité hollandaise," *ProChoix,* May 20, 2006.

16. Klaus-Michael Mallmann and Martin Cuppers, *Das Dritte Reich, die Araber und Palästina,* Wissenschaftliche Buchgesellschaft, 2006.

17. *Who Killed Daniel Pearl?*

18. Robert-Paul Wolff, Barrington Moore, Jr., and Herbert Marcuse, *A Critique of Pure Tolerance,* Beacon Press, 1969.

19. Compare Jean-Marie Kintzler's remarkable analysis, published in no. 39 of *ProChoix* and entitled: "L'État de droit face au dogmatism intégriste: la crise philosophique du modèle communautaire." Also see Catherine Kintzler, *Qu'est-ce que la laïcité,* Vrin, 2007.

20. Sophie de Ravinel, "Une deuxième proposition de loi contre le blasphème," *Le Figaro,* March 21, 2006 (on the subject of two proposed laws submitted on February 28 and March 21, 2003, by the parliamentarians Eric Raoult and Jean-Marc Roubaud).

21. Texts cited in Mohamed Kacimi, "C'est saint Paul qui, le premier, a impose le voile aux femmes avec des arguments religieux," *Libération,* December 10, 2003.

22. Abdelwahab Meddeb, "La représentation du Prophète est devenue taboue," *Libération,* February 3, 2006.

23. Patricia Briel, "Ces étranges portraits de Mahomet jeune," *Le Temps,* February 22, 2006.

24. Mahmoud Hussein, *Al-Sira,* volume I, Grasset, 2005; volume II, Grasset, 2007.

25. On these matters, see Paul Berman, *Terror and Liberalism,* W.W. Norton & Company, 2003.

26. Report on the new textbooks of the Palestinian Authority, published in June 2005 by the Center for Monitoring the Impact of Peace, page 22. The report is available online at www.edume.org.

27. Paul Claudel, *Journal, tome II,* Gallimard, Pléiade, Cahier VII, p. 92.

CHAPTER 7. THE NEW STRUGGLE OF THE UNIVERSALS

1. An example of this "association" is Daniel Leconte's investigation, filmed and broadcast by Arte on August 30, 2007, and discussed the same day by *Charlie Hebdo* and *Libération.*

2. *Le Testament de Dieu,* republished by Denoël, Paris, 1983, pp. 170–174.

EPILOGUE

1. *L'Ame de la vie,* Verdier, 2006.

2. Trans. Andrew Brown, Polity Press, 2003.

Index

Kissinger, Henry, 20
Klein, Naomi, 31, 78
Koestler, Arthur, 58, 69
Kojève, Alexandre, 97
Konwicki, Tadeusz, 103
Koran, 181, 182–83, 185, 191–92
Kosovo, 81, 133, 141–42, 143, 144
Kouchner, Bernard, 3, 189
Kral, Peter, 103
Kristeva, Julia, 72
Kundera, Milan, 102, 103, 104–5

Lacan, Jacques, 59, 61, 62, 109
La Cuisinière et le mangeur d'hommes
  (Glucksmann), 57
Lagarde, Paul de, 151
La Grande Peur de bien-pensants
  (Bernanos), 151
Lamartine, Alphonse de, 117
La Mettrie, Julien Offray de, 93
Lanzmann, Claude, xiv, 159
Larbaud, Valery, 104
Lardreau, Guy, 73
La Religion de l'avenir (Lagarde), 151
Las Casas, Bartolomé, 194–95
Lassalle, Ferdinand, 87
Lazare, Bernard, 24
Le Cancer américain (Dandieu), 124, 127
Le Carre, John, 135
Lefort, Claude, 58, 69, 102
Lenin, Vladimir, 53, 56, 69, 95, 126,
  135
Le Nouvel Observateur (news weekly), 13
Le Pen, Jean-Marie, 17, 91, 124, 128
*The Leviathan in the State Theory of Thomas
  Hobbes* (Schmitt), 95
Levinas, Emmanuel, 35, 36, 70–71, 87,
  97, 154, 183, 204
Levi, Primo, 22, 35, 165, 166
Lévi-Strauss, Claude, 202
Lévy, André, 12
Lévy, Benny, 18, 25, 71, 170
Lewis, John, 152
L'Homme pressé (Morand), 37
L'Humanité (newspaper), 25

liberalism, economic *vs.* political,
  86–88
liberal state, 90–91
Libération (newspaper), 13
libertarianism, 55, 80
liberty *vs.* equality, 30–31, 92–93
L'Ideologie française (Lévy), 123
Ligue Communiste Révolutionnaire,
  95, 172
Lindbergh, Charles, 164
L'Invention démocratique (Lefort), 102
Locke, John, 92, 192, 194
Lotta Continua, 13
Lutheran Letters (Pasolini), 36
Luxemburg, Rosa, 135

MacShane, Denis, 162
madrassas, 177
Mahfouz, Naguib, 185
Maire, Edmond, 103
Malaparte, Curzio, 13, 56, 145
Malraux, André, 11–12, 13, 17, 166
Maoism, 56
  See also China
Mao Zedong, 20, 59, 61
Marchais, Georges, 101
Marcos, Subcomandante, 14
Marcuse, Herbert, 178
market, 86–88
Marxism, 55–56, 69, 70, 81, 86, 93,
  126, 144–45, 188
Massoud, Ahmad Shah, 185, 204
Massu, Jacques, 22
Mauriac, François, 24, 25
Maurras, Charles, 24–25, 93, 123, 125,
  128
May 1968
  antitotalitarian legacy, 33, 37, 38, 40,
    55
  and Chevènement, 80–81
  and Debray, 128
  as historic event, 23–24, 25
  as reflex, 33–34, 40
  and Sarkozy, 28
  student solidarity, 101

Vacher de Lapouge, Georges, 149, 150
Vaculík, Ludvík, 103
Valois, Georges, 124, 125
Val, Philippe, 174
van Gogh, Theo, 178
Vannsak, Keng, 62
Vatican II, 154
Védrine, Hubert, 3
Vendée massacres, 20, 53
Vergès, Jacques, 141
Vichy
    as fascism, 22, 33
    as historic event, 21–22, 26
    as reflex, 33
Vietnam War, 15, 20
Villepin, Dominique de, xvii
Vittorio, Francisco de, 194–95
Volozyn, Hayim, 212, 213
Voltaire, 93, 102, 148, 151, 198, 204
von Leers, Johann, 169
Voyous (Derrida), 96

Wacquant, Loïc, 128
Walesa, Lech`, 105
Walser, Martin, 155
Walt, Stephen, 164
Walzer, Michael, 164
Werfel, Franz, 103
William of Orange, 212, 213
Wilson, Woodrow, 123, 125
Winckelmann, Johann, 102
Wolff, Robert-Paul, 178
Wolfowitz, Paul, 97
World Trade Center attacks, 34, 81, 115, 124, 173, 207
World War II, 12, 30, 119, 124, 169, 171
Wretched of the Earth (Fanon), 194

Yaqoob, Salma, 172

Ziegler, Jean, 166
Zionism, 158
    See also anti-Zionism
Žižek, Slavoj, 97

PHOTO: © ALEXIS DUCLOS

BERNARD-HENRI LÉVY is a philosopher, journalist, activist, and filmmaker. He was hailed by *Vanity Fair* magazine as "Superman and prophet: we have no equivalent in the United States." Among his dozens of books are *American Vertigo, Barbarism with a Human Face,* and *Who Killed Daniel Pearl?* His writing has appeared in a wide range of publications throughout Europe and the United States. His films include the documentaries *Bosna!* and *A Day in the Death of Sarajevo.* Lévy is co-founder of the antiracist group SOS Racism and has served on diplomatic missions for the French government.

About the Type

This book was set in Requiem, a typeface designed by the Hoefler Type Foundry. It is a modern typeface inspired by inscriptional capitals in Ludovico Vicentino degli Arrighi's 1523 writing manual, *Il modo de temperare le penne*. An original lower-case, a set of figures, and an italic in the "chancery" style that Arrighi helped popularize were created to make this adaptation of a classical design into a complete font family.